truly *Cultured*

Rejuvenating Taste, Health and Community with Naturally Fermented Foods

A Cookbook and Nourishment Guide by
Nancy Lee Bentley

Published & distributed by:
Nancy Lee Bentley
Two Pie Radians Foundation
www.TrulyCultured.com

in association with:
IBJ Custom Publishing
Indianapolis, IN
www.ibjcustompublishing.com

ISBN 978-0-9798830-2-6
First Edition

Printed in the United States of America

Table of Contents

Recipes

Preface

My childhood memories growing up on a farm in upstate New York are full of heady, often amusing stories of what my grandmother fondly called "culturing." This had nothing to do with Sunday afternoons sitting primly dressed in her parlor, learning manners and etiquette. I smelled, played in—and ate—more weird things than any of my friends ever dreamed of. There was always something brewing, souring, or proofing around our place—the rich, earthy smells of the soil, the faint, musky waft of smoking ham and bacon in our smokehouse, the potato cellar's moist, soured odors around the sauerkraut crock, the indescribably delicious aroma of my mother's freshly baked bread, to name a few.

Because I was a tomboy, my grandmother wasn't my only early childhood teacher. My grandfather Byron was one of those undeniably strong, catalyzing influences in my life, who helped me gain a greater understanding of nature, both animal and human. He was a pillar of discipline and strength, a gnarly, outspoken character, both a farmer and a politician, who had single-handedly built a diversified dairy and cash crop operation in the depression when everyone was struggling. By pure determination and hard work he had distinguished himself enough to be elected to chair of the board of town supervisors in the county, a post he held for over 25 years.

He also had a reputation as a jokester. I heard stories early on of his boastings about his superior agronomy skills. One, in particular, was

his bet with a fellow farmer and supervisor from the next town that he would be able to raise potatoes ready to eat by the Fourth of July. Most potatoes don't mature until the end of the summer. But bet he did, and the bet he won. Of course, he "planted" full size potatoes in the ground just prior to the crucial inspection.

He was my idol. From him I learned, unequivocally, "that an apple a day keeps the doctor away." I relished the few moments we spent, especially during summer vacation, sharing our daily apple break. Mind you, I didn't necessarily relish everything he attempted to teach me. In particular, another of his daily health habits, breaking a raw egg into a saucer and sliding it down his throat, still makes me shudder.

GRANDPA'S APPLE-A-DAY

My appreciation for this crusty old farmer really started one summer afternoon, in the midst of a sweaty game of hide and seek, when I was leaning into a nook in the horse barn wall just around the corner from the doorway to the cellar. I was startled to hear serious giggling emanating from the cool basement where we kept the seed potatoes and produce over the winter. Then I realized that it was Grandpa, my dad, and the hired men taking a break from haying. I had never before, and have never since, heard grown men actually giggling. Little did I know my grandpa's favorite form of daily apple was a small jelly glass of hard cider, snockered down with jokes with the hired hands before starting the evening milking.

FIRST EXCITING ENCOUNTERS

The fact that this brewed apple beverage could have such a dramatic influence over these normally strong and stalwart men raised my eyebrows and my consciousness. This was my first inkling into the power and transformative ability of fermented foods. Of course, I had to confirm the power of the drink, so after the workers left to round up the cows, I grabbed the other kids and we snuck down to see what all the fuss was about. After less than a glass, we found out firsthand why those men were acting silly. Indeed, the levity of fermented drinks has punctuated the boredom of work-a-day worlds for centuries. It certainly was a memory that stood out clearly against those boring, plastic, station wagon days of the 1950s.

Even in my early teens, I was intrigued by all things food. Yet despite my inquiring, adventuresome spirit, some things were just plain too gross and disgusting for my 13-year-old tolerance. The blackish gray pallor of just-picked creamed mushrooms, for instance. The weird, rubbery looking sediment at the bottom of our vinegar jug. The brown, spicy catsup in dark bottles that had no resemblance to the bright red store-bought kind my friends ate. Yet these were the very things that "cultured" me. Little did I know at the time, in the midst of squiggling up my nose, I was gaining an appreciation for something much deeper: the community of living creatures, dependent on each other for health and welfare, that make up life on this planet.

THE THREAD OF FERMENTATION

It was not until college that I even began to understand the full impact of the teeming life operating ubiquitously but unseen, right under our noses. When I started studying the heavier sciences like microbiology and biochemistry, I began to get a much clearer picture of just how enormous the population of microbes inhabiting the earth truly is.

The statistics from our own bodies alone are staggering. Scientists have now been able to lay out the genetic map of the human gut. What they have discovered is up to 100 trillion active microbes, representing more than a thousand species, inhabiting our digestive tract. This represents over 10 percent of our dry body weight. In this microbial mix, over 60,000 genes have been discovered; more than twice as many as found in our overall human genome, all inhabiting and interacting with our food and bodily processes, performing a myriad of services that keep us functioning.

All this is inside our bodies, to say nothing of the sheer enormity of all the processes going on in nature that are propelled and championed by microorganisms. But it has only been more recently, since I have integrated many disciplines of study, that the true significance of microbes' contribution to higher forms of life has begun to dawn on my consciousness.

In our contemporary "war on bugs" mentality, we tend to see bacteria as primitive, subservient life forms, often viewing or equating the words bacteria and disease synonymously. Yet far from outsmarting microorganisms and leaving them behind on the "evolutionary ladder," we so-called more complex, more evolved animals are literally made up of colonies and communities of bacteria. In fact, it would be fair to say that we are bacteria and bacteria are us. If this seems like a sweeping statement, you need only look at their widespread and indisputable contribution to life on the planet, from photosynthesis, oxygen breathing, and nitrogen fixation to digestion and fermentation, to realize that this is so.

Indeed, all life has evolved from common ancestors: bacteria. Bacteria were the sole inhabitants of the Earth four billion years ago, and they evolved and co-evolved through a symbiotic process of adaptation and change. Life did not take over the planet by combat but by networking. The fact that animal and plant cells originated through symbiosis, a process defined and elucidated by microbiologist Lynn Margulis and that of others, is no longer controversial. Our egos as humans might have difficulty embracing the reality that from a microcosmic perspective, plant and animal life, including humanity, are recent passing phenomena. But if we can step back and see things from a larger perspective, how can we deny our interdependence?

Yet the full impact of this interconnection hasn't been recognized or felt in our modern, sanitarily oriented world. Certainly this is evident through the hundreds of thousands of chemicals, pesticides, cleaners, antibiotics, prescription and over-the-counter drugs that we find on the market. We, as a culture, literally have a germ war mentality, continually stoked by fear of everything from terrorism to disease—and a huge industry of chemical, agricultural, and pharmaceutical giants with quick and easy "remedies" to take care of the problems.

Yet, ominous messages are on the wall. The bees are disappearing; degenerative disease is rampant. Many scientists have begun to argue that the trend of using antibacterial soap and other antibacterial products may actually cause diseases like eczema, irritable bowel syndrome, and even Type II diabetes, as well as deplete our bodies' first line of defense against disease, according to Dr. Joseph Mercola.

TRULY CULTURED

Just how interconnected are we? I mentioned earlier that we are symbiotic beings on a symbiotic planet. If we care to look, we can find symbiosis everywhere, and the illusion of separateness in nature is just that, an illusion. Our biosphere is all one piece, an immense, integrated living system, an organism in its own right.

Discovering the microcosm within and about us changes the way we view the world and life. And acknowledging that our ancestors are bacteria is humbling, even disturbing, challenging our perceptions and ideas of our individuality, uniqueness, and independence as human beings "on top of the evolutionary heap." It even violates our view of ourselves as discrete physical beings separated from—and dominant over—the rest of nature.

The reality, however, is not just that we have evolved with, through, and from microorganisms, or that they are our friends and benefactors. The fact is our very culture has been defined and built upon them. In fact, the very word culture itself is directly derived from "culture" of microbes. The lessons they have to teach us are not only legendary but crucial to our existence if we are to continue to have an existence upon this planet. Rather than seeing microbes as enemies to conquer and destroy, we would be wise to appreciate and work with these minute creatures that have become the co-creators of the rich heritage, the abundant life we so lavishly enjoy on this planet.

THE ROAD TO APPRECIATING CULTURE

In my long, rainbow ride through the world of food, agriculture, history, nutrition, health and wellness, in all honesty, it has been some of those principles, those offhanded comical or even downright disturbing little diddies that have stuck with, kick-started, kicked in, and/or contributed to the synthesis of the wisdom that seethes through these words.

As a student of brown rice, vegetables, and seaweed back in the seventies, as I sat at the feet of the icon of the revolutionary food movement, Guru Michio Kuchi, I was stunned by the shocking words of wisdom dripping from his macrobiotic lips.

"Cancer is the cure. *Civilization* is the disease."

"WHAT?!" I remember snorting to myself. "How outrageous! What a cruel thing to say."

Now that I, myself, have uncovered and embraced the proverbial Philosopher's Stone, and analogously achieved my status of being a proverbial "sourdough starter," leavening and lightening the way to health and wisdom through illuminating, time-tested but long-forgotten truths, I can see and fully appreciate this precise and pristine truth.

I hope many will begin to recognize, sooner than later, that we are inextricably linked, interconnected, and interdependent with other forms of life and that it will be through this recognition, awareness, interaction, harmony, and cooperation with these species, not against them, that we will continue to be graced with life on this planet.

Looking back, I can now say with gratitude that my road to the appreciation of culture was part of a clever, universal ploy to get me to this point. When I thought about it as I started to write this book, my whole life, in fact, has become a rich tapestry of information, interesting tidbits, and scientific, historic, and spiritual insights into the amazing, transformative world of fermentation.

Now, as a food technologist, chef, and nutrition and wholistic health expert, my understanding and appreciation for my humble beginnings, first-hand experiments and professional experiences with this fascinating subject have bubbled and grown like the proverbial soup pot on the back of the stove. So, I

now share them with you. From the ongoing sourdough starter rising in the cupboard, there has come a profound realization that all life, whether it knows it or not, owes its very existence to these beneficial little creatures we know as microorganisms. They are the true basis of culture as we know it.

The principles of fermentation are keys to help us understand our lives and the nature of things. No wonder way back in ancient times they called it "alchemy," the magic later known as chemistry.

Actually, microbes are those tiny receptacles holding bits of arcane knowledge that could be a key to unlocking the enigmas of our current health crisis. The more we learn, the more we understand the nature and reality of the fact that they are the keepers holding secret knowledge, the literal keys to our long-term survival as a species ourselves.

"Support Bacteria:
They're the only culture
some people have..."

one

Chapter 1
The Secret Keys of Cultured
Foods in Health, Wellness,
Longevity

I f you were an alien watching primetime American TV for the first time, you might conclude that we need drugs to stay healthy. Yet the deluge of pharmaceuticals in our society is actually a very recent phenomenon in the overall scheme of things.

True, today's modern pharmaceutical arsenal has saved many lives, especially those stricken with acute diseases. When antibiotics were first used, they were actually very effective in wiping out many kinds of infectious bacteria. But as we'll see from the discussion about microorganisms and their incredibly adaptable nature in Chapter 3, this has changed dramatically.

Now our health problems are more insidious and chronic. Degenerative diseases like cancer, heart disease, diabetes, and a host of other weird alphabet soup maladies such as ADHD and GERD that the medical profession has labeled as "diseases" are our predominant health challenges. The "war on bugs" mentality is rapidly losing the battle, both in the hospital and on the farm. Increasing use of pesticides, despite constant development of more potent, genetically engineered formulas, has failed to keep ahead of the bugs.

It's no accident that this is happening in both our bodies and on our farms. These circumstances are reflections of each other, an example of the ancient alchemists' principle of "as above, so below." The mineral content in the vegetables we eat, for example, is only as good as the supply of minerals in the soil. And in correlation and correspondence, this holds an essential key to unraveling the enigmas.

THE BASIS OF "DIS-EASE"

Like those morphing microorganisms, the modern definition of the word disease has changed dramatically from its original root meaning. Especially since Louis Pasteur discovered pasteurization in the last century, we've tended to look at disease as a disruptive, degenerative process in the body caused by a specific germ or agent. Yet the ancient word *disease* is actually better understood when viewed as "dis-ease," inferring discomfort or dissension on other levels, such as the mind and the body, and conflict between emotional and spiritual levels that set up the conditions for problems to develop. Health is not just the absence of disease. Health is a combination of physical, mental, emotional, and spiritual wellness, with all parts working in harmony, balance, and with ease.

Energy, like our blood, flows all around the body, carrying nutrients and waste products where they need to go. When there is a balance of energy, those processes work harmoniously, when there is too much or too little energy, imbalances result. A rush of concentrated sugar into the blood stream, for example, can lead to hyperactivity and radical stimulation of hormones, such as insulin and cortisol, leading to belly fat storage and other problems. Not having enough food can lead to low blood sugar, low energy, and fatigue—to not having enough "umph" to carry vital nutrients to the cells, to carry away waste products, or even to get you out of bed.

PREVENTING DISEASE VERSUS CURING IT

Today, there are basically two distinct camps of thinking about health that Pasteur's influence capitulated. Essentially this boils down to either curing disease or preventing it. Do you remember the old Rorschach inkblot test or the M.C. Escher painting with a grid of fishes/birds? Does the inkblot look like a pretty butterfly on a tree or a pair of spooky ghosts? Do you see birds or fishes in the Escher grid? Depending on how they are viewed, these pictures look different to each of us, and are good examples of the difference between the figure/ground relationships that applies here.

Scientists, who systematically see things from a reductionism perspective, tend to focus on the disease, looking for single causative agents, such as viruses or germs. Holistic practitioners and healers, on the other hand, tend to view things from a larger, more comprehensive perspective, placing their focus more on health. You might say that scientists focus on the "figure" (disease), whereas holistic practitioners focus on the "figure/ground" (health) relationship.

Ancient wisdom, even among primitive peoples, has consistently taught, "Everything is connected." We live in an interdependent world, in a matrix of interconnected energies and realities. Shamans and sages throughout millennia have known that sickness isn't just something that starts with the body.

I hope our current environmental problems like global warming and acid rain, combined with many other mysterious, out-of-the-blue quandaries like disappearing bees and astounding rates of autism, are helping us to get this message–that all things are connected. Optimistically, this understanding is moving us closer to a realization that no one thing causes or cures problems. Invariably, it's a combination of elements involved in the breakdown or rebuilding of health, like other parts of life. There are no quick fixes, magic bullets or bandages for polluted streams. Or for chronic degenerative health conditions that so many of us are plagued with now.

Even those old, annoyingly trite truisms we just can't seem to get away from, like "A stitch in time saves nine," remind us of the obvious: Preventing problems is invariably simpler and easier than waiting until things break down to fix them.

> Health is not just the absence of disease. Health is a combination of physical, mental, emotional, and spiritual wellness, with all parts working in harmony, balance, and with ease.

FERMENTED FOODS: THE MAGIC BULLET?

So, are fermented and cultured foods the proverbial magic bullet, the fountain of youth? Are they our salvation, the long-lost, simple key for restoring, regaining our lost health and youth?

In short, the answer is yes and no.

Do fermented foods act like site-specific pills or drugs to alleviate symptoms and cure disease? No, not usually. But are they key contributors, missing links to health? Yes. The microorganisms involved in the process of fermentation are instrumental in the foundations of health because they promote good digestion and healthy "gut flora." They are a foundation of immunity, our frontline of defense in maintaining a healthy body. And they're essential foods we're just not getting enough of in our modern diet to provide a critical, bottom-line buffer support for health.

Okay, so now you have the answer. But just because you have the keys, doesn't necessarily mean you'll know how to use them to open the door to health. Understanding the value of fermented foods isn't useful unless you can apply it to your life.

So your task will be to do a bit of exploring—and maybe working with yourself. Hopefully, this book will help you by helping you in shifting your thinking and showing you a few simple ways to improve your own health, energy, and life by incorporating fermented foods into your regular diet. The key, however, is you. You have to do it, no one else can do it for you. *You*, in effect, are the "magic bullet."

This brings up a very important principle in the holistic approach to health. You and you alone are responsible for your own health. Becoming aware of, learning about, looking at, and listening to your own body and following what it says are very basic ideas, but important in terms of finding your own route to wellness.

And you are unique. There is no one else exactly like you. And no one knows you and your body better than you. This is the basis of Metabolic Typing and one of the basic principles of the *Dr. Mercola's TOTAL HEALTH Program* Book I co-authored with Dr. Joseph Mercola, well-known for his top website, www.mercola.com and his call-it-like-it-is *E-Healthy* e-mail newsletter. Along with other key health factors, Metabolic Typing principles in this book demonstrate how to customize your food and eating to your body's unique needs. So, in reality, you are in the best position to help yourself, even if you don't have a doctorate in chemistry or aren't a trained medical professional. You don't have to be a doctor to know what is good for you. "Why not?" you may ask.

Because you have a doctor inside of you. It's often called your "body wisdom." Accessing "body wisdom" is how people have been able to know what they needed for their bodies for thousands of years, before any degrees for medical doctors were ever issued.

It's often difficult for people to hear what their body is saying, especially if they're addicted to carbohydrates, sugars, or other strong foods such as alcohol and caffeine, which set up artificial cravings and distort the body's natural hunger for what it needs. A healthy body has a natural hunger or attraction for things that are beneficial.

Fermented foods can help you restore your natural ability to hear and decipher your own body's wisdom, its natural directive toward what it needs to achieve and maintain optimum health. Fortunately, another basic part of this principle, reflecting the body's inherent ability to adapt, is "The more you eat, the more you want." Think about it. Can you eat just one chocolate-chip cookie or potato chip? The same principle applies to almost anything, good or bad. The more junk food you eat, the more you want. But the same is true of high-quality food. The more healthy food, vegetables, fruits, and quality protein you eat, the more you desire to eat these. Really.

Feedback from people who've cleaned up their dietary act comes in, almost across the board, affirming the fact that once they start eating healthier, their body naturally starts craving the good stuff. *Body Ecology Diet* author Donna Gates also confirms that in her experience with people who adopt this healthy diet heavy in cultured foods, improving intestinal health by eating fermented foods actually helps them lose their craving for sweets.

Additionally, our subconscious mind can be our ally or our enemy. It's designed to aid us in developing habits to help us simplify our lives. This can work for us or against us, depending on the instructions we give to direct it. Fortunately, we can use this fact to develop new habits and perspectives that promote good health. It takes 21 days to form a new habit. This means that there's something in our makeup that can assist us in making the transition to a healthy lifestyle, without struggling or forcing ourselves to "be good." It's a natural part of our system that we can use to our advantage, easing us into the habit of eating healthy and feeling great.

WHAT ARE FERMENTED OR CULTURED FOODS?

Fermented foods are created when the starch or carbohydrates in basic foods are broken down and changed by microorganisms like bacteria, yeasts, and molds into smaller, often more digestible components. Fermentation is an economical and simple way to preserve food for later use, increase available food, and remove the "antis" or anti-nutrients that compete for or reduce nutrition, and make food safer to eat, without electricity, refrigeration, or sophisticated equipment.

Fermentation happens naturally, often as a part of the breakdown processes in the decay of plants, especially fruits and vegetables. "Decay?" you say. "Yuck, that means rotting, doesn't it?" Well, not exactly. What distinguishes fermentation from putrefaction or rotting? Putrefaction is the decomposition of organic matter, especially protein, by microorganisms, resulting in the production of foul-smelling matter. Fermentation, however, usually involves the pre-digestion and transformation of high-carbohydrate foods. Meat naturally putrefies, wet fruit and grains naturally ferment.

The terms fermented and cultured are often used interchangeably. The difference is slight, developing via natural evolution. Fermentation is the natural process. Culturing is humans' conscious experimentation and use of the fermentation process to produce and preserve comestibles, an archaic word for edibles. Fermented foods that contain beneficial microorganisms and enzymes are considered probiotics, a broad category of "functional foods" that are beginning to attract the attention of scientists, health practitioners, and natural and commercial food companies alike. At last, scientists and technical experts are beginning to awaken to what ancient peoples always knew: fermented foods are essential to good health and longevity.

PROBIOTICS AND PREBIOTICS

Foods and supplements that contain beneficial microorganisms and support health are called probiotics. Actually a subset of a larger class of foods called "functional foods," probiotics are basically the friendly bacteria that promote intestinal health. The term probiotics comes from the Greek, meaning "for life," but it was Russian scientist Ellie Metchnikoff, who, in his 1907 book *The Prolongation of Life*, discusses the longevity of Bulgarian peasants who consumed sour milk. It is Metchnikoff who is credited with heralding the birth of probiotics.

Some of the active probiotic microorganisms include lactobacillus, bifidus, planetarum, and beneficial yeasts, such as Torula. More probiotics are being developed on a regular basis by

ARE YOUR HEALTH PROBLEMS YEAST CONNECTED?

If your answer is yes to any question, circle the number in the right hand column. When you've completed the questionnaire, add up the points. Your score will help you determine the possibility (or probability) that your health problems are yeast related.

		YES	NO	Score
1.	Have you taken repeated or prolonged courses of antibacterial drugs?			**4**
2.	Have you been bothered by recurrent vaginal, prostate, or urinary tract infections?			**3**
3.	Do you feel "sick all over," yet the cause hasn't been found?			**2**
4.	Are you bothered by hormone disturbances, including PMS, menstrual irregularities, sexual dysfunction, sugar cravings, low body temperature, or fatigue?			**2**
5.	Are you unusually sensitive to tobacco smoke, perfumes, colognes, and other chemical odors?			**2**
6.	Are you bothered by memory or concentration problems? Do you sometimes feel "spaced out"?			**2**
7.	Have you taken prolonged courses of prednisone or other steroids, or have you taken "the pill" for more than 3 years?			**2**
8.	Do some foods disagree with you or trigger your symptoms?			**1**
9.	Do you suffer with constipation, diarrhea, bloating, or abdominal pain?			**1**
10.	Does your skin itch, tingle, or burn, is it unusually dry; or are you bothered by rashes?			**1**

Scoring for women: If your score is 9 or more, your health problems are probably yeast-connected. If your score is 12 or more, your health problems are almost certainly yeast-connected.

Scoring for men: If your score is 7 or more, your health problems are probably yeast-connected. If your score is 10 or more, your health problems are almost certainly yeast-connected.

commercial dairies and food manufacturers as the awareness about these beneficials is spreading. In fact, probiotics are the fastest-growing segment of the functional foods and neutraceuticals category in the health and natural products industry.

In contrast to "anti-biotics," which destroy all microorganisms, both good and bad, probiotics, such as yogurt and kefir, and probiotic formulas, such as those sold in health and natural foods stores and sections, enhance health by reestablishing good gut bacteria. Essentially, probiotics increase production of nutrients such as B vitamins and enzymes, enhance the effectiveness of white blood cells, and reduce putrefactive bacteria. Other reported benefits include better immunological response, production of antibiotic substances, improved calcium absorption, prevention of osteoporosis, prevention of cataracts, and prolongation of life.

Prebiotics are non-digestible food products, including inulin and FOS (fructo-oligosaccharides) found in Jerusalem artichokes and other foods that promote an environment that reduces "bad" bacteria, supports and stimulates probiotic growth. Both prebiotics and probiotics help to change the pH and other aspects of the intestinal environment to promote normal functioning, absorption of nutrients, and removal of toxins and waste products.

WHAT ABOUT CANDIDA?

"Who?" you're asking. Candida is neither a Grecian goddess nor a porn star. The term "Candida" is short for Candida albicans, yeast that is common—present, in fact—in virtually everybody's systems.

As you know by now, our bodies are full of bacteria and yeasts. Even E-coli and potential cancer cells exist within all of us. Yet it's only when the conditions are ripe and the environment in the cells of the gastrointestinal tract becomes more anaerobic (i.e., oxygen is reduced) and acidic (i.e., pH is lowered) from buildup of toxins and lowered nutritional intake that these Candida-type yeasts can proliferate, turn into a fungal form, crowd out the probiotics, and start to tip the balance of our inner ecology toward the negative. Of the four varieties of Candida, Candida albicans, Candida glabrata, Candida tropicalis, and Candida krusei, it is Candida albicans that is by far the most common, causing

nearly 80 percent of vaginal yeast infections.

It's important to recognize the symptoms of Candida overgrowth. You can find simple questionnaires like this one on page 9 to help you determine if you may have a Candidiasis problem on websites including that of Dr. William Crook, well-known physician and author of *The Yeast Connection* (see www.yeastconnection.com, now run by his daughter, Elizabeth Crook). On the site, you'll find questions about your level of stress, how much or how frequently you've taken antibiotics, and whether you have itchy, oozy discharges or other symptoms.

Bottom line, you can bet that many, if not most, people have a yeast overgrowth problem called Candidiasis. But even more certain, any kind of chronic health problem is an automatic tip-off to a major problem with overgrowth of the Candida yeast in the intestinal tract. It's one of those underlying causatives, as well as consequences, of chronic digestive and immune dysfunction.

And it ain't just happening *down there*, girls! Yeast overgrowth is systemic, throughout the whole system, including the mucous membranes of the mouth, nose and throat, ears, stomach, intestines, as well as in the vagina. Nursing mothers even get yeast infections in their breasts. Eventually it can spread throughout the

"When you were born, you had a tropical rainforest in your gut. But that's been killed off in all of us long ago by everything from antibiotics and microwaves to sugar and the barrage of chemicals we've all been exposed to. Once gone, just like clear cutting the Amazon for cattle, it's a lot harder to get that beneficial eco-system reestablished."

Nutritional Consultant Rob McMaster

entire body, including the blood, the joints, and the membranes around the brain, affecting basically every system. It weakens the immune system, allowing other infections to take hold.

The fact that vaginal yeast infection products are one of the largest segments of the feminine hygiene products market is no accident. Yeast infection treatment products gained 811 percent in chain drug store dollar sales during the first quarter of 1991 over 1990, when these types of products first switched from prescription to over-the-counter medication status, according to pharmaceutical industry statistics. Sales of these medications are just the tip of the iceberg, giving you some idea of just how widespread the Candida overgrowth problem is. Not just women are affected.

Men can definitely have a problem with Candida, too, exhibiting some of the same, if not obvious, symptoms. "Yeast infections can be passed back and forth between partners in unprotected intercourse, but because yeast is frequently present anyway, a sexual partner is more likely to pick up the infection if his or her immune system is also depressed," says Dr. Philip Mead, Professor of Obstetrics and Gynecology at the University of Vermont, College of Medicine.

THE STRAW THAT BROKE THE CAMEL'S BACK

Dr. William Crook was one of the first physicians to provide a clear explanation of the proliferation and problems of yeast overgrowth in degenerative disease. One of the best examples of how Candida burdens the body is shown in the camel graphic here, from his book, *The Yeast Connection*. The graphic aptly depicts what happens when yeast overgrowth, combined with a number of other factors, congregate and together stress the body to the breaking point.

Those factors that aggravate yeast overgrowth can include inadequate digestive enzymes, lowered gut bacteria from repeated antibiotics, contraceptives and other steroids, stress, low thyroid function, diabetes or any illness, even pregnancy. Candida albicans can take over the system, aided by lack of sleep, parasites, and poor nutrition, including overly acidic pH in the digestive tract from consumption of sugars, processed foods, and too much meat consumption. Most

reprinted with permission by © Cynthia Crook The Yeast Connection and Women's Health, William G. Crook, 2003 Professional Books, Inc. www.yeastconnection.com

especially, Candida thrives when there's impaired removal of waste products and a buildup of toxicity, lowering the immune response and allowing the yeast to thrive.

It's not a conspiracy against us to keep us from enjoying bread and sweets, it's just a natural consequence, a mirror reflection of poor food and lifestyle choices, plus other stressors yielding digestive and immune systems that are off balance.

WHY SHOULD WE EAT FERMENTED FOODS

Nobel Prize winner Dr. Elie Metchnikoff was one of the first scientists to recognize the benefits of eating fermented foods. He discovered that the social groups who lived the longest regularly consumed ample quantities of lacto-fermented foods such as yogurt. He claimed that the lactobacilli in these fermented milk products were able to prolong life by reducing formation of toxins in the gut. It wasn't until much later, in the beginning of the 19th century, however, that these active components or agents of fermentation were discovered and identified.

Microorganisms, especially the friendly and

helpful lactobacillus bacteria so important to our digestive health and immunity, are the tireless workers who also produce our favorite cheeses, beer, and chocolate. These neighborly lactic acid bacteria inhabit our digestive tracts, strengthen the immune system, and help the body defend against "unfriendly" bacteria and pathogens that cause disease. Both friendly and unfriendly bacteria are always cohabitating in our digestive tract. When we are in a healthy state, the friendly bacteria outnumber the bad, keeping our inner ecosystem in harmony.

However, many of those who come from a holistic health perspective, including *Body Ecology Diet* author and founder Donna Gates, maintain that we in the "civilized" western world are destroying the delicate balance of the ecosystem that exists within— and without—our bodies. Unfortunately, our contemporary lifestyles produce a long and growing list of factors that can upset this balance. Our immune systems take a beating from all the electronic pollution, pesticides, herbicides, additives, and other chemicals routinely used in our food system, synthetic materials in our lifestyle, our fast-food culture, and our wholesale use of pharmaceuticals, including antibiotics and hormones, that are becoming routine in our world. In fact, the stress of modern life actually creates acidic conditions in our bodies.

Since bacteria are sensitive to factors like pH (acidity/alkalinity) and are adaptive to their environment, they morph to try to compensate and redress imbalances. Reduction in oxygen, for instance, from such things as chemical pollution and lack of exercise changes the pH of cells and tissues, creating conditions that invite in unfavorable microorganisms that compete with the beneficial ones we need to be healthy. The result is a constant battle for the good over the bad. These days, it looks like we humans are the ones who are losing.

BEYOND THE BUBBLY

Beyond the sheer pleasure of enjoying some of our most fabulous foods, are there other, more compelling, reasons for reincorporating traditional lacto-fermented foods back into our everyday eating?

Certainly the nutritional considerations, the sheer nutrient density of these functional foods

clearly puts them on the top of the superior, "super" foods list, making them well worth consideration as some of the world's most valuable edibles.

But even more pointedly, can cultured or fermented foods actually hold a critical key to unraveling the snarly web of degenerative diseases plaguing our civilization? This is the mess that has the medical establishment baffled and pharmaceuticals raking in unprecedented profits, with the bulk of the population sucking in and down an average of $6000 worth of pills and medical expenses per year.

In the light of our current healthcare crisis, with national and private corporate budgets about to hemorrhage because of it, and "Diabesity®" (coined from diabetes and obesity) our number one national health problem, doesn't it make sense to at least spend some time investigating the potential that these simple and lowly foods have for addressing underlying health challenges we're facing as a nation and the world?

We'll take a more in-depth look at this in Chapter 5, but if you survey the current degenerative disease map and connect the dots, a disturbing picture emerges. Despite recent advances in mapping the human genome or DNA, and despite the medical and drug establishment's current practices of turning hangnails and overeating into bona fide new diseases, opening markets for new drugs to "treat" them, while continually maintaining the need for more research to find cures, there actually is a potential solution right under our noses.

When you examine some common denominators and statistics, it becomes obvious that we are beginning to apprehend the knowledge through which we can actually identify and scientifically verify a common etiology, a bottom line theory and basis for disease, most especially for the overwhelming incidence of degenerative disease we're experiencing in our current culture.

What are the most common over-the-counter drugs? Antacids. Yeast medications, another huge indicator of degenerative disease, are a reflection of the underlying and related problem of Candida overgrowth, and are also near the top of the list. A fellow nutritional researcher, Neil Voss, has demonstrated that 90% of patients tested in a small clinic in the West do not digest protein very well, if at all. All of these point to widespread, almost universal problems with digestion, which leads us directly to our immune systems.

Digestion is close to 80% of our immunity. In a healthy gut, the bacteria outnumber the body cells by a factor of 10 to 1. They are implicitly and inexorably involved not only in digesting and processing our food, but in producing the enzymes to break down food and in providing a buffer of healthy nutrients that form our bodies' first line of defense against disease.

As I stated earlier in the chapter, lacto-fermented foods are the single best and most effective way for replenishing and supporting the beneficial bacteria that insure digestive health. If this is true, why aren't we hearing more about it and why aren't doctors and the medical establishment recognizing and recommending this commonsense approach to improving health?

Here are a few facts. You draw the conclusions.

- With the exception of high margin varieties, fermented foods are inexpensive to produce. Like other food commodities such as grain, they can't be marked up much, can't support high-profit margins, and so are difficult for commercial food processors to profit from.

- Doctors have busy schedules, they spend an average 7 minutes per consultation, and need quick, bullet-point solutions to address their patients' health problems. Seeking deeper causative factors in disease conditions requires more time than is normally allotted.

- Doctors don't have time to talk with or educate patients about nutrition.

- Drug representatives are a major source of information for doctors. Doctors rely on drug representatives to keep them updated on the newest advances. Doctors may be looking only at symptoms treatable with the promoted drugs, and not truly 'seeing' the patient.

- Food and nutrition are not reimbursable medical expenses. Doctors can't profit from nutritional recommendations.

- Reviving old solutions does not make for lively marketing and advertising copy. Cultured food is not a snappy topic.

- Fermented foods are less easily controlled or tracked than drugs. The double blind controlled research study model is the medically accepted protocol. Research money for acceptable studies comes primarily from pharmaceutical coffers. Culturing foods is as much an art as a science, a melding of science and art.

- Terrorist food security fears have continued to fuel and reinforce the current "kill the germ" warfare mentality. Culturing foods relies upon the beneficial workings of, not on vilifying, microbes.

- Growing microbial resistance to antibiotics is an impetus for redoubling efforts to find the magic pill to solve our rampant, out of control and out of balance ecological disasters, which promotes the out-of-control path, and our journey into the wilderness of poor digestion, poor nutrition and compromised health.

- In short, little money or incentive exists to study the benefits of cultured or fermented foods. Government agencies, like the FDA, are under-funded, pressured, and influenced by transnational corporations and have no major incentive to look at, focus on, or study fermented foods.

- The bottom line is that the prevailing government and industry stance amounts to the conclusion that we cannot afford to find a low-cost solution to degenerative disease. In reality, though, we cannot afford to ignore this fact: lowly, unassuming fermented foods are a key to solving our short- and long-term health problems.

Although cultured foods are starting to regain attention, they are still largely underestimated and

> "We have seen the future of medicine and the future is food."
>
> Dr. Mitch Gaynor, New York Strang Center For Cancer Prevention

ignored in favor of drugs and chemicals. The fact remains, however, that our long term health and survival literally depend upon our waking up to this. The old margarine commercials from the 1970's nailed it: "It's not nice to fool Mother Nature." We will, ultimately, find out it is neither nice nor wise.

Even more subtly hidden than a needle in a haystack, among the plethora of single bullet solutions that can theoretically extract us from our current degenerating health and lack of wellness, are those slivers of wisdom we could well use to help us liberate ourselves from the overfed and undernourished curse of our modern society. Let's tease out the "culture" slivers.

HOW MUCH FERMENTED FOOD DO WE ACTUALLY NEED TO EAT?

Everyone knows what happens when you eat too much fermented food. Bingeing on alcohol, cheese, pickles, or brats can produce some devastating digestive distress! Getting the wrong kind or amount of fermented foods can profoundly affect how you feel.

However, the right amount of fermented foods aids in the digestion and enjoyment of the rest of your meal, especially when it is high in protein, fat, or grain, reports food expert Anne Marie Colbin, author of *Food and Healing*. This, no doubt, is one of the reasons why cultured foods are often served in small portions, on the side of the plate as condiments, adding a dash of complementary flavor and a small but potent digestive assist.

NAS/NRC (National Academy of Sciences/National Research Council) has not established a minimum daily requirement for fermented foods. Yet these nutrient-dense foodstuffs have been an essential part of many cultures' daily dietary regimen for literally tens of thousands of years.

So, how can we improve our consumption habits? The problem many of us have is that we don't necessarily crave the right kinds of fermented foods. Research shows that your individual preferences and constitution can affect your receptiveness to eating fermented foods. In fact, your preference for or repulsion toward fermented foods can be an indicator of the health of your digestive system, thus your overall health. How is this so? As adaptive as the human organism is, we become habituated to certain tastes and textures in our repertoire of the things we consider fit or good to eat. This is culturally, socially, religiously, as well as economically influenced. But all else being equal, it has been discovered, through Ayurvedic and other disciplines, that certain metabolic or constitutional types will reject foods they actually need. This is, of course, highlighted today by our overzealous craving for sweets.

In general, we do not often acknowledge or adequately credit the body's own wisdom with leading or directing us to make choices that will benefit our health. It is our built-in guidance system, if we listen to it. Most of the time, when it's not drawn into artificial addictions, the body tells us through our cravings for certain foods what we need to stay healthy. What's interesting and a little ironic is that although some people love fermented foods, often those whose digestive systems are compromised, who need fermented foods the most, actually dislike the taste.

CULTURED FOODS TO THE RESCUE

Traditionally lacto-fermented and live cultured foods can help us restore our body's natural digestive health and its ability to right its imbalances. They can also put us much more in touch with what's going on in our systems.

Because of their composition, cultured, fermented foods can have a major impact on many of the nutrition, disease, and health problems common all over the world. Two key ways they do this are through their ability to reduce anti-nutrient factors, and to improve the digestibility of foods.

In addition to making some nutrients more available, fermented foods can actually synthesize some new nutrients. Microorganisms in these foods may contain enzymes or other biologically active components, improving their nutrition. And isoflavones and antioxidants such as genistein, occurring in certain soy foods that have been enhanced by fermentation, can bind the excess estrogens so common in breast cancers. Some bacteria in natto, another traditionally fermented soy food similar to miso (a fermented soybean paste), produce increased levels of Vitamin K2, often low or lacking in women with osteoporosis.

> "They say tofu is the 'food of the future.' I say, let's keep it that way."
> Swami Beyondananda, Steve Bheerman

Eating fermented food to stop the gastrointestinal problems that are a basis of many degenerative diseases is not just "new-age" wishful thinking. The prestigious medical journal *Lancet's* June 2006 issue included a study by Johns Hopkins researchers who concluded that probiotics effectively treat acute diarrhea and antibiotic-associated diarrhea in adults and children, and are especially helpful in international travel.

Studies on humans and animals show that consuming fermented soy miso also reduces risks of cancers, provides protection from radiation, and strengthens the immune function. This fermented soybean paste also reduces free radicals and enhances the alkalinizing, antiviral nutrients, such as linoleic acid and isoflavones, involved in maintaining soft skin, reducing hot flashes, and preventing aging.

Unfermented soy products, on the other hand, do not exhibit these properties and are high in such digestive anti-nutrients as phytic acids, which are also found in wheat and other grains.

This is an important distinction, verifying the wisdom of Asian and other cultures who have consumed fermented soy products for centuries. They did not, as a rule and despite popular belief, consume many soy products that were not fermented. If unfermented soy such as tofu was eaten, it was generally for short periods, emergencies, when food supplies were low, usually with meat.

Soybeans, in the Western world have generally been regarded as animal food. But even Japanese and Chinese cuisines did not use all the soy milks, tofus, soy analogues, and other processed soy products that now take up much of the shelf space in natural food stores and supermarket health food sections. We may have cleverly discovered some isolated nutrient benefits to these foods, in our typical "magic bullet" medicine style, but in the final analysis, our poor health will eventually prove that "soy is not a health food."

Likewise with bread. Wheat and domesticated grains were only incorporated into human diets a mere 10,000 years ago—a relatively short blip in the history of Homo sapiens. These "new" grain foods were transformed into bread, but only after being soaked, sprouted, and/or fermented to reduce and remove the phytic acid and toxic gluten that undermines digestion. Our modern practice of simply grinding grains into flour and quickly puffing them into standardized white loaf, with yeast instead of sourdough, will someday be seen as short-sighted. It has been good for our industrial food production system, but not so healthy for ours.

Did these ancient cultures know something we don't? Yes, they knew from trial and error that eating unfermented grains and beans was neither viable nor sustainable for their longtime health and longevity. As Sally Fallon points out in *Nourishing Traditions*, "We now understand that their process of fermenting grains and beans before eating them neutralized phytic acid. It also neutralizes enzyme inhibitors and breaks down gluten, sugars, and other difficult to digest elements in grains and beans. And these nutritional benefits don't apply exclusively to humans. Herbivores often have as many as four stomachs, as well as an extremely long intestinal tract, allowing fermentation to take place within their bodies after they have eaten."

We humans each have only one stomach! Hmmm, perhaps we weren't designed to eat unfermented grains and beans…

YOU CAN NEVER DO JUST ONE THING

Back to our basic principle of natural health and disease. It's been said that you can never do just one thing. Everything is so interconnected that whatever we do, whether it's throwing a stone or planting a seed, sets in motion a whole series of actions and reactions that ripple outward. For example, a butterfly flapping its wings in South America affects the wind currents in the North American Pacific.

Likewise, it's never just one thing that causes health problems, but rather, a carefully choreographed dance of factors working in harmony within our body and being that creates the "ill-ness." Although we don't generally view health problems, or any kind of problems for that matter, as being "in harmony" with our welfare, it is a fact that bothersome, uncomfortable symptoms such as pain, fever, inflammation, and infection are actually doing us a favor.

"What? Are you kidding?" you're saying. It's true. These are nature's basic ways of trying to get our attention, letting us know that our equilibrium is off—that circumstances have tipped us over into an unbalanced inner ecosystem that impairs and impedes our body's normal functioning. Once again, this underscores the importance of observing and listening to our body and the clues and feedback it's constantly giving us.

The fact that conditions such as Candida are natural, predictable outgrowths of unwise lifestyle choices is not something we generally want to celebrate, but we should. We are all in charge of our bodies, and we were designed to be able to be in charge of our bodies. We have simply forgotten this.

REMEMBERING WHO WE ARE

So a big part of regaining and maintaining our own health and the potential for healthy longevity is remembering. That would include both "re-membering" our parts or our members as well as recollecting or "remembering" who we are. Often this involves helping our bodies to remember what a healthy state is by becoming conscious about and clearing away the blocks or distractions to hearing what our bodies are saying. Certainly when we've eaten too much, or consumed too much of the wrong kinds of foods, or eaten contaminated food that produces food poisoning, our body tells us loud and clear that something's wrong. The goal in regaining and maintaining health is to be sufficiently in touch with our internal workings, to know ourselves and our bodies well enough that we can sense when things just are not right. Most of us can already do this, but we may rather not listen.

Of course, the optimum goal is to respond to what the body says with lifestyle choices that promote good, functioning digestive and immune systems and good health, a margin or buffer of resiliency to shield us from disaster. Interestingly enough, the nutritional support that fermented foods offers creates an unexpected phenomenon in the "body talk" department. The body can actually "crave" or develop an appetite for what's good for it, even if the taste of the food is unfamiliar or even odd. "I can't believe how much better I feel since I started drinking kombucha (a traditional fermented tea drink)" says mother of two and Smart Foods Healthy Kids Chief of Belief, Kelly Corbet. "I just love how it makes me feel, so soothing, energizing," she says, her hand on her stomach. "It really helped me when I was nursing, boosting my energy and almost replacing the sleep I lost. It kind of takes a bit to get used to the taste, but now I actually crave it." Just one example of how your tastes can automatically change (in the direction of what your body needs, for the better) when you improve your diet with healthy and fermented foods.

You've no doubt heard it said that people take better care of their cars than their own bodies. Certainly, when your car starts making loud, radical noises, you pay attention. How about your own body? Do you listen to yours, especially when it's not screaming or clanking at you? The reality is, our bodies are always "talking" to us. Whether it is gas or creaky joints or the feeling of delight and deep satisfaction from eating a really delicious, nutritious meal, our physical bodies are continually giving us feedback.

> "Food is one part of a balanced diet."
>
> Fran Liebowitz

For example, have you ever been in a restaurant and noticed someone biting into a sandwich, then watch as they immediately itch the underside of their nose? This itching reaction may actually be the body announcing an allergy or sensitivity to wheat. But how many of us even notice or are conscious of the fact that this is a body signal, let alone register the connection that the body knows and is trying to communicate its own inability to handle this specific food?

The trick is in hearing what your body is really saying. Now it's true, an upset stomach can come from a number of sources. When my gut aches, was it too many doughnuts or the pain of guilt or resentment? There certainly is a big difference between an acquired craving for something like doughnuts or choco… now, wait a minute, don't even go there! We all know that chocolate is its own major food group—just leave it alone! So, back to the doughnuts…there is a big difference between an

acquired craving or appetite for doughnuts and the body's hunger or call for more nutritious spinach or beets. "Is there such a thing," you're saying "as a craving for spinach?" Maybe Popeye had it, but typically, in our culture, the sugary starch and the salt are the squeaky wheels that drown out or overshadow the body's many cries for what it needs.

Just another verification of the fact that, as a culture, we have really gotten out of touch with our body wisdom. I've said it before and I'll say it again: a tuned in, healthy body naturally hungers for what's good for it. Following our tongue alone, and eating only for taste or for other reasons, has obviously gotten us into a lot of trouble.

I've been saying this, in fact, since I was a green nutritional newbie in this business. As a recent graduate from Cornell University's esteemed Foods and Nutrition program, I was an organizer for the very first Earth Day in NYC back in 1970. Six years later, I was quoted in a lead article in the *Miami Herald*, saying, "We can't continue indulging our taste buds, eating anything and everything only for taste, and expect to live to a ripe old age." Now it's become an obvious reality.

Certainly, the perversion of our natural "sweet tooth" through a deluge of high-density, low-nutrient, chemically-altered and artificial sweeteners hasn't helped the situation. High-fructose corn syrup is now our number one sweetener. Researchers at the University of Georgia have demonstrated that because high-fructose corn syrup does not raise the blood sugar like regular table sugar or sucrose, it tends to promote a "the more you eat, the more you want" craving. Meanwhile, sucrose increases the production of insulin and the hormone leptin, which regulates appetite and fat storage. Natural sugars also suppress the hormone ghrelin, which signals feelings of satiety or fullness.

However, chemically derived fructose (as opposed to the natural sugar in fruit) does not chemically trip a switch to help suppress appetite. This is why some scientists are suspicious that high-fructose corn syrup is subtly but insidiously addictive, setting up a "forward feeding" response that fools the body into wanting more, instead of

and its corresponding moniker "The Staff of Life." You might say addicted. After all, modern refined, processed, high glycemic, sugary, starchy bread and bakery products (and soft drinks) are everywhere, outnumbering other nutrient-dense food choices such as whole, natural fruits and vegetables. And we've certainly dived into breads and other foods with gusto and abandon, gobbling and gulping them down insatiably.

Not only have we been taught and conditioned to view bread as the very mainstay of life, we have adopted this belief and have had years of consuming it day after day to reinforce this. So naturally, we have a powerful momentum, our bread habit, to overcome. *The Earl of Sandwich*, who popularized the world's worst food combination—a slab of meat slapped between two pieces of bread for the road—has made our mobile, eat-on-the-run culture possible. But some nutritionists think he should have had a V-8™.

These days the word bread carries many different meanings in our culture. And often, these aren't related to the original food itself. One of the classic definitions for bread is "something that nourishes; sustenance." Another definition, in line with our more expansive view, is "food in general, regarded as necessary for sustaining life." Frankly though, in my opinion, with the exception of a few wonderfully dark and nubbly, organic, artisan sourdough loaves, bread definitely "ain't what it used to be."

Today's mass-produced, spongy white bread is a pale reminder of the original hearty and life-sustaining food. Unfermented, it's practically an indigestible blob of starch. Did you know that the Egyptians were credited with making the first breads? You probably wouldn't have recognized their versions, because you would have been slurping them instead of buttering them. The first bread made by these Mediterranean dwellers was more liquid than solid, more like a thick beer than a solid loaf. That bread had life. In contrast, today's loaves…it's a *wonder* we've been able to subsist this long on them.

Meanwhile, beer is bread. Bread is beer. Even today, you can make bread from beer or beer and other fermented foods like kvass with bread—even with hard, leftover, stale bread you wouldn't feed your dog. You'll find recipes in Part II. The microorganisms, especially the yeast in traditionally

In our quest and dedication for achieving the perfect silhouette, that classic hard body, or optimum age-retardant health, have we lost our zeal and appreciation for the simple, delightful pleasures of eating really good food?

made bread and beer, are the same. They literally give it life.

So, if you're really sick or you're just plagued with that achy nagging feeling that you aren't as healthy as you know you should or could be, if you are craving breads or sweets, you very likely have a problem with Candida albicans. And you may find yourself going more than one day without bread. At least until you get your digestive system back in functioning order.

THE PLEASURES OF WINE AND CHEESE… AND BREAD

But ask this nutritionally-devoted author whose German heritage still keeps her salivating at the smell of just-out-of-the-oven bread, when will we be free to recapture the memory, the taste, and the sheer, abandoned joy of eating grandma's freshly baked homemade rye bread, drizzled with buckwheat honey, washed down with a cup of mint tea just before bedtime, while reminiscing with delight about the fun the family had that day raking the leaves or picking strawberries? Grandma knew what real culture meant.

When again, if ever, will we be able to do this? The answer: when we can slice off a warm, moist, freshly baked hunk of that savory, dark crusty whole grain bread, slather it with rich, creamery raw butter, nestling a pungent, soft, sticky wedge of grass-fed brie into the melting paradise and devour it—without thinking about calories, our bills, or tomorrow's carpool. When we can sit on our back porch, sipping the neighbors' homemade beer along with our friends, watching the sunset and planning who's going to be growing the opal basil for the pesto you'll all be so gratefully enjoying on your bruchetta next summer. When we can just be.

In our quest and dedication for achieving the perfect silhouette, that classic hard body, or optimum age-retardant health, have we lost our zeal and appreciation for the simple, delightful pleasures of eating really good food? In our double-duty, e-mail checking, TV watching, "take out" frenzy, have we missed the essence of what it means to be truly nurtured and nourished by our food? Does continual eating out of boredom or distraction or obsession or guilt or fear, instead of out of true hunger, blunt our ability to extract the pleasures and sustenance from food? Will our reluctance to simply stop, sit down, and eat—perhaps because the food itself is largely lifeless and uninteresting—eventually take us out?

In *The Yoga of Eating*, author Charles Eisenstein shares his experiences after a decade of dietary exploration and self-experimentation in the endless pursuit of the "perfect" diet. "I decided to try something different. Instead of trusting any outside authority, I would trust my own body—no matter what it lead me to. The decision opened up whole realms of realization and discovery about the untapped potential of the body and its senses, about the relationship between manner of eating and manner of being, and about the spiritual aspects of our corporeal selves."

"Most importantly," he continues," my practice, which is called *The Yoga of Eating*, freed me to enjoy, for the first time in memory, the uninhibited pleasure of food accompanied by a growing wellness and physical vitality." Eisenstein uses the word "yoga" in a very general, not a religious sense, to mean a practice that brings one into greater wholeness or unity. And his exercise seems to have liberated him.

UNLOCKING THE TRUE SECRETS TO HEALTH AND WELL BEING

In its simplest form, the word "health" means the absence of disease. Even as early as 1940, the World Health Organization (WHO) described health as the "state of complete physical, emotional, and social well-being, not merely the absence of disease or infirmity." Interestingly enough, considering the conservatism of this international health authority, this widely accepted definition was expanded in the 1970s and 1980s to include intellectual, environmental and spiritual health. The balance of all these components is based on the principle of self-responsibility.

This sounds like an excellent description. And it is actually quite enlightened, considering the source. Yet actually, there's a wide disparity and much lip service in the medical

In the final analysis, health is not a destination, but a journey.

establishment, embodied in this description, between the words and the reality. From the medical perspective, there is a sharp distinction between the terms disease prevention and health promotion. Disease prevention, according to the medical professionals, focuses on "protecting as many people as possible from the harmful consequences of a threat to health (e.g., through immunizations)" as quoted from the World Health Organization's website. Health promotion, on the other hand, "consists of the development of lifestyle habits which healthy individuals and communities can adopt to maintain and enhance the state of well-being. The ultimate goal is the optimization of health."

Yet, while the words acknowledge that the individual is responsible for his or her own health, the attitudes and the reality in hospitals and doctors' offices are actually quite different. Most practicing physicians don't have time or the inclination to assist the average person with nutrition or making necessary lifestyle changes. Furthermore, doctors are often overloaded with patients and feel a responsibility to get them in and out of the office with something that will address the immediate problem, a magic bullet, as it were—namely a drug—in the shortest time possible. Admittedly, the WHO itself, as well as standard dietitians and nutritionists, shows bias toward the remedial and therapeutic, even in its so-called nod to "preventive health." This international body, echoing the sentiments of the medical profession, sees preventive services being "fulfilled by health providers."

In the final analysis, health is not a destination, but a journey. It's what we do every day, not in sporadic bursts, that makes the ultimate difference in the quality of our life. The encouraging thing is that it is under your control. Change your mind; change your health. Likewise, if you change your habits, you can change your life.

You are more than just a mouth, just as you are more than just a bundle of habits. A favorite expression in my house is: You know you're not that body, i.e., you are more than just a human machine. You are the interaction of your body, your mind, your heart or emotions, and your spirit/soul. And even if you're not completely feeling like your "good old self," you're always more than just a container for Candida. Food, not drugs, is still the most dependable way of nourishing your body back to health. And that applies to fermented foods versus supplement sources for promoting healthy gut flora and immunity, as well. Besides, they're much more enjoyable to consume.

In the final analysis, though, nourishing yourself is as important as nourishing your body. Many things other than what we put into our mouths nourish us—the soft arch of a rainbow, the smell of a baby's skin, the nurturing glance of gratitude in our mother's smile.

But for many of us, undoubtedly and indisputably, true nourishment also includes savoring and enjoying the cornucopia of sinfully delicious, high calorie, and these days, almost verboten gourmet foods like bread and cheese, wine and beer. These are sacred victuals in our culinary emporium that just happen to be fermented and cultured, as well.

As fermented foods expert Sally Fallon pointedly asks us in her traditional foods bible, *Nourishing*

> After all, partaking in food, especially embodied in the savory, succulent, tantalizing flavors of our favorite cultured, fermented foods, is one of the penultimate acts of bliss. Eating is an act of love. Let's reconnect with our passion for eating only the best, the healthiest and the most delicious.

Traditions, "Could it be that by abandoning the ancient practice of lacto-fermentation, and insisting upon a diet in which everything has been pasteurized, we have compromised the health of our intestinal flora and made ourselves vulnerable to legions of pathogenic microorganisms?" Like the $2.97 gallon jars of dill pickles Vlasic sells at a loss at Wal-Mart, are we undermining our health, and even our economic well-being by our insistence on "more, faster, cheaper?" And who can deny the pure, unadulterated joy of diving into a batch of gooey macaroni and cheese, savoring the rich, creamy textures and indescribable flavors of melting brie or garlic chevre and a glass of Merlot, gorging on

caramel nut cheesecake with coffee or rich, tempting chocolate truffles? Is there anything more sensuous and delectable?

After all, partaking in food, especially embodied in the savory, succulent, tantalizing flavors of our favorite cultured, fermented foods, is one of the penultimate acts of bliss. Eating is an act of love. Let's reconnect with our passion for eating only the best, the healthiest and the most delicious.

To this food and nourishment scholar, cultured foods are the epitome, a virtual communion of flavor, nutrition and life, holding the promise of reconnecting us back to place and our source, replugging us back into who we truly are.

23

In the glossary that accompanies this book, you'll find a complete list of technical terms related to the fermentation and culturing process, and more in-depth discussion of the science of this process in Chapter 3, page 39. You can also find answers to some of the common questions about fermentation, such as those pertaining to rotting and alcohol, in the FAQs, page 37-38. Find community profiles of Fermentation at Work throughout the book. Lots of other useful info, including over 120 recipes for making and using fermented foods can be found in Part II along with Sources and Resources, and Notes on Ingredients and Equipment. For even more info, www.TrulyCultured.com

As a student I loathed history, at least the chronological dating part, and found any way I could to re-view and approach it from any other perspective than just a collection of facts. To my delight, I found that studying history from the perspective of food turned it into a fascinating and delightfully interesting topic. In fact, my favorite course, in pursuit of my Foods and Nutrition Degree at Cornell University, was the Cultural Aspects of Food and Nutrition.

Looking at the world and its development through the window of food and nutrition changed my attitude completely. Studying geography and classifying regions of the world by cooking oils instead of man-made boundaries, for instance, put a completely different light on the subject. Suddenly, history became exciting, giving new meaning and depth to the mundane focus on food for survival. Taking the time to understand human evolution from a culinary perspective, I have concluded, offers the potential to enrich our lives and impart wisdom that extends way beyond the facts and data we pull out to be able to converse intelligently. It can help us find our way.

AN AWESOME ASPECT

In many ancient cultures, fermentation was treated with a kind of respect and awe that is almost religious in quality. "This kind of reverence pervades indigenous and older societies. Each life form, whether a cactus, stone, or yeast, is viewed as an expression of the sacred, with its own intelligence, awareness and sacred nature."

As Jessica Prentice speculates, perhaps the Kingdom of God referred to in biblical texts, is likened to "leaven", the word describing the action of the sourdough that raises the bread and brew, because leaven is alive and sacred, and because leaven has its own intelligence that is, in itself, an expression of deity.

Or is it the reference to the magic and mystery of the process, which is something we can't see with the naked eye, can't easily measure, quantify or capture, or even really understand, but that is nevertheless completely real and true and potent?

Or perhaps its biblical reference and comparison with the Kingdom of God comes from the fact that it is something that uplifts, that brings lightness to man's being, ever pushing him heavenward to higher understanding and consciousness.

The mysteriousness of the message of the "Parable of the Leaven" in historical texts reminds us of the mystery of leavening itself. Perhaps that is the true message: like religion and spirituality, it is something we can marvel at, and experience, and know to be true, but in the end, it is and always will be a mystery.

OLDER THAN FIRE

One of my first surprising discoveries in college about the phenomenon of fermentation destroyed my long-held belief in man's early accomplishments. I was amazed to learn that fermentation, not fire, was likely man's first foray into the transformation of food we think about as "cooking."

This is natural for fermentation to be first, because it is a natural, transformative process that happens almost spontaneously when sugar and water, for example, get together in the right proportions and are left alone, even for a few hours. But even more surprising was another myth-buster I learned only recently about the same subject: it's entirely likely that *elephants*, not humans, were the first to discover fermentation. This, too, seems uncannily bizarre, but actually quite logical, when you think about it.

Mead, the first known of all the fermented beverages, is basically honey and water left to its own natural processes. Elephants were likely the first to experience this delight when, after a rain, these clever creatures discovered that hollowed out old logs used by bees as protection for their honey-filled hives became the source of a most enjoyable and entertaining beverage. Humans saw a good thing and followed.

> I was amazed to learn that fermentation, not fire, was likely man's first foray into the transformation of food we think about as "cooking."

FROM NATURE TO CULTURE: FERMENTED BEVERAGES

Ironically, surmises *Wild Fermentation* author Sandor Katz, fermented beverages may well have been one of the primary incentives for man's transition from being a nomad to taking up life as a more settled, sedentary creature. This is because fermented beverages, for the most part, require time and stable conditions to produce in any quantity. So it's entirely possible that such beverages could have been a powerful impetus for our ancestors settling down to live in one place. Here, we see a recurring reference to fermentation as a major brick in the foundation of man's evolution and development.

According to *History of Food* author Maguelonne Tousssaint-Samat, mead, "the child of honey, the drink of the gods," was so universal that it can rightfully be called the ancestor of all fermented drinks. Honey ale, the common name for mead, was popular for thousands of years, enduring longer in countries where grapes did not grow and grains for ale-making were sparse.

Indeed, cultural historians like anthropologist Claude Levy Strauss equate the practice of making mead with humanity's transition from nature to culture. Human knowledge of fermentation actually existed long before history was being recorded, but the origins of employing it to produce beverages and food are lost somewhere in antiquity. There are indications, though few written records, that the art of culturing fermented foods originated in PreVedic times in the Great Indus Valley of India, between 9,000 and 10,000 B.C.

Artifacts from Egypt and the Middle East suggest that fermentation was known from ancient times in that region of the world as well. The Egyptians, credited with originating beer, believed that Osiris, god of agriculture, actually gifted man with the precious beverage. According to Egyptian myths, one day Osiris made a concoction of barley germinated from the sacred waters of the Nile, got distracted, and forgot it. Returning to the crock sitting in the sun, he discovered that the fermented liquid inside was so good that he bequeathed it to mankind for fun and profit. The Egyptians subsequently perfected the process of producing beer and became famous for their export brews.

Early clay tablets carrying some of the most ancient texts in the world, that were found in what is now Iraq or lower Mesopotamia, tell the story of the Sumerians who settled there and became good at farming in the Tigris-Euphrates River valley after The Great Flood. In a story very similar to the Old Testament record, Gilgamesh, the Sumerian equivalent of Noah, is quoted as saying that he gave the workmen building his ark "ale and beer to drink, oil and wine, as if they were river water." These beer makers dating back nearly 5,000 years worshipped Ninkasi, goddess of beer.

Babylonians, whose great civilization followed the Sumerians, left us the first true written recipes for making beer from barley and wheat. They were obviously sophisticated with this process because their records are very explicit about specific harvesting and soaking procedures and the importance of using the purest possible water.

Babylonian beer was cloudy, thick, and soupy. Edible beer? Drinkable bread? This led to the saying "beer is bread, bread is beer." Pliny mentions sauerkraut in his *Natural History* but also comments about the Iberians and Gauls, who used the froth skimmed off the top of fermenting beer to make bread without sourdough starter.

JOHNNY-COME-LATELY: GRAINS AND DAIRY

The Babylonians were also apparently masters at producing fermented milk, for their archives reveal a highly developed system for animal husbandry and souring of milk products. Cultured milk products with names ranging from dahi, kumis, yogurt, buttermilk, and leben have been produced by almost every civilization, but a great many were developed by nomadic Asian cattle breeders. The ancient nomadic Turks, it is believed, first made yogurt, although Chomakow and others attribute its origins to the Balkans. But no matter under what names, where or how they first emerged, fermented milks have been one of the most ubiquitous of all cultured foods.

To put things into perspective, the absence of early records or artifacts from South Asia, compared to substantial documentation of Neolithic cultures from 6,000 B.C. in the Near East, Central Asia, and even Africa, has lead to overemphasis on the latter's cultural practices, including the processing of grains and dairy products. Lest we reinforce the myth that grains and dairy products have dominated our foodways forever, the reality is they have only been consumed in any quantity for under 10,000 years, a mere blip in the screen of humanity's existence.

We have to remember that for roughly two million years prior to the dawn of civilization, Homo Sapiens existed on a Paleolithic diet. Nomadic

hunter-gatherers, Paleolithic humans primarily ate meats, seeds, nuts, fruits, and greens, whatever and wherever available. Cultivation of grains and domestication of animals happened gradually, as people discovered multiple uses and benefits for the labor involved. Interestingly enough, the word "culture" itself, with its many meanings and connotations, is derived from the Latin *colere*, which means to cultivate.

And while dairy products were some of the early cultured foods, these were often first prescribed as medications. Butter was used for burns and other conditions by the Egyptians. Dairy products such as soured and fermented milks were prescribed by the Roman historian Plinio for stomach and intestinal problems, even as a spermicide.

Of course, in the cradle of civilization and before the advent of refrigeration, warm, moist conditions hastened the process of fermentation, so it's no surprise that most milk products were consumed soured or "clabbered." And certainly no less surprising, in that they were thus more digestible. Is this possibly why we read almost nothing in historical records about dairy being consumed in its fresh state?

So man's diet certainly wasn't low on carbohydrates, but grains and dairy were latecomers in our dietary repertoire. Considering their history and anti-nutrients, it's logical that these foods would not have survived this long had they not been fermented. Through long periods of trial and error, people from many diverse cultures learned that grains and dairy had properties that created too many digestive and other disturbances, and unless fermented were not conducive to optimum health and long life. This is a lesson we have forgotten, and to our own peril. The effect, evidenced by the degenerative diseases plaguing the planet, is that we've inadvertently sawed off the proverbial limb we are standing on.

While many tend to think of fermented dairy as one of the primary and original types of fermented foods, it appears from recent archeological findings that early man had alternative sources for prebiotics to promote intestinal health. The Chinese and a few other civilizations, for example, never adopted milk products into their culture at all, although they fermented a number of other foods, including beans, nuts, rice, and fish.

In *The Prehistory of PreBiotics*, paleobioticist Jeff Leach demonstrates the widespread consumption of tubers such as onions and agave, high in the nutrient inulin, the most extensively studied of the indigestible prebiotic carbohydrates. Leach illustrates, "studies have shown that inulin-rich plants dominated the dietary intake of our ancestors in various regions from the African SubSahara to the American Southwest dating back tens of thousands of years." In fact, as much as 60 percent of caloric intake may have come from such sources, as the presence of huge numbers of massive stone ovens used to roast these roots to make the inulin more available proves that not only did these people know about the importance of prebiotics for health, they were numerous enough to be called; inulin farmers."

RICH HISTORY OF FOODS TRANSFORMED BY CULTURING

The history of foods transformed by culturing is rich and way more voluminous than space or time permits sharing here. Chronologically, the earliest types of fermented foods were mead, beer, wine, leavened bread, and cheeses. These were soon followed by East Asian fermented foods, yogurt and other fermented milk products, pickles, sauerkraut, vinegar, butter and a host of traditional alcoholic beverages. Cultured meats and fish, from Chinese fish sauces and pastes through a wide variety of European cured sausages and other charcuterie, developed in tandem with settlement, growth in agriculture, and mechanization. Our beloved spices, chocolate, tea, and coffee delicacies were discovered in remote lands after massive sailing ships enabled global exploration.

As civilization grew, so did the sophistication of production methods. The Middle Ages saw more cultivation of fermented foods on a mass scale, including breads and alcoholic beverages. Through the Middle Ages, honey was the sweetener of choice, although figs, dates, grapes, and even occasionally sugarcane, as well as grains, were used both as sweetener and as substrate or basis for fermentation.

But not surprising in a way, it has consistently been women who were the master breweresses.

By the time the settlers were making their way across the North American continent, fermentation was commonly used to preserve and augment many foods. Rows of tasseled corn, signaling the edge of the frontier, were routinely turned into hogs and whiskey to increase the value of the crop to market. Pork and venison were the most common meats, invariably dried, brined, or cured.

Beer was very popular in the colonies. Even children drank it as a beverage with breakfast, lunch, and dinner up until about 1825. But cider—mostly apple, but other types as well, including pear and peach—was this fledgling nation's favorite beverage. It was cheap and plentiful and also yielded a most delightfully intoxicating beverage for quaffing hefty, hardworking thirsts. Tea, coffee, and chocolate, the last of the fermented beverages that made their way into the civilized markets of Europe after Columbus and DaGama's voyages, were brought by those who could afford them to the New World. Their expense and exclusivity both stoked and symbolized the revolutionary protests over taxation at Boston Harbor.

ALCHEMICAL TRACINGS: THE PHILOSOPHER'S STONE

Widespread industrialization of fermented foods was not possible until the process could be accurately understood. So it wasn't until Anthony Van Leeuwenhoek demonstrated the use of the microscope and the presence of microorganisms in the 1600s that the scientific basis of the process was revealed.

Before this time, alchemy played a significant role in many cultures, as the state-of-the-art knowledge or discipline for explaining the mysteries of the universe. Alchemists were the first to set up real chemical laboratories in which they worked out many of the basic methods still being used in the modern lab. Many were distinguished scholars, doctors, clerics, and scientists (even Roger Bacon was reportedly among them). Like shamanic predecessors to the modern physician, alchemists were the forerunners of our modern chemists.

We find the subject of fermentation mentioned early in alchemical writings, in the context of the search for the elusive Philosopher's Stone, a key or prized activator in the alchemy process. The basic tenents of alchemy held that all metals can be transformed into one another through a series of chemical operations, based on Aristotle's principle of prime matter. Alchemists believed that metals were closely related to each other based on and emanating from common "vapors," alternate but intertwined planes or phases of existence. Other systems, such as the Asians', had similar archetypes acknowledging energetic dichotomies such as fire, water, air, earth, wood and metal. The idea was that these elements could be changed into each other through transmutation by certain procedures with the help of the Philosopher's Stone, also envisioned as an elusive elixir or potion that acted as a fermenter or catalyst in the process. The Philosopher's Stone acted in the same way that the leaven or yeasts, the essence of fermentation, hastened and initiated the making of bread or the brewing of beer. The process of fermentation was supposed to have a purifying and elevating effect on the bodies involved. This precisely mirrors the physical act of fermentation.

ALCHEMICAL ANALOGIES

It's interesting that both medicine and alchemy flourished alongside each other in the Middle Ages. Yet the leading medical elite, students of life, seemed to have more interest in the ability of the Philosopher's Stone to cure disease than, as purported, in its ability to turn base metals into gold. For this they were aptly ridiculed and marginalized by the encroaching leagues of reductionists, followers of the mechanistic worldview espoused by René Descartes.

The key point about the alchemists and the Philosopher's Stone that is and has been so consistently missed—even today when viewed from the strictly bottom line, mechanistic, reductionist, chemical/physics viewpoint that is so rampant in modern science—is that the process of turning metals into gold was really an analogy, a mirror of spiritual principles–identical invisible processes– nevertheless happening on other, imperceptible levels of existence.

This is a very important principle for understanding arcane, but nevertheless applicable knowledge, including the alchemist's dictum "As Above, So Below, As Inside, So Outside" that can be extrapolated and applied to the larger current worldview.

SOLVING A GREAT MYSTERY: A VITAL QUESTION

For millennia, fermentation was regarded as a mystic, mysterious life force, until Western science attempted to analyze and explain it, which resulted in a huge and prolonged debate in scientific and medical circles.

The ancient theory of spontaneous generation, espoused by Pliny the Elder and long held back in time by the Romans, was first used to explain the phenomenon of fermentation and other natural processes. This theory held that life forms could spontaneously and independently generate or arise by themselves, out of decomposing material, without the involvement of any reproductive process. This theory was even used to try to create mice out of wheat and other bizarre replications.

The alchemist's view, characterized as *vitalism* and based on the teachings of Hippocrates, sharply contradicted this. These proponents of vitalism maintained that living organisms owed their existence to a "vital principle" or life force—called chi, ki, or prana–in different cultures, and that this life force was distinct though not separate from physical and chemical forces. Essentially, they maintained that life processes were not explainable simply by the laws of chemistry and physics alone, and held the view that the spiritual cannot be separated from the scientific. Life is interconnected and the whole is greater than the sum of its parts.

Essentially the debate that raged on for years circled around whether the process of fermentation, now becoming increasingly important with the rise of commercial breweries and bakeries, involved live or dead organisms. Gradually, the members of the scientific community in Europe during the eighteenth and early nineteenth centuries had begun to recognize that yeast was a living organism. But how it functioned remained a controversy.

Meanwhile, paralleling the rise in scientific explorations during this time, René Descartes had started promoting his remarkable new view that all natural phenomena could be relegated to mere mechanical processes, paving the way for an era of "chemical reductionism."

Once the microscope was discovered, chemists of the day fully recognized the presence of what were called "animacules" in fermentation, but basically chose to ignore their significance. The German chemist Joseph Von Liebig, a nineteenth-century pioneer in the development of chemical fertilizers, led the fray, staunchly maintaining superiority of the chemical over the biological.

"Most contemporary biologists and other scientists still take it for granted that living organisms are nothing but complex machines, governed only by the known laws of physics and chemistry," points out Rupert Sheldrake, author of *A New Science of Life*, a researcher in the fields of morphic resonance, a holistic, qualitative, and quantitative scientific theory that is starting to put a foundation on the alchemist's vitalism. This new paradigm discipline disputes that everything in the universe can be explained from the bottom up, recognizes the existence of organized hierarchies at every level of existence that cannot be understood in isolation, and validates, through quantum physics and biological sciences, that the whole really is greater than the sum of its parts.

Assuming, as author Sheldrake says, that you somehow have all the chemicals, and know all the sequences and the precise timing of the many processes involved, you still can't create life. You can't create life in the test tube without having the blueprint of another previous life form to start with.

PASTEUR PARTS THE WATERS AND MICROBES GARNER THE NOBEL PRIZE

Louis Pasteur, whose name became the root word for pasteurization, was a chemist living in nineteenth-century France. He conclusively showed that bacteria cause souring of milk. His investigations into the process of fermentation, funded by an industrialist in Lille who hired Pasteur to solve problems in his beet root plant, led to revolutionary discoveries and eventually the development and adoption of his general germ theory of infectious disease. This theory essentially maintains that the body is sterile and that specific external micro beings invade the body and cause specific diseases.

Pasteur's methodical study of beet root fermentation contradicted the chemistry establishment's dominant view at the time that fermentation was primarily a chemical rather than a biological process. Pasteur successfully established once and for all that lactic acid fermentation is caused by living organisms, opening up new vistas in the fields of biochemistry, microbiology, and fermentation.

Unfortunately, Pasteur also incorrectly identified fermentation as "life without air" and produced some other generally unpublicized disasters. His "Silk Worm Cure" cut the production of silk in half, and his rabies vaccines in Europe were nothing less than disastrous. In 1956, the *Journal of the American Medical Association* reported that the Academy of Medicine in France found that Pasteur's rabies vaccinations "may be followed as much as 20 years later with a rare form of psychosis." But this wasn't all Pasteur apparently got wrong.

Meanwhile, progress was being made in the lab, and in 1897, German chemist Eduard Buechner showed that even dead, ground-up yeast was capable of fermenting sugar solution, producing carbon dioxide and alcohol. Essentially, Buechner was cracking the code to proving the existence of the enzyme. Buechner won the Nobel Prize in 1907 in chemistry, opening up a new era in the studies of enzymes and fermentation. While his discoveries were significant, the honor, as we will see, went to the wrong man.

Most of us have been conditioned to believe in Pasteur's germ theory of disease. After all, it's been drummed into us again and again that we need to be worried about germs. This perspective, summed up by health pioneer J.I. Rodale and aptly described in an *Idaho Observer* article, is simply: "Germs live in the air, and every once in a while get into the human body, multiply and cause illness. Nothing to it at all. All you have to do is kill germs and disease is licked."

Yet, as we have said, germs and bacteria are everywhere. If Pasteur's theory of invading disease carriers is true, why doesn't everyone get sick?

The fact is that germs are not the enemy; they are responsive soldiers who come in to clean up the dead and dying members on the battlefield. They are drawn to and rally around diseased tissue. Pressed into service, bacteria digest or break down dead matter—not live, healthy tissue. Same with pests, they don't attack healthy plants, they are attracted to and invade the weak plants in the field, the ones that don't have proper nutrients or have become devitalized. This puts new light on the fact that we currently have such a problem with pests in our food production and distribution system, a problem that is getting consistently worse, not better. All the time, this is reflecting the adaptability of microorganisms and their hosts to morph into forms that help them survive even bombardment with lethal poisons.

In fact, bacteria and germs are actually trying to help organisms survive. Highly adaptive, changing in response to the pH or terrain of the environment, their adaptive capacity is one of their essential strengths, and is an analogous key to understanding the integrated processes of life on this planet.

THE OVERLOOKED AND UNPUBLISHED

In the mid 1800s, Western medical science was faced with the choice of taking one of two paths. Focus and emphasis on the figure or the ground, the germ or the environment. It's becoming increasingly clear, based on the proliferation of lifestyle-induced degenerative diseases today, that our scientific experts have us going down the wrong one.

As we've seen, Pasteur is credited with discovering and proving that microorganisms were the basic catalysts in fermentation. Though a scientist, he had no background in life sciences, yet interestingly enough was given the credit for the germ theory of disease, which has become the basis of modern medicine. However, Pasteur was not the only scientist studying this phenomenon at this time in history, nor were these discoveries entirely his.

Antoine Béchamp, whose name almost no one recognizes, was a contemporary of Pasteur's in France. A genius of considerable accomplishment, Béchamp was a Master of Pharmacy, Doctor of Science, Doctor of Medicine, Fellow and Professor of Physics in Medicine and Toxicology at the Higher School of Pharmacy in Strasbourg, Professor of Medical Chemistry and Pharmacy at the University of Montpelier, and Professor of Biological Chemistry and Dean of Faculty of Medicine at the University of Lille.

Béchamp, through years of work and experiments, actually solved the mystery of fermentation, though he never received the credit due him for identifying it as a process of digestion

All parts of the natural, cyclical patterns of life and death, the survival of the fittest, the revolution of the seasons, are ultimately embodied and mirrored in the process of fermentation. One man's meat is another's poison. One animal is food for another— exactly what happens in the etiology of life cycles involved in the fermentation process. Fermentation is the part of the natural life cycle process that accelerates or completes the breakdown of waning life back into the elements, back to the soil. Ashes to ashes and dust to dust.

and adaptation by microorganisms. Ironically, in a book aptly titled *The Enigma of Ferment*, written by noted microbiologicalist Ulf Lagerkvist, there is not one mention of the works or significant discoveries of Antoine Béchamp, his day may yet come.

Béchamp's theory maintained that every living thing rose from what he termed microzymas (tiny enzymes), the fundamental units of the corporeal organism or the body, the indestructible part of the cell we now associate with the bacteriophage that change and adapt in response to their environment or cellular terrain. With innate intelligence that communicates genetic information to the cell, these tiny entities respond to produce either life-giving or death-giving pathogens, depending on the pH of the cellular terrain. In healthy cells, the microzymas provoke harmonious aerobic fermentation, such as grapes fermenting into wine or beneficial gut flora proliferating through fermentation in the gut wall. In a diseased condition, characterized by low oxygen, malnutrition, acidic pH, stress, and built-up toxins, the microzymas signal the cells to accelerate the breakdown process, returning the beyond-repair cells back "to the dust" to complete the life cycle.

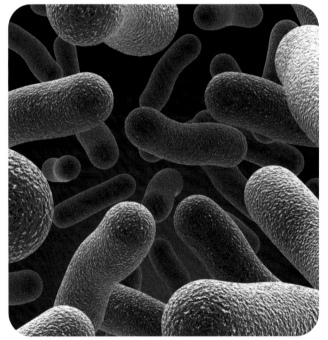

Béchamp's investigations and scientific mind unraveled the mystery of both fermentation and the disease process, showing that it isn't the bacteria or viruses themselves that produce disease; they are an aftermath of diseased tissues. Germs respond, change, or evolve into yeasts, molds, viruses, fungi, and other morbid microforms that eat away at the necrotic tissue, acting as a clean-up crew. Germs don't produce the disease any more than mosquitoes cause a stagnant swamp or rats create garbage, notes

research scientist Gary Tunsky in *The Battle for Health Is Over pH*.

Béchamp's theory placed all of the responsibility for disease prevention on the individual and his lifestyle. Ideally, individuals themselves should be charged with the responsibility and empowered with the ability to proactively resist disease by taking care of themselves. Unfortunately and practically, there was no money to be made from this approach.

Pasteur's theory (with the emphasis on theory), on the other hand, took power away from the individual and shifted it to outside experts like doctors and drug companies who could "take care of" the inevitable problems that would arise from abdicating responsibility for individual health.

Béchamp was a quiet, humble man who eschewed the limelight and painstakingly went on about pursuing his work quietly, while Pasteur, an inveterate crusader, became more and more popular—using Béchamp's discoveries, including fermentation, as his own. Pasteur, it turns out, had "borrowed" Béchamp's earlier discoveries about micro beings and the nature of life and presented them as his own—but with flawed understanding—to the French Academy of Science. While Béchamp's careful observations led him to understand that the condition of the medium or the terrain—the environment of the body or test tube or plant—determines whether or not microorganisms are present and operative, Pasteur, unfortunately, missed this critically important fact.

Coupled with his popularity and the powerful financial and political influence Pasteur had over Béchamp, this led to the cover up of Béchamp's work and the adoption of Pasteur's germ premise as the "law of the medical land," a theory that medical researcher Peter G. Tocci and others have called "extremely lucrative, yet superficial and dangerous." "Western medical science went along with Pasteur's theory because it opened the door to creating the more profitable tract, laying the foundation for growth of the world's medical and pharmaceutical industries," says Dr. Blaze Welch of Sandpoint, Idaho. Since this time back in the mid 1850s, there has been an unswerving bent on developing new drugs to attack and kill the "disease invaders." The result has been an epidemic of cancer, sickness, and degenerative diseases—at once catered to by and spawning a very rich and powerful pharmaceutical industry, with the highest profit margins of any industry today, even oil.

In 1998 alone, the pharmaceutical industry grossed $182 billion in drug sales worldwide. Yet, it took approximately $183 billion to treat adverse reactions from all those drugs, Welch notes. Today $275 billion dollars are spent on pharmaceuticals, which average, as an industry, 19% profit margins, compared to 5% for the rest of the Fortune 500. "We are miserably losing the battle against viruses and bacteria. Antibiotics, pesticides, and herbicides are not working. We need to take a different tack, because this approach is obviously NOT working," he concludes.

In both cases, the bacteria and the pests are predictably doing their thing, if you understand them from Béchamp's holistic perspective, morphing and adapting as they are so good at, trying to clean up the increasingly toxic world that has become a reality inside and outside our bodies.

The British Medical Journal has stated that only one percent of all scientific research papers that

> Béchamp's investigations and scientific mind unraveled the mystery of both fermentation and the disease process, showing that it isn't the bacteria or viruses themselves that produce disease; they are an aftermath of diseased tissues. His observations led him to understand that the condition of the medium or the terrain – the environment of the body or test tube or plant – determines whether or not microorganisms are present and operative. Pasteur, unfortunately, missed this critically important fact.

explore medicine are scientifically sound. So, if this is also true, then not only are allopathic doctors with their self-created (iatrogenic) diseases incorrect in their understanding of the basic nature of disease, they are basing 99 percent of their conclusions—therefore their diagnoses and treatment of their patients—on flawed science.

On his deathbed, Pasteur admitted that Béchamp and his disciple, Claude Bernard, were right. Acknowledging that he had usurped his colleague's work, he admitted that in his ignorant zeal he had incorrectly interpreted and applied this essential knowledge: the germ is nothing, the cellular terrain is everything. But few heard this confession. The path was already set.

Fermentation's Many Functions and Benefits

FUNCTION	DESCRIPTION	SOME EXAMPLES	BENEFITS
Preservation	"Bi-preservatives" that retain nutrients and prevent spoilage of perishable raw materials	Lactic and acetic acid, alcohol from grains and other starches, dairy, vegetables, fruits, meats, fish, poultry	Low cost, energy efficient method to increase food shelf life, safety and security;
Flavor Enhancement	Development of unique and savory flavors; improves bland tastes and mellows sharp flavors	cheese, wine, sausages, sauerkraut,	Improves taste, texture, edibility, enjoyment of most prized foods
Reduction in Anti Nutrients	Breakdown of allergens and other factors that impede digestion	Phytates, gluten, in grains; noxious bacteria in intestines;	Increase digestive health and immunity
Digestion/ Predigestion	Presence of digestive enzymes which breakdown foods	Carbohydrates such as those in grains, Proteins such as casein, gluten in milk and dairy products; curing stomach aches, diarrhea	Increases digestibility and absorbability of these foods, especially by lacto or gluten sensitive individuals
Nutrient Availability	Increases availability/bio-availability of beneficial nutrients, ionized simple sugars and minerals	Amino acids, vitamins B & C, minerals	Increases absorption of nutrients, decreases bone loss
Nutrition Enhancement	Synthesis and enhancement of essential amino acids and vitamins	B vitamins, Vitamin B-12, Vitamin C, anti-oxidants, Hydrogen peroxide	Improved transport of oxygen, immunity, health and well-being, feeling good.
Prebiotics and Probiotics/ Functional Foods	Increasing good bacteria and/or improving conditions for their growth	Live lacto-fermented cultured foods such as Kefir, yoghurt, kombucha, acidophilus or bifidus supplements, inulin	Promotes and enhances gut health/ protect the intestinal mucosa, prevent diarrhea and constipation
Detoxification	Beneficial microbes breakdown unwanted or dangerous pathogens and contaminants,	Food and water, GIT, "bad bacteria", oil spills, toxic waste, other contaminants	Purifies and preserves foods, beverages, and things in the environment;
Immunity	Lactic acid bacteria inhibit pathogenic organisms	Reduce putrefactive bacteria, help white blood cells fight disease	Improve digestive function and health of intestines, immunity
Salvage of Waste Foods	Transformation of raw, unusable and/or manufactured by-products	Soy akara, coconut and peanut meal, groundnut meal, tapioca waste, fruit peelings, bones, hides, loc	Increase access to quantity and quality of foodstuffs available for consumption; improve accessibility of foods for low income populations
Production of both Food and Fuel	Fermenting grain for ethanol, then feeding to livestock	corn, barley in beer production	resource efficiency, more digestibility, less entropy
Seed for Community Development	fermenting and culturing are ideal activities for small groups or food circles, sharing products	sauerkraut, salsa, natural sodas, kombucha, cheese, sourdough breads	easier and more efficient, accomodates busy lifestyles, healthier local food, fun and fellowship
Archetype for Cooperative Co-existence	reexamining our relationship with microbes	shift from germ warfare to Gaia theory	more peace, harmony, appreciation for the community of all life

Frequently Asked Questions

What's the difference between fermented and lacto-fermented foods?

Fermentation happens spontaneously under the right conditions when sugars or starches and water such as in fresh fruit are left to their own devices. But not all fermentations are created equal. Lacto-fermented foods, a regular part of human food since prehistoric times, are produced through pH lowering lactic-acid fermentation by lactobacillus bacteria, stimulated by such agents as salt, whey and wild yeasts from the air. Also called live cultured foods, these are vital foods, still containing health promoting bacteria that have not been destroyed by heat or chemicals that help to replenish and maintain healthy gut flora and digestion. Pasteurization kills these beneficial bacteria.

Much fermentation today is classified as industrial fermentations, produced by yeasts such as baker's or brewer's yeast. These are more alkaline, alcoholic fermentations producing carbon dioxide and alcohol, such as in many commercial beer and breads. While microorganisms, namely yeasts, are the active agents, they are not like the healthy live lacto bacteria.

Don't all fermented foods produce alcohol?

Not all fermented foods have alcohol. Fermentation of starches and sugars can produce alcohol, but usually and primarily during the secondary or later stages of the process, from other associated microorganisms, such as when the larger yeasts get involved. So, naturally fermented yogurts and sourdough starter would contain the live and healthful lacto bacteria, whereas commercial beer and breads leavened with yeast would produce the not so healthful, but entertaining alcohol.

What is the difference between fermention and rotting?

Fermentation is a natural breakdown process, where starches and sugars in the presence of water are converted to carbon dioxide, water and lactic acid or alcohol. Rotting or putrefaction is a similar disintegration process that happens with protein products like meat.

Why make cultured foods at home when I can just buy probiotic pills like acididophilus in a health food store?

Expense, for one. A typical one month's supply of high quality probiotics in a health or natural food store (with 50 billion active bacteria) can cost $50 dollars or more, compared with the pennies it costs to create your own natural probiotics by making simple sauerkraut or yogurt in your own kitchen or food circle. Research studies show that you get a lot more benefits from eating the foods than from taking pills or capsules. Besides, with current, unsustainable, unpredictable fuel oil supplies and encroaching international food regulations, there's no guarantee we'll continue to enjoy access to supplements. Learning how, getting into the habit of making homemade cultured foods may be the only way you'll be able to acquire the healthy probiotics you absolutely need to insure your immune health.

I thought all sauerkraut was good for you. What's wrong with regular commercial pickles and sauerkraut available in supermarkets?

While many of our favorite foods are cultured, not all are equally healthy. Commercial fermented foods are pasteurized, and are required to be if they are shipped across state lines. Only a few states currently permit distribution of raw processed foods like milk, cheese or sauerkraut. Pasteurization kills the beneficial lacto-bacteria, one of the most important benefits of these traditionally fermented foods.

Making pickles and sauerkraut? I'm really busy. These fermented foods will take a lot of time and energy, won't they?

You might be surprised to find out how very simple and easy it is to make your own cultured foods. While some are complex with many steps, like aged cheeses, many are unbelievably simple to produce at home, only requiring time – a few hours, days or weeks on their own – to go through the fermentation or culturing process and be ready to eat.

Fermentation at Work

Great Lakes Brewing Company

Pat and Dan Conway have successfully created another living, breathing "food circle" on their way to creating the perfect beer. Owners of Great Lakes Brewing Company, one of Cleveland's simultaneously hottest and most sustainable establishments, the Conway brothers have managed to create a successful local microbrewery and popular "meet and eat" establishment on the shores of Lake Erie that exemplifies their commitment to sustainable business and lifestyle, delicious food and distinguished brew.

What they've created is a closed loop system, an integrated brewery and natural farming system that mirrors natural ecologies, even though this is clearly a business entity. And although this has developed and evolved since its founding in 1988, Great Lakes Brewing has become a seed around which a whole local, food community that's not only environmentally aware, but committed to achieving a zero waste operation, has and continues to develop.

The brewery and restaurant itself were built retrofitting an old building that has become part of the revitalization of the downtown area. The business operates cycling energy and air for cooling and heating through a cogeneration system with a natural gas and biodiesel generation back up plant, produced further using grains in their brewing process. They also supply "spent" grains to Zoss, their local spent grain bakery to produce cracked barley beer bread and pretzels for their menu, to a local vermiculture operation producing sustainable fertilizer, a local mushroom grower for producing the shitake and oyster mushrooms they use in their restaurant, and to local organic farmers who feeds the transformed grains to livestock, producing the natural and organic beef, pork, chicken and cheese they serve. They use the "low fills" in their ice creams and soups, and get their organic vegetables for GLBC Brewpub from Kentucky Gardens, their innovative, passive solar-powered greenhouse, and weekly vegetable baskets from the local Common Ground community garden project.

"Besides, our beer delivery truck and "fatty wagon" shuttle to the fair run virtually free fuel on recycled cooking oil processed by one of our subsidiaries, Burning River fuels, which filters waste cooking oil and sells the fuel back to us and others" says Mark Hunger, manager of Brewing and Quality Control. "In terms of carbon footprint, the carbon is grown the year before instead of thousands of years before…"

"In terms of being a marketing tool, without a doubt people patronize our business and the restaurant because of our commitment to sustainability, which was one of the main reasons we started this place," Hunger continues, having just described the big all day music and environmental festival Great Lakes just sponsored the weekend before, outdone only by their annual Burning River Fest. But of all the things they do, their outstandingly delicious beer is tops, a Great American Beer Festivals gold medal winner 7 times.

Great Lakes Brewing Company
2516 Market Avenue, Cleveland, Ohio 44113
216-771-4404 www.greatlakesbrewing.com

People all over the world have been using microorganisms—bacteria, yeasts, and molds—for centuries to produce a wide variety of fermented foods. A literal testimony to the wonders of the world teems beyond the naked eye–From butter, sour cream, and yogurt, to pickles, sauerkraut, sausage, and cheese–these small creatures are responsible for creating the world's favorites foods.

And the list is extensive. There are over 80 types of foods throughout the world that reap their character and popularity from the mysterious process of fermentation. Most people probably don't realize that many common and favorite foods, including bread, butter, and beer, coffee, tea and chocolate, whiskey and wine, soy sauce and spices, as well as a host of weird, not always appealing concoctions, count themselves in the category of cultured or fermented foods.

But the fact that they are found all over the world—sometimes with only a different name—shows that these foods are universally acknowledged and utilized. Cultured, fermented foods and beverages now make up a large and important part of the food industry. Next to alcoholic beverages, fermented milk products such as yogurt are the largest sector of the industry, accounting for about 20 percent of all fermented foods worldwide.

And, according to growing consensus of experts in the field, the importance of cultured or fermented foods will only continue to grow. As we recoup and access more ancient and indigenous knowledge, as well as learn to identify more microorganisms and technologies that can be adopted for mass and small-scale commercialization, we increase the potential for meeting the growing quantitative and qualitative food needs of the world.

Even the technical and scientific community acknowledges the vast wealth of knowledge on the subject much of which is indigenous and still undocumented passed down in oral tradition through the generations and the centuries. From the production of new probiotics and other functional neutraceuticals, through the reclamation of nutrient-rich wastes and sources of new, ecologic, economic biofuels, the ancient world of fermented foods continues to open new vistas for improving the quality of life in the future.

WHAT EXACTLY IS FERMENTATION?

We've discussed the benefits of fermentation, as well as its speckled history, but what exactly is fermentation? Actually, man's first foray into preserving foodstuffs was dehydration, drying the captured beast or excess berries in the sun. The second oldest method of preservation was fermentation, a natural biological process that was probably, as we have seen, in use even before primitive man discovered how to use fire.

Various common and technical definitions have been developed for the fermentation process, based on the prevailing knowledge on the subject at the time. Technically, fermentation is a chemical transformation of various organic materials into smaller compounds by enzyme catalysts produced by microorganisms such as bacteria, molds, and yeasts. This is a biochemical process, brought about by anaerobic (without air) or partially anaerobic (reduced air) oxidation of carbohydrates.

The word fermentation itself is derived from the Latin verb *fervere*, meaning "to boil," probably because the bubbling, gurgling action of the process resembles boiling liquid. It is very likely that the first fermentations were a combination of trial and error, accidents evolving out of the need to preserve food for later consumption. Impure salt or sea water were probably used to promote development of the characteristic acid conditions required for the process, although it's unlikely those doing the experimenting had any real understanding about what was causing these reactions.

Lacking knowledge about the process, the tiny creatures that aided it, or how to control it, early man essentially just learned to live with foods infected by microbes. Often this meant dealing with foods with unacceptable appearance, slightly off or even rank foul odors, rendering the would-be edibles into everything from unappealing to downright dangerous to eat. Frequently these reactions produced toxins, some of which we know were lethal. Probably only occasionally did these "infections," by tiny microorganisms (that could be neither seen nor detected) produce beneficial changes, actually improving the looks, texture, and, most importantly, the taste of many foodstuffs.

Likewise, human beings themselves were also evolving, adapting to live and coexist with the microbes in their environment. At some point, they two worlds morphed together. That's when the symbiosis we enjoy or endure with these tiny microscopic beings became a reality.

A WORLD OF FLAVOR AND FUNCTION

Throughout the centuries, and still today, fermentation has been one of the most important methods for preserving foods. Today we understand the microbiology involved in the natural process we call fermentation, but in former cultures, this phenomenon was considered to be magical, even mystical. What couldn't be explained then was credited to the gods, such as Dionysus, the Greek god of fermentation.

Our modern knowledge has dissected and digested the fermentation process down to one that, if not completely controllable, is at least more scientifically understood. Fermentation completely changes the character and experience of many foods. It enhances the flavor of some foods, making mild or bland foods taste richer, tastier, or stronger. It tones down or mellows out the flavor of other foods. In fact, it can enhance not only the flavor but also the texture, appearance, and aroma of the foods we eat. It can definitely improve the whole eating experience.

Fermented foods are all favorites on our "Love to Eat" list. They include cheese, chocolate, tea, bread and butter, pickles, olives and all types of condiments, yogurt, coffee, sausages, beer, wine, ale, and yes, even chocolate. And the reality is that they are easily within our reach, not just in specialty stores.

As Sandor Katz, author of

Wild Fermentation, one of the friendlier books on the subject, says, "Fermentation is easy. Anyone can do it, anywhere, with the most basic tools. Humans have been fermenting longer than we've been writing words or cultivating the soil. Fermentation does not require vast expertise or laboratory conditions. You do not need to be a scientist to be able to distinguish specific microbial agents and their enzymatic transformations, nor a technician maintaining sterile environments and exact temperatures. You can do it in your kitchen."

HOW DOES FERMENTATION WORK?

There's nothing special about cabbage, salt, and water. But combine them in the right proportions, under the right conditions, and you have sauerkraut, one of the most popular of all cultured foods.

While the principles involved in all fermentations are similar, these reactions are complex, involving a series of microbes working either together or in succession to achieve various characteristic results. These conditions contribute to create an ecosystem where different microorganisms compete for substrates and survival. How these play out determine whether the fermented product goes into your mouth or into the garbage.

Breathing and respiration are often considered the same thing, but actually they are two separate processes. Breathing is how a living organism exchanges gases with its environment. Respiration occurs in all living cells, involving the breakdown of organic molecular bonds to release energy packets the cells need for fuel. Fermentation generally employs anaerobic respiration, chemical reactions without oxygen. Cellular products and sugar interact to produce combinations of ethyl alcohol, carbon dioxide, and lactic acid as their end products.

Lactic acid fermentation is the type carried out by lactic acid bacteria. Sugars are converted entirely or nearly entirely to lactic acid (homolactic acid fermentation) or to a mixture of lactic acid, acetic acid, or other compounds (lactic acid fermentation). Lactic acid bacteria represent only .15 to 1.5 percent of all microflora involved in these reactions, yet their importance is enormous.

The three primary types of microorganisms involved in typical fermentations are bacteria, yeasts, and molds.

Various bacterial families are present in foods, often involved in spoilage. However, the lacto-bacteria, as discussed, are the overlooked beneficial type active in fermented foods that are so important for digestive health.

Yeasts are unicellular organisms that reproduce by budding. Larger than most bacteria, they generally activate in later stages of spontaneous fermentation and produce enzymes that promote desirable chemical reactions, including the leavening of bread and the production of alcohol and invert sugar.

Molds, while often maligned, are important both as spoilers and preservers of foods. Many, such as the aspergillus species, are often responsible for undesirable toxins and spoilage. While they do not play an important role in desirable fermentation of fruits and vegetables, oxygen-requiring molds add flavors and enzymes to food, and are responsible for some of our favorites, including the ripening and delightful flavors of cheeses.

The culturing of vegetables like sauerkraut and kimchi, for example, are simple fermentations. Fresh vegetables harbor numerous and various types of microorganisms, mostly dominated by aerobic bacteria, yeasts, and molds. Fermentation happens spontaneously when vegetables are cut, salted, or placed at a temperature between 18 and 20 degrees Celsius (64.4 and 68 degrees Fahrenheit). Principle bacteria commonly involved in these types of fermentations are such species as leuconotstoc mesenteroides, pediococcus acidllactil, and lactobacillus planetarium.

SPONTANEOUS (WILD) FERMENTATION

There are four recognized phases of spontaneous, or wild fermentation:

Pre-treatment, in which raw materials are graded, cleaned, and treated with lye and salt.

Heterofermentation, a gaseous phase that occurs during incubation of the ingredients at temperatures between 18 and 20 degrees Celsius (64.4 and 68 degrees Fahrenheit). This phase can be recognized by the characteristic bubbling and fizzing that signals the release of carbon dioxide and other products such as acetic acid, sugars, and ethers.

Homofermentation, an evolutionary stage in which the final pH or acidity of the product lowers to an acidic 3.5 to 4.0, lactic and acetic acid comprise about 2 to 3 percent, and there are no sugars remaining in the mixture.

Post-fermentation, a maturing phase in which active fermentation slows and subsides, and flavor, texture and other characteristic changes continue to occur.

Wild fermentation usually occurs within three days. On the fourth day, the increasing acidity irradiates pathogens. After this, any secondary fermentations, usually involving yeasts and producing alcohol, happen. Active growth has stopped but chemical reactions like maturation of flavors continue.

TAMING THE WILD FERMENTATION

Control of fermentation reactions depend on a number of factors, including the particular raw materials used, the climate or environment, the use of salt and other additives, the specific production processes utilized, and storage conditions.

This is how fermentation reaction sequences often occur. Usually, small, fast-proliferating bacteria are the first to grow. These are followed by yeasts and then molds. Basically, these microorganisms, with their narrow and specific food, temperature, and pH requirements, proliferate until their byproducts stop further growth. In essence, they get bogged down in their own waste products. Then, the next set of microbes, usually larger such as yeasts, start to feed on the waste as food. And so it goes. One species becomes food for the next, epitomizing the cycle of life and death. Vinegar, for example, is made both by yeasts from the air and from acid-forming bacteria. The yeasts convert the sugars to alcohol, which is the food for the acetobacter, or fruit-loving bacteria.

Fermentation is a quasi-controllable process, and food producers and processors spend millions working on perfecting their brews and cultures, trying to bring them to the masses. Although certain brew masters stake their reputations on branding the consistency of their products, fermentation is an inconsistent process. Talk with any microbiologist or fermentation specialist and he or she will tell you, though they work hard to achieve consistency and stability within the lab or commercial food factory environment, the process is really more of an art than a science. In fact, commercial food processors keep food technologists very busy studying and experimenting with developing strains of microorganisms and techniques to more consistently standardize their yields.

Technically, anything that is brined in a solution of salt is fermented. Yet in reality, that is where the similarities in fermentation end. Or begin.

There is, indeed, a big difference in fermented foods. A quick look down supermarket shelves and coolers reveals plenty of foods that have been treated through the process of fermentation, or something akin to it. However, not all foods like pickles and sauerkraut we normally identify as fermented foods are created or end up equal, especially when it comes to nutrition or what savvy nutrition professionals term nutrient density.

Essentially, nutrient density is the relative degree or percentage of nutrients in a food, compared to the number of calories or energy in that food. The higher the nutrients, the greater the nutrient density. The higher the calories, the lower the nutrient density. So, liver and dark leafy greens, for example, have a high nutrient density. Deep-fat-fried starches, like potato chips, and other high-sugar and/or high-fat "foods" like processed snacks and sodas without many vitamins or minerals have a low nutrient density.

Note that this is essentially true, despite the soft drink industry rhetoric and marketing of their new "healthier" products. Synthetic vitamins or neutraceuticals added to soda pop don't make them or you "smarter." They're still junk food, on the bottom end of the nutrient density scale.

But there are additional key differences between most commercially produced fermented foods available today and the old-style lacto-fermented foods. The really healthful kinds are what we call traditionally lacto-fermented foods or live, cultured foods. That's because they are produced chiefly by the action of lactobacillus species of bacteria. The fermentation reactions produced by these bacteria yield a variety of end products. The resulting acids, primarily lactic and acetic acids, are the healthiest, most desirable kinds from a health perspective—and the ones often lacking in our contemporary diet.

These acids are also destroyed by heating or pasteurization. So, virtually all commercially produced fermented foods have lost a lot of their essential benefits because they have been heat-treated, by law, in order to be transported through interstate commerce. And they have been heat-treated for practical purposes, as well. A jar of live, lacto-fermented pickles, still bubbling with vital lacto-bacteria, could potentially explode in a store.

Thus, the few truly lacto-fermented foods that are available commercially can be found, usually with some effort, in small, retail operations that produce small batches on a frequent basis, such as open vat pickles in a kosher delicatessen or from large crockery vats at a farm store. The other option is to produce them at home, or even more wisely cooperate with others to produce them together to share.

PROBIOTICS AND PREBIOTICS

As noted in Chapter 1, probiotics are foods or supplements, such as yogurts, kefir, and kimchi, containing faorable bacteria that may directly alter the composition of the intestinal or gut bacteria flora. Technically defined, they are "live microorganisms, which administered in adequate amounts confer a beneficial physiological effect on the host," according to the Food and Agriculture Office of the World Health Organization. Probiotics can be found in all unpasteurized fermented foods.

Prebiotics are beneficial bacterial promoters. Prebiotics are defined as materials that alter the bacterial composition of the gut by changing the environment in the intestines, making it more hospitable for friendly, health-giving bacteria to grow and develop. Some examples are inulin-rich foods such as onions, agaves, and Jerusalem artichokes, as well as supplements such as FOS (fructo-oligosaccharides). Prebiotics promote the growth of probiotics.

Both prebiotics and probiotics are considered members of a nutrient-dense class of foods and neutraceuticals called functional foods. They are being heavily researched and developed for their proven and potential health benefits including cholesterol reduction, protection from gastrointestinal disease, improved immune system response, and resistance to disease.

Probiotic supplements are available in health and natural food stores. These are also produced in large quantities in commercial facilities through modifications of the same process. Currently in the worldwide probiotic market, there are over 80 products that are being marketed for these specific health benefits, over 50 of which are from Japan alone. Europe boasts over 45 plants that manufacture fermented and cultured dairy products, with France, Germany and Sweden producing 25% of the world's supply of all fermented milk based probiotics.

But there are many benefits, including expense, to acquiring the friendly bacteria that support intestinal and immune health from fresh, live foods instead of expensive supplements. Both currently have their place in maintaining health today, but with encroaching international regulations and

impending restrictions on the availability and potency of nutritional supplements, there is no guarantee about the future. As far as nutritional insurance for the future, you are wise and smart if you take the time to revive these age-old traditions involving fermented foods.

This may mean cooperating with your friends or members of your local "food circle," your Community Supported Agriculture project, slow food group, or health or environmentally-friendly neighbors to learn how to make and share these simple, nutrient-dense foods together in your homes or a local church or community kitchen. And besides, it's great fun! The results are delicious, satisfying—and rewarding in many nourishing ways—for everyone.

EXTRAORDINARY MICROORGANISMS

Microbiology is the study of all microorganisms. The magical agents of fermentation are these tiny, microscopic organisms that create profound changes in foods, transforming fluid milk into solid, savory wheels of cheese or bunches of succulent grapes into sweet or woody astringent wine. Even tall stalks of field corn are transformed in silos by these minute but mighty processors to become a cow's habitual winter meal, the feed called silage or ensilage. So is compost. Undeniable but unexploitable working class microorganisms are tireless workhorses that carry out a number of biological life processes, and in the process just happen to create new things to eat.

Yet as amazingly competent as they are, microorganisms, unlike plants, cannot make carbohydrates from CO_2, water and sunlight. They need something to feed and grow on. They need a host for their survival and growth. Carbohydrates are their favorites.

INTRODUCING:
THE GOOD, THE BAD, AND THE UGLY

Interestingly, these little critters possess a "double edged sword." Ironically, while microorganisms are constantly, ceaselessly providing delicious and nutritious foods for our enjoyment, they are at the same time our adversaries, especially of the food industry that consistently seeks mastery over them and its quality-controlled production processes.

Fermentation produces changes that are both

advantageous and disadvantageous. Initiated by the action of microorganisms, fermentation occurs naturally, often in the decaying process of fruits and vegetables. This wild or spontaneous fermentation happens naturally from yeasts and other microbes in the air.

Contamination of foods that are being fermented can happen through unclean utensils, molds, or other foreign materials getting into the mixture. Some contamination can make you sick, and some are just disgusting. But weird, darkened films or layers are not always a reason to throw the whole batch out. Cheese is made from mold, so sometimes all you have to do is cut off the outside. Learning about the process through first-hand experimentation and experience is almost a pre-requisite, and definitely increases your knowledge and confidence in this area.

Putrefaction, often thought of as rotting, is a similar, but distinct process. In fact, a form of fermentation, it is the breakdown of proteins, instead of carbohydrates.

Development of alcohol, considered to be the ultimate goal by some and a killing scourge to others, is another potential byproduct of the fermenting process. Not all fermentations produce alcohol, contrary to a popular notion. Alcohol is normally produced by yeasts in secondary fermentations that go on in the later parts of the fermentation cycle. The goal for those seeking the health benefits of lacto-fermented foods is to consume them before they develop alcohol. Young beers consumed after only a couple of days of fermentation are historical examples of such pre-alcoholic ingestibles.

Chemists and food processors work hard to control the process so that only the desired bacteria and other microbes grow and multiply. This naturally suppresses others. Take the differences between pasteurized and unpasteurized milk, for example. Unpasteurized milk will spoil naturally, producing a sour taste and a product that can be used in baking to improve texture of certain breads. Pasteurized milk on the other hand, spoils with a non-desirable type of fermentation reaction that produces a nasty, unpleasant product to throw in the garbage. Pasteurizing and homogenizing milk destroys the integrity of the product, changes the configuration and alters or denatures many of the proteins. Pasteurized milk actually putrefies.

The reason for the difference is that pasteurization, despite being a very important process to destroy pathogenic microorganisms, changes the environment so much that if pasteurized milk is left unrefrigerated, the undesirable microorganisms start to grow before the desirable ones. And despite another common notion, pasteurized milk is not immune to contamination by pathogenic organisms. Studies have shown, in fact, that raw milk has more protective benefits than heated, treated pasteurized milk. Organic Pastures, a California dairy legally selling raw dairy products, has demonstrated through constant laboratory testing that, even when inoculated with pathogenic bacteria at night, the raw milk is virtually and consistently free of pathogens by the next morning. Raw milk, not pasteurized, possesses a protective, anti-bacterial buffer—another of nature's secrets.

Most food spoilage organisms cannot survive in either alcohol or acid environments. This is undoubtedly the reason your grandmother easily canned high acid foods like tomatoes, but had to be especially careful about canning low acid fruits or vegetables like apples or pears. This is good in that the end products of these reactions can actually prevent a food from spoiling and extend its shelf life.

The same principles are operating whether we're looking at desirable or undesirable spoilage. The result all depends upon pH, moisture, and the environmental conditions surrounding the microbes. Once again, we have another demonstration of these amazing creatures' closely guarded secrets, their ability to respond and adapt. Their *responsibility*, so to speak, something we can learn from them.

ENZYMES AND THEIR INDISPENSABLE SERVICE

Although we still do not understand the fundamental mystery of fermentation, we do know, thanks to the work of biochemist J.B. Sumner, that enzymes are protein catalysts, the key instigators or initiators of these amazing reactions.

Thanks to the hard work of a number of scientists in the 1800s and 1900s, we now know that enzymes are intricately involved in the miraculous process of fermentation. All the modern sciences, including microbiology, biochemistry, mycology, bacteriology, and industrial fermentation technology, collectively share a focus and interest in the nature and working of enzymes. That's because they are an integral part of virtually every biological reaction known.

Enzymes exist in all living things, from plants to animals. They are complex proteins, produced by living organisms to carry out specific biological reactions. These protein complexes drive all types of reactions that make life as we know it possible. Thousands of enzymes, both inside and outside the body, are the instigators of literally billions of reactions every day, from your muscles firing to the conversion of your steak into energy or fat, to the release of hormones when you are being chased by a wild animal or running to catch a plane.

Known as catalysts, enzymes initiate and control reactions, rather than being used up in reactions like vitamins. They are very sensitive to changes within the cell, such as fluctuations in temperature, pH, moisture, ion strength, and concentrations of minerals. Examples of enzyme activity are in the beer-making process, with the conversion of barley to malt, and in cheese making, with the action of rennet, an enzyme in the cow's stomach responsible for coagulating the milk into the pre-aged solids we enjoy as cheese. The first cheeses were accidental discoveries of the nomads who found that the milk they carried in animal skins after a long journey of heat and jostling had become solid from the action of the rennet enzyme in the milk.

Enzymes are very specific in how they work to create changes in the body and nature. They are proteins designed with a folded three-dimensional structure that work through a very precise, finely tuned patterning of parts. Enzymes basically operate through a system that looks very much like a lock and key type of mechanism. Specific proteins must fit precisely together with others in order to unlock or release the desired reaction. Each can catalyze only one type of chemical reaction.

While there are thousands of types of enzymes, microbial enzymes are the chief instigators in the fermentation of fruits and vegetables and some other foods. There are actually very few pure culture ferments; they are almost always the work of more than one microbe. The changes that occur during the culturing process—whether it's the production of beer, the ripening of cheese, or the rotting of road kill—are caused by the enzymes liberated by these microorganisms.

Some of the foods usually said to be fermented are actually cured by the enzymes naturally inherent in these foods. The enzymes originate from three sources: those produced by the microorganisms involved in the fermentation, those native to the food, and those produced by the microflora that happen upon the unfermented food.

A good fermentation is one in which enzymes produced by the fermenting microorganisms play the primary role. A bad fermentation, which might smell putrid or make you sick or create an inconsistent result in a food factory, can happen from the wrong kind of contamination or changes in temperature or pH that disrupts the enzymes or the co-enzymes, allowing other organisms like molds or fungus to interrupt or take over the process. Not all bad fermentations are harmful or lethal. Some can actually produce delicacies.

Because of their makeup, fermented foods can have major impact on many of the nutrition, disease and health problems that plague the world today. The F.A.O. emphasizes, "It is essential that the knowledge of their production is not lost. There is danger that the introduction of western foods with their glamorous image will displace these traditional foods."

Yet despite technological advances in this arena, even the new designer enzymes being developed and used by the food industry cannot displace or decipher, but only hope to attempt to replicate, the wonder of nature's unique and closely-held mysteries. Time will tell whether genetic manipulation of enzymes and other food additives currently in vogue by the commercial industry will prove to be as safe, effective, beneficial and sustainable as their natural ancestral counterparts inherent in the "untampered with" processes of this age-old natural technology.

SECRETS UNDER LOCK AND KEY

While microorganisms have been studied and identified, codgeled and corralled, they still remain mysterious creatures, even to the scientific community. And they are sorely underestimated. Cells live in an environment that is constantly in chaos, challenged by continually changing conditions to which they are forced to adapt or die. Whether in the gut or the soil, the same principles apply. These basic units of life are master adapters, although we don't know exactly how they accomplish this.

Processes and systems in nature are designed with checks and balances that keep everything functioning in balanced cycles or circles. Microorganisms are an integral part of maintaining this balance, which we call homeostasis. The term homeostasis is used by physiologists to mean the natural maintenance of static or constant conditions in the internal environment.

These simple, tiny living creatures are concealing some very significant fundamentals about cellular adaptation, the secrets to life and other arcane wisdom, intuited by alchemists but, which the scientific community with all its knowledge has missed, skipped over and taken out of context, too often for its own usury. Louis Pasteur was not the first and certainly not the only scientist of his time to devote significant energy and resources to the study of microorganisms in an attempt to help explain and thus create a better world. His work has paved the way for countless advances and innovations, yet his errors have cost us much.

We are not merely chemical machines at the mercy of haphazard outside germ invaders. We are living, breathing, and respiring beings, mini-ecosystems ourselves, with a much more complex design that includes intimate interdependence with the physical as well as the spiritual, the micro and the macro levels of existence. Instead of analyzing, trying to dominate and supersede the supremely intelligent design of a flawlessly balanced natural system, substituting cheaper but lifeless parts that are mere plastic imitations of the master, we need to look with different eyes past the shallow, egotistic isolation and narrow self-interests of a bottom line that has no agenda but its own survival and profit.

It's time to restore the ecology of our bodies, just as we are finally "getting it" and attempting to begin restoring the ecology of our planet. One thing is for certain, we won't be able to do it unless we stop trying to control, dominate and kill microorganisms and start recognizing, respecting and cooperating with these unseen but undeniable sages.

Instead of "shuffling deck chairs on the Titanic," we can and must look and listen for the deep lessons and gifts right before our eyes in the natural world that contain the true wisdom we're seeking. Like the humus of the soil, also created by microorganisms, we need to become more humble about our place in the world and learn from and how to co-exist in harmony with it, especially with the multitude of micro creatures who hold the very key to our lives and survival. Our lives literally depend upon it.

Fermentation at Work

Caldwell Bio Fermentation

Caldwell Bio Fermentation is an innovative Canadian developer of lacto-fermentation cultures, products and technologies which support community fermentation projects. The company, pioneered by Gary Caldwell and Microbiologist Tony Savard, has partnered with Agriculture Canada Research to develop and market five fermentation technologies for the production and support of live cultures designed for small scale operations, including one which inhibits proliferation of yeasts and molds.

Caldwell produces live cultured packaged products such as sauerkraut, fermented vegetable salads, kimchi's and lacto-fermented juices, including fermented fiddlehead fern and garlic condiments which are currently available in consumer packs through their website and other venues in wholesale quantities under the BioLacto and Deep Root labels.

But a main focus of their work, according to owner Gary Caldwell, is providing single and mixed lactobacterial strains customized for their producer clients needs, with average annual production of no more than 200 tons of fermented vegetables per year. This can be easily produced by a mere three full time workers, visible at Caldwell's new demonstration pilot production and testing facility in their Montreal location, a functioning prototype model including a farm-based plant and Centre d'Interpretation or learning center, which they hope to expand to other areas. In 2008, Caldwell will begin retailing lactobacterial starters in small containers capable of yielding 10-20 lbs of live fermented product, ideal for small co-ops, families or food circles.

Caldwell Bio Fermentation Canada, Inc.
189, de la Rivière Rd., Martinville (Quebec) Canada J0B 2A0
Tel: (819) 849-2000 Toll Free 1-877-849-9941
info@biolacto.com; www.biolacto.com

Fermentation at Work
Common Health Products

Carmen Morano is the larger than life head of a large family. Forty people large, they live and work together on a 120 acre farm just over the New York State border in Bellows, Vermont. The Basin Farm produces food for their own family, plus grows and mills spelt, an ancient grain, that they make into sourdough bread and distribute. This devout family is part of a rather large and growing network of similar communities in New England and vicinity called the Twelve Tribes of Israel, which follows Biblical dietary laws and run restaurants and cafes all over North America.

They not only grow their own vegetables, goats and grains, they are also a retail distributor for BioLacto and Deep Root live cultured products made by Caldwell Bio Fermentation, which they retail through mail order sales. When Caldwell delivers they often take back daikon radish and cabbage that Common Health raises for Caldwell. Now that's what you call a real food circle.

"It's a teaching process from garden to table," says Carmen Morano. "Our children get an education from doing and working with us. They play with real babies instead of dolls. They're well fed and nourished, gain many skills that enable them to be competent and productive adults, and look people right in the eye when they talk with them. They're one of us and it shows."

"A lot of people are saying we're on the cutting edge. But we're just doing what makes sense. As people have more medical problems they're looking for something different. Some other way than what the medical people are saying. Our bodies are designed to be eternal. When they're well fed and healthy, they can reject a lot of the problems that are cropping up all over the place now."

When asked about the quiet success of this astounding group of people, Carmen responds, "People see that we care. We care about the vegetables, the spelt, the soil, We restore buildings, work together in unity. Where do you see that today? You don't have to listen to us. Come for a visit or stay with us. We're all about kingdom living, putting words into action, putting action into our words, loving and taking care of each other. Nothing fancy."

Common Health Products/ The Basin Farm
Common Health Products, PO Box 108, Bellows Falls, VT 05101
802-376-8959
Carmen@CommonHealthProducts.org

one

Chapter 4

The State of Our Health:
Modern Food and
Agriculture Systems

Fermentation at Work
Ontario Kombucha Cultures

Master kombucha makers Patricia Meyer-Watt and Joseph Nunno in Toronto are sharing their knowledge and experience with making KT, as Joseph calls it, through demonstrations to others members at their quarterly meeting of the Weston A. Price Foundation chapter. "I love teaching people about kombucha and sharing it," says nutritionist and chapter leader Patricia. Sometimes the presentations are lectures, some times participatory, but members usually go home with a small mushroom or "scoby" and instructions or a jar with a ready to ferment starter sample.

At the same gathering, some people in the group bring their raw milk or kefir, sourdough breads, krauts and their own particular cultured specialties, which they may trade and share.

"Fermentation is the best," says chapter leader and local organizer, Ann Denny. "I've been literally drinking kombucha, raw goat's milk kefir and cream kefir almost exclusively for the last three weeks as an immune builder and I feel fantastic on it. It has been contributing to the healing of a very long-standing chronic health issue of mine and I'm happy to 'testify' to anyone I talk to about it," says Ann, a traditional foods enthusiast who recently compiled the first Canadian WAP shopper's guide to local, organic and traditional foods.

"I'm trying to eat local foods," says Patricia, "the 100 mile diet, as they say. It's a way for me not to buy foods from a package or bottle, but then I can have my kombucha in a bale top grolsch bottle. And it's so nice that it's nutritious, as well. A double whammy!

In Ontario, Patricia and other Canadians are combining this natural community building culture with other local and healthy fermented foods in creating greater connections for supporting health and working together, goals of the Weston A. Price Foundation chapter to which they belong in Toronto.

Ontario Kombucha Cultures
Toronto (Downtown), Ontario WAP Chapter Patricia Meyer Watt (416) 653-7112
b-healthy@rogers.com; Ann Denny, ann.denny@gmail.com Toronto
(East): Joseph Ouimet (416) 439-4753, joseph67x@yahoo.com

We in the U.S. have a reputation as the *best fed* nation, the breadbasket of the world. The reality is closer to (something like) we are the *most fed* nation in the world. While we have enjoyed the most prolific, productive food and agricultural system of all time, it doesn't necessarily mean we have created the most optimum or ideal one. There have been many obvious and not so obvious trade-offs. To understand the anomalies, we need to take a quick look at how our modern food system developed.

The mechanization of agriculture, facilitated by the development of the seed drill, the tractor and chemical fertilizers promoted by chemists such as Justus Von Liebeg, have enabled this nation to produce an unprecedented amount of crops, particularly grains.

Since the disciples of Rene Descartes' mechanistic worldview, our modern agricultural systems have been increasingly moving in a straight line trend toward the reductionist, the simple, the quantifiable. The industrial model that was adapted in the eighteenth and nineteenth centuries has also been wholeheartedly applied to agriculture, as well as medicine. This has led to a chemical reductionist mindset, with its concurrent germ warfare viewpoint, espoused and adopted by agricultural leaders starting back with fertilizer chemist Justus Von Liebeg.

What has resulted is a production agriculture system that emphasizes volume, quantity and yield, over quality and value, exemplified by U.S. Department of Agriculture Secretary Earl Butz' "Get big or get out" slogans that have pushed farmers to plant "hedgerow to hedgerow" since the end of World War II, abandoning traditional conservation practices.

The doctrine of comparative advantage, which concentrated agricultural production in areas of the country most suited to growing particular crops to reduce production costs, became the norm, while access to cheap and plentiful oil supplies provided the logical rationale to then ship products all over the country to consumers, instead of producing these crops locally, close to home, as had been traditional practice up until the 20th century. This, in turn, facilitated more specialization, as the functions of production and consumption became separated.

The green revolution's plant breeding and scientific research from the land grant colleges were 20th century miracles that were going to "end starvation and save the world." Yet, in the process, somehow "the cart got before the horse." We did not speed up the increase in sheer volume of crop production simply because we needed more food, but because that is what we knew how to do, notes farm historian, Wendell Berry in *The Unsettling of Agriculture: Culture and Agriculture.*

Where the root word "agri" used to be associated with culture, (agriculture), it's now associated with business (agribusiness). Now instead of agriculture, we have agribusiness.

Rural social changes and specificity also mirrored the changes in agriculture. In the early stages of this country, farms were a way of life, made up of homes and lands that functioned as a complete unit. The household wasn't merely a unit in the economy of food production, it was an integral and major part of it. The family that owned and worked the farm lived on it and from it. Consumers of food were also producers or processors or both.

But as things evolved, explains Berry, "the collaborators purified their roles – the household became simply a house or residence, purely consumptive in its function, the farm ceased to be a place to live and a way of life and became a unit of production – and their once collaborative relationship became competitive. Between them, the merchant began to usurp the previous functions of both household and farm, becoming increasingly both a processor and a producer.

Increasingly, farmers and their families were forced to work outside the home, farms stopped producing a variety of crops and livestock, and stopped being a balanced diverse ecosystem. The farm and household ceased to be a cohesive unit, a production-consumption-recycle system or circle. Instead, it became a production-consumption chain, a *food chain*, as it is often called today, where one part has no connection with the other except for economics.

Our standards and our values have also changed. The collaboration of household and farm in America was never, according to Berry, sufficiently thrifty or careful of soil fertility. Perhaps because of the unprecedented existence of the frontier and the apparently unlimited abundance of resources in this, The Land of Promise, homesteaders and farmers never adopted the kind of frugality and reverence toward the land that characterized the attitudes of rural farmers and rural dwellers on other continents.

"And so an enterprise that once had some susceptibility to qualitative standards from standards of quality, personal taste and preference on one end and good husbandry at the other, has come more and more under the influence of standards that are merely economic or quantitative. The consumer wants food to be as cheap as possible, the producer wants it to be as expensive as possible; both want it to involve as little labor as possible. And so the standards of cheapness and convenience, which are irresistibly simplifying and therefore inevitably exploitative, have been substituted for the standard of health (of both people and the land) which would enforce consideration of essential complexities." Berry continues.

"To treat every field, or every part of every field with same consideration is not farming, but industry." The attitude of kindly use as a concept favored by Berry and other ecological stewards depends upon intimate knowledge, the most sensitive responsiveness and responsibility. As knowledge, (hence use) is generalized, essential values are destroyed. As the householder evolves into the consumer, the farm evolves into a factory – with results that are potentially calamitous for both. The movement from the farm to the city involves a radical simplification of mind and of character," Wendell Berry notes.

Farms are ecological systems, and by their nature complex, delicate, finely balanced natural systems that are like food circles or cycles. When farmers started using large quantities of N, P and K (N =

nitrogen; P = phosphorus, and K = potassium) processed chemical fertilizers, to fertilize the fields, instead of the traditional fermented or composted manures and feedstocks left over from the harvesting process, the circle was broken and the balance of ecology shifted in the land.

Traditional composts, which have been the economical, ecological, age-old mode of recycling and returning nutrients to the soil and a natural safeguard for preserving the circle of life, are another product of fermentation. The best organic and biodynamic farmers of the day are once again using these techniques to restore the vitality and the humus – the living matter full of lifegiving microorganisms that hold the soil together – so essential to healthy plants, food and environment.

We now know that use of large quantities of synthetic minerals such as nitrogen, phosphorus and potassium that have been routinely employed by industrial commercial agriculture for over 50 years, produce accelerated growth of crops, but have other side effects. For one thing, use of these synthetic fertilizers tips the ecological scales and disrupts the balanced interplay with micronutrients and other macronutrients, as well, causing all kinds of long-term havoc.

There are many examples, and the subject is too huge to do more here than scratch the surface. Protein percentages in wheat have dropped close to 5% in a few short years. In the blink of an eye, we are losing the critical six precious inches of topsoil that took millions of years to develop. And now a literal Pandora's box has been opened with the widespread, yet untested and unlabelled influx into the system of genetically engineered crops, seeds and additives. "Frankenfoods" and genetic abnormalities, rural suicides, contamination and obliteration of entire

> We have lost our humility, as we have lost our humus, when it comes to our place in the sacred land that supports our very life.

species are just a few of the bizarre and disastrous consequences that are already presenting in this freakish, huge, unregulated experiment on the human race. All thanks to an abandoned allegiance to progress and the god of the bottom line.

With the exception of a small but growing number of ecologically-minded farming stewards, our relationship with the land has become strictly usury, and we have become its dominators, trying to make nature conform to the dictates of the mechanical business model, instead of working in harmony with it. We have lost our humility, as we have lost our humus, when it comes to our place in the sacred land that supports our very life.

And we will only just touch once again here upon the fact that the ecology of the gut mirrors the ecology of the soil. That is to say, what is happening in our farmlands and agribusiness production systems is mirrored in our bodies.

Farm families used to routinely produce their own cultured and fermented foods as an important part of their total food supply for the year. As discussed previously, there is a big difference between the bulk of commercially available foods such as pickles, olives and sausages, even yogurts and cheese that are produced now industrially using fermentation, and these more traditionally produced lacto-fermented foods that contain the healthy bacteria.

How do you tell the difference? Technically, anything that is brined with salt or has gone through the fermentation process — the breakdown of carbohydrates through the action of bacteria, yeasts and molds is fermented. However, just because something is fermented, doesn't mean that it's healthy or alive with the life-enhancing probiotics

The biggest difference between commercial and traditionally lacto-fermented foods is processing, using heat to be exact. Any food that is shipped interstate is required by law to be heat-treated or pasteurized. While pasteurization has been effective in destroying many pathogenic or disease causing organisms, pasteurization effectively kills off *all* microbial activity, both detrimental and beneficial.

MODERN COMMERCIALLY FERMENTED VERSUS TRADITIONAL LACTO-FERMENTED FOODS

Processing makes a big difference in fermented foods. The really healthful kinds, what we call *traditional lacto-fermented foods* or live, cultured foods, are produced chiefly by the action of the lactobacillus species of bacteria on carbohydrates. The resulting acids, primarily lactic and acetic acids are the healthiest and are present liberally in all traditionally fermented foods.

However, the current commercially processed fermented foods are not the same animal. Today, virtually all commercially produced fermented foods, and any that are moved in interstate commerce, are legally required to be pasteurized, which effectively kills off the beneficial bacteria. Even our popular yogurts have been pasteurized. Any active cultures must be added after the heat-treating process, and they are only active for three to four weeks, at most.

The effective health and nutritional difference between modern and traditionally lacto-fermented foods is enormous. While there are copious quantities of ingredients for charcuterie—delicacies known to have been preserved or improved by fermentation— only traditionally lacto-fermented foods contain the really beneficial bacteria that impart the excellent, health-giving properties to the foods.

Unfortunately, with the exception of frequenting a few old-time delis, purchasing imported varieties, and seeking out a few isolated domestic brands, traditional lacto-fermented foods are not available on a wide-scale basis. You will be hard put to find these in supermarkets and mass-market retail outlets. We are left to make them at home in our own kitchens, or to join together with friends and family to create and share them among those in our local circle. This is actually easier, and, as we'll see, more fun than you might think.

Foods that are actively fermenting produce CO_2 gas. So one big difference is a level of activity. If you were to leave a jar of actively fermenting lactic acid pickles at room temperature on the counter, they will continue to ferment and produce CO_2, possibly blowing off the lid, or exploding the jar, explains Pickle Packers International executive Richard Henschel.

This, of course, is why all shelf-stable pickles and other fermented foods are pasteurized. While making them easier to ship and sell, pasteurization kills off the bacteria, including any healthy lacto-bacteria, the principle advantage for eating these cultured foods. Many cheap pickles are simply pickled versus being fermented.

Of course, wine and beer are fermented, but these have also gone through secondary fermentation, which produces alcohol. So while they may contain other healthy factors such as anti-oxidants or beneficial neutraceuticals such as resveratrol from grape skins and seeds, they do not contain live, beneficial lacto-bacteria. Refrigeration, high heat pasteurization, vinegar and alcohol, along with other factors, deactivate, slow or halt the natural fermentation and enzymatic processes.

Fermentation is naturally an inconsistent (chemical and biological, transformative) process for preserving and developing unique characteristics in many foods. It's almost more of an art or craft, as evidenced by the term "brewmaster," used to describe a knowledgeable, accomplished beer-maker, for example.

So, over the years, in order to more precisely control processes, large-scale commercial food producers developed standardized techniques and elaborate manufacturing systems that yield more consistent results. For the most part, they aim for consistency and higher yields, not healthful product results. And, as in all businesses, whether manufacturing tires or Tilamook cheese, the overarching goal is producing products as cheaply as possible and selling them for as much money as possible.

As a result, there are actually a large number of cheap, knock-off products that basically masquerade as fermented foods. The really cheap versions of foods may not be fermented at all, as I discovered when writing the "Incredible Health Benefits to You of Traditionally Fermented Foods for Dr. Joseph Mercola's E-Healthy News," which appears on his

website, www.mercola.com. The cheapest, spongiest white breads, for example, while injected with yeasts, are forced or accelerated with chemicals to create CO_2 to leaven or raise the product for a short 10-15 minutes, but are far from what you could call healthily fermented.

Many cheap store brand yogurts, heavily sweetened with high fructose corn syrup or artificial sweeteners, are barely more than thickened puddings, and rely on the term yogurt so you will think these brands are healthy, and buy them. There is no claim about active cultures, because, for one thing, sugars and other chemicals kill the live bacteria. The cultures may have been live when added, but don't last.

Commercial yogurts, even organic ones, are pasteurized, and the active cultures are added *after* the heat treatment. As such, even in yogurt that is plain with no added sugars, the active cultures only last approximately four weeks. So, many are not really very healthy, despite the marketing claims that the healthiest yogurts and cultured dairy products are the raw dairy brands, the sharp, tangy flavored ones that still have active bacteria. If it tastes sweet but bland, chances are very high that there is no active culture present.

Most commercially-canned, California-style black olives are not generally fermented, but simply treated with lye to remove bitterness, packed in salt and canned. Olive producers can now hold olives in salt-free brines by a solution of chemically-produced acetic and lactic acids, sodium benzoate and potassium sorbate, a long way off from the simple, homestyle lacto-fermented techniques that have long characterized these normally delicious, health-promoting foods.

Many inexpensive soy sauces you might find in fast food oriental take-out shops, for example, are literally chemically altered soy, caramel syrup, sugar and water, with other colorings and flavorings added. There is no life in these soy sauces, and there never was.

Each fermented or cultured food has specific, unique requirements and production methods.

Today, there are a wide variety of food manufacturing ingredients and nutritional supplements produced through large-scale industrial fermentation.

Enzymes, used in thousands of applications, as well as probiotic and prebiotic supplements such as acidophillus and bifidus available in health and natural food stores, are cultured or fermented in large factories. Enzyme technology is widely used in the beer and wine industries, as well as in the baking industry. Enzymes are used for everything from decreasing the gumminess of breads to changing the starches in beer. Hydrolases are the most common enzyme classification used for food processing, and are responsible for clipping large molecules into smaller ones, changing the consistency or performance of food. Some soy-type condiments, such as brands identified as liquid aminos, are processed soybeans in a liquid form that use enzymes to hydrolyze the proteins instead of subjecting them to fermentation.

And enzyme biotechnology companies, the fastest growing segment of this industry, are constantly developing and refining more uses for these industrially applied, biological catalysts.

With increasing concerns about health, some enzyme biotechnology products are being used to replace chemicals considered harmful, such as bromates. However, many of these enzymes are themselves, genetically engineered. The industry is perplexed about this subject, worried that consumer skepticism and rejection of genetic engineering technologies will thwart their unbridled research and expansion, while still trying to maximize production and reduce costs.

It's probably not that surprising that our culture has traded many of the benefits of these normally healthy fermented foods for the convenience of cheaply mass-produced, easily shipped, shelf-stable products that are available, literally, anytime, anywhere.

YOU'VE TRIED THE REST, NOW TRY THE BEST

So the best-cultured products from a health perspective are live, cultured foods, in short supply commercially these days. These good ones will contain the active lacto- and other bacteria that enhance your digestion and health. You may be able to find some in ethnic neighborhood shops or delis.

Open barrel pickles ("overnights") are also produced in some retail stores, stored in vats or barrels so that the escaping gas is not the problem it presents when the pickles are packaged or sold in individual containers.

The trend toward high-end, self-serve olive bars is another encouraging sign. These olives are often lacto-fermented, not pasteurized, and thus generally healthier.

Some imported and domestic cheeses that are made from raw, unpasteurized milk are still alive. One cheese aficionado who manages the cheese department in the largest whole foods chain confided that while they may be labeled as pasteurized to comply with U.S. agricultural importation regulations, many imported cheeses are actually still raw. This is not a reason for concern. On the contrary, raw cheeses, like other raw dairy products, have powerful built-in protective buffering mechanisms that automatically kill pathogenic bacteria. If properly handled, raw cheeses can be marketed and sold if they are aged a minimum of 60 days.

Naturally lacto-fermented sodas and soft drinks are a new and delicious food trend, substituting healthy, refreshing live beverages for the cloyingly sweet and deadly, acid "mega-gulpers" that use the liquid poison high fructose corn syrup (HFCS) to create addictive consumption. Can you find any soft drinks, even healthy ones that are not sweetened with HFCS?

There are increasing numbers of rural farm stores and retailers who sell raw, lacto-fermented foods in the network of traditional food producers and consumers created through the Weston A. Price Foundation (www.westonaprice.org). You can also read about these Fermentation at Work projects, (see Table of Contents for page numbers) innovative entrepreneurs around the country who are successfully creating community-based food circles™ or food community with a fermentation project focus, such as bakeries, community kitchens, and other groups making artisan cheeses, kombucha, natural sodas and fermentation cultures, that lend themselves very nicely to being produced by a cooperating group of friends or partners.

Commenting on the still limited availability of these traditionally crafted edibles, Sandor Katz points out in his new book, *The Revolution Will Not Be Microwaved*, "To be sure there are niche brands, which are still living foods, available in health food stores, but then freezing or refrigeration is necessary.

This is rather ironic, since a major motivation for fermenting foods in the first place was to preserve them, in the days before refrigeration."

FOOD SAFETY AND SECURITY

As we became more removed from the land and from the source of our food, safety issues became more of a concern. When you live far away from, and are not familiar with the source of your food, when you don't know where it comes from, you have to be more concerned about its purity and safety. If you get your eggs from the farmer down the street, you know the condition of the henhouse, and how he treats his chickens.

Pasteurization has resulted in the widespread production, processing and distribution of foodstuffs that are grown or produced in one area, then shipped to another area for sale and consumption. And pasteurization has certainly saved many lives from consuming deadly microorganisms. However, as clinicians and food historians together point out, the scrutiny and preoccupation with cleanliness, safety, security and sterilization of our food has become so obsessive that it has obscured issues of food quality and taste, as well as true healthfulness. Incredulously, Pasteur's germ theory has become close to a curse on the food supply.

Safety and security issues have now risen to unprecedented prominence in our value system and world. Ironically, food safety and security issues have become yet another concession to business that, almost absurdly, has sacrificed health. The preoccupation with clean and safe food has certainly been exacerbated as of late by the events of 9/11/01, early on in the new century. Now issues of HAACP (Hazard Analysis and Critical Control Point) and ISO9000 (Good Manufacturing

Practices) take up more time and money than research about how to make products be healthier or tastier. As the focus on volume production and liability has increased, the focus on diversity and quality has decreased. The sad reality is that we've traded food quality for food safety.

FEAR AND FORSAKEN PLEASURES

Food terrorism and security issues have become of paramount importance to food manufacturers and processors, dominating the technical and food science agenda. Recently, an invitation to a food science seminar focusing on the logistics of nanotechnology arrived in my mailbox.

Food scientists see the emergence of nanotechnology and the ability to work at increasingly smaller levels of matter as one of the most exciting research areas in decades. This is based on the improved ability of researchers to image, measure, model, control and manipulate matter at dimensions of 1 to 100 nanometers, where novel interfacial phenomena introduce new functionalities. Now creation of rapid detection methods and single-molecule sensors that detect changes in food quality, including being able to detect (or insert) contamination in the minutest of quantities, has become their new preoccupation. Is this more fascinating to most food scientists than just developing new flavors or healthier content?

This is not to say that these professionals are not scrambling to meet the new accelerating demands of consumers who want healthier food products and are voting with their dollars. The food scientists' approach to "healthier food" is to isolate the active component, develop a cheaper synthetic replica and then splice the me-too neutraceutical to the food's genes, creating "vunder" foods that can be then labeled with claims for their nutritional superiority.

This is far from most consumers' perceptions of healthy food as whole, natural and untampered. And further than ever from the real answers, the inescapable conclusions that increasing numbers of scientifically trained, consciously creative and wholistic-oriented individuals have been seeing for a long time.

It is looking in the wrong direction. "Stop, lift your head up from your microscopic, sanitized, segmented view of the world and look around," I want to say to my colleagues. "You will see that we need to start looking and acting from a larger, global and wholistic perspective, with eyes that see the complexities of the bigger picture, not the ions of smaller parts." Thus, we need to look up and around, then back into the past, then forward, not to the next quarter, but far into the future. And then examine our hearts.

With most people, it seems, common sense "left the building" long ago. Unless we start thinking and communicating with whole, connected brains and healthy hearts connected to the earth and to each other, about our common heritage, our collective welfare, and our future together, living in harmony with other beings, big and small we may not have the luxury of looking at all.

Whether it's weight control, toxicity, or terrorist tampering, there's an undeniably pervasive cultural atmosphere of anxiety about food. Fear and worry have become so intertwined with eating that teens and even girls as young as six years old worry about their appearance and fitness. One evidence of our body-obsessed culture is a study reported in the *The British Journal of Developmental Psychology* of 80 little girls between ages 5 and 8 who were interviewed by a university research team. It was found that 47 percent of the girls wanted to be slimmer, and that most of them thought being slimmer would make them more popular. These are children as young as six wanting to be thin.

The study concluded that a substantial number of pre-adolescent girls are dissatisfied with their bodies and wish to be thinner," while also pointing out that 5-year-olds exhibit little dissatisfaction with their bodies. The factor of peer pressure beginning at school is obvious, but can this be all? What about the much reported 'obesity epidemic'? Does all this fear-inducing media coverage of our weight problems and the obsession with being fat, losing weight, being skinny like models, coupled with all the weight-loss products promising quick, svelte results, send so much of the wrong message that by age 6 our daughters are already saturated with the propaganda, and feel fat?

It would be wonderful if this preoccupation with weight and fat were enough motivation to propel these girls into developing fitness habits that would get them moving. But overwhelmingly, like most children their age, they spend an average of eight hours a day watching television.

It's ironic that so much preoccupation with weight doesn't appear to be getting us healthier. Or happier. Instead of enjoying our food, our fear sets us up for periodic catapulting into the polar extreme and binging or gorging for satisfaction. We've made food, especially fats, our enemy. (Just as we've made microbes and bacteria our adversary we feel compelled to kill.) Yet, as I often remind attendees at my workshops and talks, FAT is not a four-letter word, it's THREE letters. (Yes, I think we need to lighten up about the subject.)

WHAT'S WRONG WITH THIS PICTURE? ISN'T IT IRONIC?

Irony is an expression used in writing to convey an opposite or contradictory meaning, often sarcastic or sardonic in tone, to emphasize a big contrast. When you look at the statistics about our current food, agriculture and health situation, it's truly *ironic* that we, in the most coveted nation in the world, are suffering from these so-called diseases of civilization.

Isn't it ironic that we in the U.S. have the highest standard of living on the planet, yet we are plagued with degenerative diseases, much more than other westernized nations?

Isn't it ironic that due to scientific advances we in the U.S. have for the most part, successfully eradicated most infectious diseases within our borders, yet have not been able to forestall major problems with degenerative diseases like cancer, arthritis, heart disease, obesity and diabetes?

Isn't it ironic that degenerative diseases are almost completely related to and dependent upon lifestyle choices here in the U.S., most particularly diet and nutrition?

Isn't it ironic that in the U.S., a higher income is no guarantee of improved diet or improved health?

Isn't it ironic that we in the U.S. have the most productive food and agriculture system in the world, as well as the reputation as the *best* fed nation in the world. We might be the *most* fed nation in the world, but can hardly be considered the *best* fed nation in the world.

Isn't it ironic that we in the U.S. spend the most on healthcare, yet only rank 72nd in overall health rank?

Isn't it ironic that despite such an advanced medical system, improved diagnostics and other technologies, we in the U.S. have a national healthcare budget that is projected to bankrupt our economy by 2019?

Isn't it ironic that we in the U.S. are spending an unprecedented amount of time, energy and money focusing, stressing and worrying about our diets, exercise, our weight and health with such poor ROI (Return On Investment.)

Isn't it ironic that if business were run like this "healthship," it wouldn't be tolerated, or more likely, would go out of business. The problem is that business is at the bottom of it. And because of the bottom line, we in the U.S. have left out a key, core, center of this acronym: health"steward"ship

Isn't it ironic that we in the U.S. annually spend $6,000 per capita for pharmaceuticals from the largest industry in the country, for the most part alleviate symptoms, but do not address the root causes of disease?

Isn't it ironic that once we in the U.S. give in to the medical assumptions and start relying on pharmaceuticals for our health, we start a cycle of imbalances that finds us being forced to take drug after drug to counteract the problems caused by drugs? Ironic, or insane?

Isn't it ironic that the search for a clean, safe and secure food supply has gotten us to a place where we in the U.S. are almost afraid to eat, and so worried about being poisoned from without, that we are not listening, missing that fact that we are inadvertently and unconsciously poisoning ourselves from within?

Isn't it ironic that our "kill germ warfare" mentality is undermining the very health of our nation, and that we in the U.S. are warring against the very organisms that can solve our problems and save our personal and planetary health?

Isn't it ironic that, despite the benefit of centuries of wisdom from traditional cultures, we in the US have stubbornly clung to a scientific model that is based on a shaky, incomplete conclusion?

Isn't it ironic that we in the U.S. have access to simple, inexpensive and easy-to-achieve answers for solving these health problems, yet blindly cleave to the hope and promise "they'll find a pill for that?"

FERMENTATION: THE MISSING LINK

The answers to our current health dilemmas are complex. Yet we continue to look to science and medicine for simple, convenient one-shot answers to these problems. The reality, though, is that we are deluding ourselves when we irrationally continue to look outside ourselves for answers; when we continue holding out hope that they will be solved by simple, single-bullet solutions, either drugs or scientific discoveries, developed by so-called "experts." To climb out of this mess, we have to stop looking outside of ourselves for the answers.

While any single cause is out, we can use the powers of observation to help us find a clue. Of course, there is never a problem if we choose to not look at it. However, if we step back and examine the whole from a larger vantage point, we can see trends and a trail that leads us back to some unavoidable facts, followed by some simple, commonsense solutions.

These are predicated or preceded by a couple of basic assumptions. First, he who refuses to learn from the past is doomed to a dismal future. Secondly, we are responsible for our own health.

The overall health of our soil and our bodies is inextricably linked. Our food, agricultural and health systems have all suffered from a single-minded focus on quantity and bottom line over quality, flavor and health.

Ecological diversity is a protective key to balance or homeostasis, inside and outside our bodies.

Digestive health is the biggest single determinant of immune health.

Poor nutrition and poor waste removal lead to build-up of toxicity, lowered pH and changing the ecology, the microorganisms. This is true in the gut, as well as in the soil.

Even overweight or obesity alone can cause inflammation, recognized as a major factor and a common marker of all degenerative disease. Fat cells act like immune cells and secrete inflammatory factors like histamines and cytokines that lower the immune response.

Unchecked, these conditions lead quickly and inevitably down a slippery slope to other health problems.

Fermented foods are an age-old, time-tested remedy. One obvious and clearly helpful choice that can have a profound impact on our physical and environmental health. Fermented foods are protective and rejuvenative, helping us to restore our digestive health and thus our immunity, our nutritional status and our well-being.

Fermentation is not only a missing link in our individual physical health; it represents the bridge that helps us span the gap and the holes in our collective ecological, social and spiritual health, as well.

For our social ecology is suffering just as much as our physical and environmental ecology.

A reflection of our isolated, dissipated and very busy culture increasingly filled with individual cell phones, internet and divorce, multiple jobs, hardship, aches and pains, dissatisfaction, depression and drugs despite our wealth and abundance, we are not living an overall healthy, balanced life. Just as people are hungering for real food, they are hungering for real meaning, community, fellowship and fulfillment, a sense of belonging and peace in an increasingly alienated world.

As a young person growing up in the sixties, I witnessed first hand the part that food played in the revolution that characterized Woodstock and the Hippie Generation. The hippies, what a funny name, were as much into healthy food as they were into psychedelics and rock music.

Your memory may be dim, but those long-haired freaks were the ones who started the first food co-ops and buying clubs, scooping beans and grains out of barrels, in an attempt to get back to the land, to real food, to real life. They were all about breaking out of old stifling molds that held our consciousness as a nation into a bland, boring, 2.5 children-per-family, station wagon mentality in which everything – people and food and life —was bland and boring, all the same. Hippies *were* the sixties revolution.

It was all about breaking out of the old chains of plastic food and plastic slipcovers, stifling conformity that kept us imprisoned in one-track thinking and life. Ironically, mass-produced food and fast food eating has us imprisoned in another kind of trap today. This one is a quick, cheap, convenient - burgers-and-French-fries processed food death trap.

Fermentation at Work
Three Stone Hearth

Three Stone Hearth is a Community Supported Kitchen run on traditional, local food principles and plenty of fermentation! This worker-owned cooperative offers seasonal nutrient dense foods on a weekly basis to homes and families around the San Francisco Bay Area. Like other community supported agriculture and food initiatives that characterize the budding local food system developing all over the country, participants enjoy a weekly opportunity to taste the fruits of the seasonal harvest and the members pure joy and dedication in transforming delicious, nutrient dense foods into resplendent meals and healthy take home treats.

They might be using time tested lacto-fermentation techniques, but this food circle" is keeping up with the times. Members can register online and sign up for weekly food orders, posted a week prior for pickup on Fridays. Their main menu changes weekly, highlighting the nourishing traditions of a different part of the world. Plus, their weekly pickups always feature a variety of their many lactofermented specialties, such as Broths, Crunchy Cereals, Oatmeal, Kombucha àla Larry, Sourdough Whole Wheat Crackers, Beet Kvass Tonic, Coconut Sweets, Coconut and Red Palm Oil, Celtic Sea Salt, Traditional Breads, Pastured Eggs, Raw Claravale Milk, Local Farmhouse cheeses. The day I checked in late summer, this was their menu for the next week:

Three Stone Hearth
Sample Late Summer Menu
Summer Vegetable Minestrone Soup with Beef
Cream of Summer Squash with Marjoram (dairy free!)
Baked Polenta with Greens, Eggs, and Cheddar Cheese
Wheatberry Salad with Juliette Tomatoes and Basil
Tomato Sauce Bolognese
Italian Pickled Vegetables
Herbed Parmesan Flat Breads
Caesar Dressing
Live Culture Cheesecake with Fresh Mission Figs

Food can be picked up directly from their kitchens, delivered direct to door through a local Planet Organics Delivery service, Pedal Express bicycle service, or through a neighborhood pickup cluster, made possible by subscribers who rotate the task of picking up their orders with their neighbors. Because they believe in using the most sustainably-raised local produce possible and supporting small-scale, local, ecological, and pasture-based farmers and ranchers, they pay a premium for their ingredients, which are transformed and produced in their kitchens by worker owners, volunteers and students who are in interested in learning the art and craft of producing these treasured foods. They also hold monthly church supper-style dinners, offer classes and workshops periodically to help members master making these foods, sometimes taught by co-worker/owner chef, Jessica Prentice, author of *Full Moon Feast*.

"It is our goal at Three Stone Hearth.. that you are paying as close to the true cost of the food as possible —- the true cost of growing it, of processing it, and the true cost of distributing it. For your own health and the health of the planet and our community, we believe in putting your money where your mouth is, and investing in REAL FOOD," says worker/owner Larry Wisch, the Larry in Kombuchu àla Larry. And from the smiles on their faces and the health of their children, it looks like it's working – and worth it.

Three Stone Hearth
415-846-8217
www.threestonehearth.com, info@threestonehearth.com

So now we've reached a crossroads where we look on the other side of the terrain. If you only look at the state of our health discussed in the previous chapter, you'll probably conclude that things look pretty bleak. In reality, the picture is quite a bit brighter, thanks to the unprecedented and undeniable groundswell of current interest in diet, nutrition, health and fitness that has been ramping up steadily since the 1990's.

Americans, especially the baby boomers and GenX'ers, appear to be beginning to wake up out of their sleepy, lackadaisical processed foods buying and oblivion toward food and health. Taste is still king, or queen, of the royal North American palate, and convenience a requirement de rigueur. Still can be observed a more decided shift in the behavior of Americans when it comes to their goal to eat healthful foods. Despite nutritional confusion, conflict and seductive food images bombarding the average American television viewer, some citizens have taken more responsibility for themselves and are determined, one way or another, to be or to become healthy.

According to the National Institute of Health, $75-$125 billion is spent (annually) on indirect and direct costs due to obesity-related diseases. In the 30 years between 1970 and 2000, the average intake of vegetables worldwide increased from 60 kg to over 100 kg per person. 180 million people, two-thirds of the American population, routinely take nutritional supplements, and over 60% of them have tried complementary and alternative medicine.

SUSTAINABLE, ORGANIC, HEALTH AND NUTRITION EXPLOSION

Organic foods have been growing by a phenomenal 20% annually since 1997, and one in ten dollars now is spent on organic and natural foods. Around 80% of U.S. and European consumers report they are concerned about food and health issues. Two-thirds have taken active steps to eat more healthily in the past year alone. Eating fresh food is the key cited as important by a staggering 90% of the people polled.

From virtually nothing in 1980, to ten years later in 1990, organic foods accounted for roughly 4% of new products. By the year 2006, 7% of all the new products launched were labeled as organic or certified organic. This remarkable growth in the availability of products marketed or perceived to be healthy is seen clearly in sales figures. Organically grown foods in the US grew from an $18 billion market in 2000 to a $32 billion market in 2005, a whopping 43% increase. European sales grew from $15 billion Euros to $25 billion during this same time.

And whether they can afford them or not, 80% of consumers surveyed in a recent survey by the Food Marketing Institute and *Prevention Magazine* believe organic foods are healthier than conventional foods. Other surveys show that even low-income consumers who cannot afford them think organically grown foods are healthier.

At the same time, general consensus of what is considered healthy is changing. It isn't just about losing weight, exercising or taking vitamin and mineral supplements. Today's prevailing consumer values are simultaneously reflecting a much broader, as well as a more definitive, discerning viewpoint that prizes personal and environmental health, balance, and sustainable, even holistic concerns and choices. More people are realizing that they are out of balance.

Local: Common sense informs that broccoli grown closer to home is fresher and more healthful than broccoli grown on the west coast and shipped cross country. This preference for locally grown produce is pervading the North American shopper's consciousness, and in some cases, local is becoming the new organic.

Organic: Today, the words *healthy food* are synonymous with the word organic in many consumers minds. While the term natural, as we will see, has virtually no legal definition, it is used liberally by a plethora of commercial wanna-be product manufacturers trying to make themselves over as healthy.

Healthy Gourmet: While not yet a widely used industry term, healthy gourmet certainly epitomizes the blending trend of nutrient and high-end flavor-heavy comestibles available in supermarkets, natural food and specialty food stores. Discriminating eaters, whether slow food aficionados, professional chefs or educated, high

DPI university professors, know that the most delicious food also happens to be the most nutritious. No accident here. A simple brix meter, an instrument used by professionals to measure sugar content, will quickly tell you which food is the most tasty – and nutritious. Not coincidentally, the higher the mineral content, the higher the brix or sugar level, and the higher the flavor of a plant or food. Voilà.

Sustainable: While most consumers, even organic food shoppers except the hard-core devotées, probably couldn't give you a literal definition of this term, they are certainly conscious and discerning about their preference that their food be produced sustainably. Sustainable infers a conscious effort to be aware and to exercise resourceful, energy-efficient and environmental strategies in seemingly different areas of economy: healthy lifestyles, ecological lifestyles, alternative healthcare and personal development. Sustainability is a term that extends the scope of the healthy umbrella to the land and growing practices that reflect the values-based perceptions and viewpoints of America's 50 million "cultural creatives." These are considered to be LOHAS Consumers.

Eco-Food Labeling: Food packaging has carried nutrition labels for years, and now we are seeing the emergence of a different kind of label. No, not listing the protein content, but the item's ecological footprint. Initiated by some consumer goods manufacturers such as Timberland's "Our Footprint" label on shoeboxes, as well as UK's Tesco, search for a universally accepted and commonly understood measure of the carbon footprint on their products, the food industry is starting to adopt new legislation and practices which would include "country of origin" and other source information. Some food retailers already label their local, organically grown produce with the names of the farms where it originated. No small feat, a recent *Boston Globe* article quotes an academic researcher who envisions food labels listing not only nutrition but also "relaying their carbon emissions along with their fair-trade credentials." A question in such a scheme,

however, is: how meaningful this kind of information (especially too much information), will be to consumers.

Fair Trade: This movement is another associated market-based segment approach to sustainable development reflecting social justice values. It seeks to empower disadvantaged producers and to protect the environment for future generations, encouraging U.S. consumers to adjust their shopping list, thereby giving industry a nudge in the right direction, which helps make a positive difference. Fair Trade products have grown dramatically in the marketplace, which proves consumers are voting with their purchases for sustainable, ethically-sourced goods. Country-of-origin labeling, now being implemented in the food industry, is another related trend.

Eco-Greening: Another related and amalgam term that integrates active political and lifestyle choices reflecting green politics and green consumerism, typifies the process of incorporating "green" products and processes into one's environment, such as the home work place and general lifestyle. These green qualities include but are not limited to, reduced toxicity, re-usability, energy efficiency, responsible packaging, recycled content, intelligent design, responsible manufacturing techniques, and reduction of personal environmental hazards.

Environmentally friendly companies like Green Home have developed a rigorous approval policy that allows consumers to qualify each product based upon the above criteria as they apply to specific product categories. Carbon footprint, mentioned above, is an associated and relatively new marker term utilized by this growing segment in an attempt to quantify and assess fees for individual and corporate environmental impacts, then proactively funding and seeding green energy initiatives such as solar and wind power in an attempt to help restore ecological balance.

LOHAS: Consumers epitomize these values. See the website, http://lohas.com. LOHAS means Lifestyles of Health and Sustainability, and "describes an estimated $208 billion U.S. marketplace for goods and services focused on health, the environment, social justice, personal development and sustainable living." The consumers attracted to this market have been collectively referred to as Cultural Creatives and represent a sizable group in this country. Approximately 16% percent of the adults in the U.S., or 35 million people, are currently considered LOHAS Consumers." Furthermore, "… focus on Personal Development, with the ultimate goal of achieving his or her full human potential, is of utmost concern to the Cultural Creative. The current growth in this market group strongly supports the notion that spirituality is no longer relegated to the New Age periphery, but is undeniably migrating to the center of mainstream cultural awareness."

LOVOS is an acronym for Lifestyles of Voluntary Simplicity, which refer to consumers who are oriented to health and sustainability similar to LOHAS, but differing from them in their critical consumption attitude and criticism of consumerism. LOVOS are a partial, not distinctly separate group within LOHAS that gave important impulses as trendsetters to an ecologically-sustainable lifestyle. It is an essential characteristic of LOVOS that environmental awareness is in agreement with environmentally suitable behavior. From the point of view of marketing, LOVOS is considered a marginal phenomenon which is often neglected; but in terms of the society impacts, LOVOS comprises a futurable potential. It exemplifies the evolving holistic viewpoint, blending into the emerging spiritual values and consciousness that accompany this ideology. It reflects individual responsibility and choices beyond "Think Global, Act Local" to "Live Simply So Others can Simply Live." Population carrying-capacity is definitely an unavoidable discussion in this scheme of things.

"Natural," "Zero Trans Fat" and other Eco-Obscenities: The food industry is responding, although not without wincing resistance. Consumer upsurge in devotion to healthful food and lifestyles is a strong testimony to the power that consumers have in affecting and changing the trends, what is available and what is possible even though consumers, as a rule, are still the most unorganized and victimized of all segments in the food system. Whether organized or not, consumers and their dollars count. Within the last five years, since the astounding growth in natural and organic foods, the food industry has finally come around and is sitting up straight, awake and alert in their boardroom chairs, finally getting it that the "health food" trend is no fleeting fad. Whereas a bunch of long-haired counterculture revolutionaries calling for more healthful food could be easily dismissed in the late sixties, the food industries in the nineties could no longer ignore the millions of mothers and others who became dedicated organic and natural food shoppers, especially when it came to their kids.

The industry has not only responded, it has dived in with astounding fervor. The trade shows held by the commercial food industry now surprisingly resemble natural food shows. And for the past three years, the Organic Trade Association's annual All Things Organic Show has been held concurrently with four other major food industry sector shows, including produce, exports, and fancy foods at the mammoth Food Marketing Institute's annual food industry universe show in Chicago. The industry is crazed with the 'healthy' buzz.

Nutrition sells. Not because commercial food is actually substantially more nutritious, but because of extensive corporate promotion and marketing, consumers are led to think so. Public perception and awareness on the subject is definitely up. Essentially the food industry has taken three approaches to increase sales to take advantage of the groundswell of consumer passion about health and healthy food.

"HEALTHIFYING" AND TECHNOFOODS

First, food manufacturers' lobbyists have gone to great lengths, as nutritionist Marion Nestle explains in *Food Politics*, to protect its own interests by influencing government programs dispensing dietary advise about food and nutrition to the public.

Second, the nutritional and dietary supplement industry, which not only gets approximately 70% of its raw materials from the pharmaceutical and chemical industries but is surreptitiously controlled by them, (despite the appearance and existence of many cottage-y mom and pop independent health food stores), has developed into a niche market with so much clout that it has been able to leverage market demand into, up to this point, unfettered marketing of its products. This is rapidly changing.

Third, the food industry has launched a dual supplementation or subtraction approach, enhancing or reformulating foods and beverages with health claims and benefits that go beyond the food's original nutritive qualities. This ranges from enriching and fortifying foods with vitamins, minerals, herbs or other nutrients, to reducing the calories, fat or sugars by substituting artificial ingredients, even creating new categories of "functional foods" and their often bio-identical "neutraceuticals."

Although these approaches may seem to be advantageous, the majority of them are still focused narrowly and based on that old familiar rationale of trying to isolate things down to pinpoint their active parts or elements. This is very similar to the medical model. Based on the presumption that the health or protective benefits inherent in fruits and vegetables, say, come from one particular nutrient or component, the industry also reasons that if a little is good, then more will be better. This leads to the standard practice of amping up the amount of any isolated, replicated synthetic vitamin or a concentrate of phytoestrogens, for example. As Nestle and other nutrition professionals point out, this is clearly flawed logic, since being healthy is really dependent more upon dietary patterns or habits than single nutrients or foods. And this quantitative industrial "magic bullet" approach widely misses the mark by failing to acknowledge the complexity and dynamic interaction of nutrients in foods.

Of course, much of manufacturer "healthifying" is purely marketing spin, and just about as real as that made up word. Unbeknownst to most consumers, trans-fats are essentially a problem generated by the food industry, inadvertently produced through adding hydrogen gas to vegetable oils which makes the oil shelf-stable (and one molecule away from being a plastic). The industry though, with the skill of a magician's sleight of hand, has whisked the curtain away to reveal an amazing feat: another shiny new, synthetically manipulated table spread that now appears pristine and healthy, without any of its nasty "trans fats," as if they were doing consumers a favor in removing some inherently bad part of the plant. Vegetable oil corporation executives must certainly be smiling at their near-flawless coup, because their "zero-trans fat" scam has netted them millions of dollars.

Actually, they've been smiling for years, since their successful wholesale and widespread marketing of cheaper and more easily stabilized mono-and poly-unsaturated oils accomplished through an elaborate and expensive campaign to get doctors to endorse these new, manipulated plastic fats and vote "thumbs down" to the traditional saturated fats that have been consumed for millennia, and are, we know now, actually beneficial and necessary for good health. You can and should read the politics and history of this tawdry story in *Know Your Fats*, by Sally Fallon and Mary Enig, to get a birds-eye view of yet another sad story in the saga of "civilized" food supply, now flipping a trans-fat liability into a marketing advantage.

As a result of the big push to produce and market the proliferation of processed and or completely fabricated "techno foods," the public is confused. All this one-upmanship in nutritional claims makes it difficult for consumers to determine the true nutritive value of normal, everyday whole foods, blurring the distinctions between foods, supplements and drugs. It is also increasingly challenging to protect consumers from harmful substances in foods, and most of all, it really increases consumers' confusion about exactly what is the most healthful way to eat.

This is so ironically epitomized and perpetuated in Michael Pollan's *The Omnivore's Dilemma*, as pointed out by Weston A. Price Foundation President, Sally Fallon, in her Summer 2007 issue of *Wise Traditions* Presidential Message. Pollan is so correct about the dark and dirty politics and polemics of industrial agriculture and the industrial food complex, yet still so short sighted, tripped up and blind-sighted, paddling the wrong way down the vegetable oil river of myths perpetuated by the very system he so accurately dissects and roasts. Once again, we're placing bets about what, when the truth comes out in the final analysis, will ultimately be revealed about the ultimate wisdom of the truly cultured, old fashioned, traditional way to eat, including reliance on animals for nutritional and ecological balance.

WADING THROUGH THE HYPE

Although they may not understand the science or the technical specifics, consumers' sixth sense is getting surprisingly acute. Take "Frankenfoods," for example, the pejorative slang assigned to genetically modified foods. Consumers all over the world are becoming more vocal in their skepticism and opposition of genetic engineering and the indiscriminate use of genetically modified ingredients in processed food. Western Europe and Scandinavia have been much more adamant about prohibiting BST/BGH and other genetically-engineered compounds from their food

> It would be nice if the Food and Drug Administration stopped issuing warnings about toxic substances and just gave me the names of one or two things still safe to eat.
>
> – Robert Fuoss

supply, even rejecting US beef because of the hormones and potential problems with our genetic manipulation of feedstocks.

One of the first issues in this fight is over labeling. While the industry and through its pressure, the government continues to maintain the ruse that GM foods are safe and there is no difference between bio-engineered tomatoes and regular hybrid varieties (thus tomatoes "don't need to be labeled"), consumers continue to be skeptical. When polled, even the man or woman who doesn't give a flip about eating organic food, is staunchly outraged and vocal about their right to know whether food in the market has been genetically altered. This interesting bit was revealed by Good Morning America's ABC news segment on GM foods in November 2006. In short, these shoppers clearly would not being buying GM foods, if they were labeled so that they could tell the difference. They have good reasons to refuse GM foods.

"The challenge is to transform human laws to match natural laws, not vice versa," says Center for Food Safety Director, Attorney Andrew Kimbrell, one of the leaders in the anti-GMO movement. But try to tell that to the industry. Though this mirrors consumer sentiment, it's still a small voice crying in a wilderness of corporate food executives, such as the 800-pound organic gorilla, the natural foods industry tag given to describe Wal-mart's instant status as the world's largest organic retailer once they decided to carry a few items. They're all busy now salivating to profit from consumers' willingness to pay more for what they consider to be 'healthier.'

Problems with pesticide and antibiotic resistance have been increasingly surfacing for a number of years. Genetically engineered foods, on the other hand, are a whole another set of problems. While corn, soy and other grains have been hybridized by seed companies since 1926, when the first commercial seed corn company, Pioneer Hi-Breds, founded in Des Moines, Iowa, tried to try to take advantage of hybrid vigor of the new genetically engineered seed stocks. The hybrid seed are an entirely different class of tinkering. The potential problems are staggering, even though they are just beginning to surface. The most in-depth animal study on genetically modified food published to date was performed on test rats. The results include pre-cancerous stomach growths and smaller brains, livers and testicles. This study was later published in *Lancet*, and shows severe damage from consumption of genetically modified foods. Read Jeffrey Smith's *Seeds of Deception* or his new, definitive *Genetic Roulette* at www.seedsofdeception.com, or call toll-free 1-800-717-7000.

While the term "organic," or more accurately "organically grown," carries legitimate and hard won standards — thanks to a small group of us dedicated healthy foods crusaders in the mid-1980's — the term "natural" has no standards whatsoever. "Natural" is truly meaningless; since it carries no legal definition or standards, it is loosely, liberally and profusely scattered on food labels by commercial food companies feigning 'healthy hats.' In reality, the word natural is almost an eco-obscenity to serious foodies, reminiscent as it is of the late 1960's advertising slogan of one of the major oil companies that maintained by discarding old car hulls on the ocean bottom, they were creating new homes for fishes.

Just as in the case of trans fat, we as consumers have become righteously skeptical about food marketing and labeling claims of products from the large corporate conglomerates. And rightly so. For the bottom line is always the holiest to corporations, and consumers are getting hip to the fact that these food cats can't be trusted, no matter how 'healthy' they portray their products to be. Especially since buyers have been tipped off far too many times by repeated occurrences of the "Whoops, we were wrong about that" corporate excuses for out-of-the-blue mysterious discoveries of problems with chemicals, ingredients or drugs that were rubber-stamped by the FDA and rushed onto the market with inadequate or no testing. Only five or ten years later these products may be found causing cancer, or sterility or immune dysfunction. Cyclamates, Vioxx, DDT, hydrogenated fats, Thalidomide, genetic engineering, to name just a few.

Mark my word, many more such discoveries are coming. With the shortsighted injection, one by one, of short-term tested (if at all), 80,000 chemicals into the food system, you don't have to be a biochemist to realize we are dealing with a time bomb that has been ticking for too long. No wonder the average American is distrustful, and saying in reference to nutritional labels, "if I can't pronounce it, I don't want it."

But as in all things, what goes around eventually comes around. Here is a bit of what is just now coming around:

A July 4th, 2007 article in the International Herald Tribune revealed published findings of a consortium of scientists that challenge the traditional view of the way genes function, a discovery that calls into question the very principles upon which the $73.5 billion dollar global biotech industry is built. The exhaustive, four-year effort, organized by the United States National Human Genome Research Institute and carried out by 35 groups from 80 organizations around the world, surprised researchers when they found out recently that the human genome might not be a tidy collection of independent genes after all, with each sequence of DNA linked to a single function, such as a predisposition to diabetes, heart disease or sound vocal cords. Rather, genes appear to operate in a complex network, and interact and overlap with one another and with other components in ways not yet fully understood. According to the Institute, these findings will challenge scientists "to rethink some long-held views about what genes are and what they do."

The presumption that genes operate independently has been institutionalized since 1976, when the first biotech company was founded. In fact, it is the economic and regulatory foundation on which the entire biotechnology industry is built. Known as the Central Dogma of Molecular Biology, this mechanistic "one gene, one protein" theory held that each gene in living organisms, from humans to bacteria, carries the information needed to construct one protein. It has been the basis for recombinant DNA and a whole industry that as of 2005 has patented more than 4,000 human genes in the United States alone, a small fraction of the total number of plant, animal and microbial genes that are now "owned" by corporate interests. This new information dawning is likely to have repercussions far beyond the laboratory.

Commonsense alone could tell you that we were bound to have problems. Antibiotics that were once considered miracle drugs did greatly reduce the probability that people would die from common acute bacterial infections. But of course, doctors didn't yet know that the genetic material responsible for antibiotic resistance moves easily between different species of bacteria. Over-prescribing antibiotics for virtually every ailment has given rise to "superbugs" that are now virtually un-killable. Now they know. And "Gee, we didn't know," is about all they can say. No apologies, no accountability, and NO bandages for this one.

By the way, genetically modified crops can carry an antibiotic effect that will also promote the development of "superbugs." See Jeffrey Smith at www.seedsofdeception.com.

DISCERNING THE TRUTH

Of course, ignorant consumers are still no match for the power and might of the dollars behind sophisticated corporate marketing, psychological and subtly manipulated scientific research and development efforts to subconsciously and even subliminally hit consumer hot buttons with alluring emotional images and rhetoric, further reinforcing the lie that "things, including consuming their quasi-healthy foods" can make you happy, healthy, slim and beautiful.

Or for the immense, but yet undetected bulldozer of health in the process of steamrolling all things healthful in the name of food safety and security and, ironically, consumer protection - the regulation proposed by and promoted by WHO (World Health Organization), Codex alimentarius.

The website spells out (in a confusing manner)

international food rules that are in the process of being adopted to standardize food and supplement laws in line with drug law, and to declare foods to be drugs, therefore regulated as are drugs. European countries have already seen some of this happen; for instance, in Germany, simple supplements (zinc, for example, like you would take for tissue health), has increased many times in price, the equivalent of $74 dollars for a small bottle. And now, zinc is not available for purchase "over the counter." The consumer must have a doctor's script and present it to a dispensing pharmacist. Make no mistake about it, this WILL TAKE AWAY access to the plentiful selection of nutrient-dense supplements that are still, as this is written, available on natural food store shelves.

There are definitely forces in this world not wanting this kind of information publicized. Yet, the fact remains: this is happening NOW. This is not time to cower in the corner. It is time to get alert, become educated and get in gear.

FERMENTATION HAPPENS

We may not have the luxury of being able to depend upon supplements to maintain our health. But we will always have fermentation. Fermentation happens. There have been brief and fruitless efforts, known as prohibition, trying to control the production of alcoholic beverages, but it is virtually impossible to control or limit this ubiquitous phenomenon.

Of course, the industry and the government are quick to do the semantic shuffle in an effort to stay ahead of consumers and keep them in the dark. For instance: new legislation and procedures in the almond industry. As of September 2007, all almonds on the market are required to be pasteurized (by either heat treatment, short blasts of steam or dry heat, or chemical fumigation with a carcinogenic chemical that's used for manufacturing bowling balls and foam seat cushions, as well as insecticide), a remedial, preventive, knee-jerk measure in response to small outbreaks of salmonella that occurred in the California almond industry in 2001 and 2004. That's all I have to say about it.

Except: almonds, unlike many other crops, are 100% pollinated by bees. In fact, almond crops

heavily rely upon and work the thousands of bees that are trucked in every year to perform this necessary task. Now we have a REAL problem with the bees disappearing. Almonds are cultivated in the dead and lifeless soil of the San Joaquin and Sacramento valleys where they are heavily sprayed with pesticides, herbicides and fungicides.

Perhaps this sounds good to the unaware, especially with the scare about food safety and "terrorist tampering." But we should ask, who are the terrorists?

As Bill Maher acerbically nailed it when interviewing Tommy Thompson, exiting Secretary of Health and Human Services, after Thompson's comments about the susceptibility of our food supply to terrorist attack: "Heck, food terrorists are no problem. Everyone knows the food industry's already beaten them to it, making our food way more toxic with chemicals than the so-called terrorists could ever manage, making people sick so their buddies, the pharmaceutical companies, can come back with drugs to keep us alive, but barely functioning." Mr. Thompson seemed more than just a little bit uncomfortable with this truth torpedo.

Who is studying the bigger picture and connecting the dots? Don't count on your government or the food producers; they're looking down at the bottom line.

But everything circles. Everything that goes around, comes around. You can't eat money. "They" can't even eat money. And though it is my overarching aim to do away with "We" and "They" dichotomies, hopefully that's what these "food" manipulators will find out, and will enjoy eating it

when the bottom drops out of their bottom line. Such blasphemy, and coming from a consultant who works in the industry. But someone needs to say it. Don't shoot the messenger. The writing's been on the wall for a long time, and now all hell is starting to break loose. The system is dying.

All natural systems, and even apparently the artificially colored and artificially flavored commercial food system, operate in circles. You can't do just one thing, and it's not nice to fool Mother Nature. They said it themselves. Now the circle is coming back around like a boomerang, and will strike the myopic, narrowly focused, money-motivated big-food, ag and drug conglomerates in their backsides. Like Pasteur, they've missed the point and the boat, as well.

Consumers are saying - nay, shouting: "We want delicious, good, old fashioned, nutritious REAL food." I would say "whole" before the food" but now that word's been blemished, too, and this time, unfortunately by the top retail purveyor of natural and organic foods in the industry. But it's almost as though ignorant consumers somehow just know, just sense, that the line, (read "lie") we all are being fed about the low fat saga, for one example, is a lot of baloney – that is, chopped up, ground up, chemically-treated and manipulated from low-value foodstuff, artificially fattened with GM foodstock. Their noses and taste buds, as jaded as they have become from low-nutrient, low fat food, simply refuse to believe the moralistic shaming of their bodys' unquenchable lust for and enjoyment of rich, fatty foods — the nutrient dense, naturally high fat animal products that native cultures couldn't quantify or identify, but knew and understood in their bones and in their bodies were infinitely and undeniably nurturing, essential to their health and their well-being.

Money talks. For awhile. Remember, though, "time heels all wounds."

A CULTURAL RENAISSANCE AND REVIVAL

But there is also another new food revolution, a fermentation, a fomentation in food, eating philosophies and lifestyles going on all over the world, really. It amounts to a cultural revival, a revolution, in effect, around food and the environment, far surpassing the 1960's hippies back-to-the-land, back-to-the-beans-and-grains movement that we knew as the Woodstock generation. Now hand in hand, generation to generation, people all over are reclaiming their connection to food and the land in many exciting and hopeful ways. And these are just a few of the monikers:

A RAINBOW OF DIETS – AND OPINIONS

vegetarian	food sovereignty	beer activists
lacto-vegetarian	food gleaners	biofuels/biomass
quasi vegetarian	fresh foods	gene action
vegan	local foods	slow food
fair trade	live cultured	small scale
fair labor	foods	sustainable
ecoexchange	nutrient dense	traditional foods
ecoboomers	foods	LOHAS
food justice	raw foods	LOVOS
food security	slow foods	light eaters

There is a literal rainbow of popular diets and philosophies, books and websites that encompass a wide diversity of opinion about what is the best way to eat. Diet, health, and cookbooks abound. The fitness industry is one gigantic reflection of the trends. The number of self-help books in the health and wellness category, now the largest category of non-fiction book sales, keeps climbing every year, as people look away from the medical paradigm toward being more in charge of their lives and true preventive health.

Yet how can the average consumer who wants to lose weight and be healthier know what's real and what's Memorex®? Is low-fat better, or is it actually dangerous? Is soy really a health food or is a smoke-screened health menace? Does cholesterol really matter that much and is low cholesterol actually more problematic in the final analysis than high cholesterol? (A mute point, from a larger perspective, since your body produces more cholesterol every day than you could easily consume.) This point is, it's still a confusing scene out there, and no wonder some people just throw up their hands and say, "Heck with it all, it doesn't matter, everything causes cancer." Hmm.. Considering Michio Kuchi's seemingly caustic, enigmatic comment… "Cancer is the cure, civilization is the disease," this seems (somewhat and eerily) prophetic.

WHOM TO BELIEVE?

The divisions and the debates in contemporary diets, food philosophies and regimens is no less confusing, almost rivaling religious wars. This is almost dizzying. Appalling really, when you consider how much information, ignorance – and sheer need — there is out there.

"Food is the vehicle with the most potential for personal and planetary transformation."
~David Yarrow "Closing the Food Circle", NY State's, first organic conference, Ithaca, NY, November 1984

The government and the medical establishment physicians are telling us one thing, like eat 9-16 servings of grain a day, which I, myself and many evolved food and nutrition professionals, as well as countless numbers of tuned in crunchy people surpassed in the seventies' on our way to understanding what true nourishment and nurturance is. Makes me think of the "Is Martha Stewart Living?" Parody's first issue with its article and recipes for making "90 grain bread."

TRADITIONAL VERSUS MODERN DIETS

While established modern dietary practices keep shifting, almost as much and as fast as the panoply of fad diets that populate the airwaves and the bookshelves, traditional diets have withstood the test of time. Dentist Weston A. Price's survey and documentation of traditional diets in the 1920's revealed with photographic clarity and word, the effect of modern processed foods on the health, dentures, facial structure and even fertility of so-called primitive tribes of traditional peoples all over the planet. *His Nutrition and Physical Degeneration*, a classic text on the subject, showed the devastating effect of modern processed foods had, even within one generation on the health, fertility and vitality of early man.

Fats, a hot topic of debate across the entire nutritional and dietary spectrum, are still a quagmire of politically and economically motivated half-truths and outright lies, mostly trying to convince us that the cheaper to produce grain and vegetable oils are inherently better for us than the most costly, yet nutrient dense animal fats.

Yet, the sad but unadulterated truth is that the good old fats – the naturally saturated butter, lard, and coconut oils, as well as the high essential fatty acid extra virgin olive and flax oils, – it turns out, are actually the healthier. We hear the gasps, especially about the saturated part. But once again, the truth in the end will out. The fact is, traditional cultures before the aberated culinary dogmas of the later half of the 20th century, deeply valued, prized and literally devoured the rich fats and the organ meats of animals grazed on green grass. They never ate lean meat, in fact they sought out the fattest animals and relished the fat along with the muscle meat or later

drowned it in butter-rich sauces, but only after they had savored the fattiest parts of the animal – the *foie gras*, the organ meats, and the marrow gleaned from the bones.

"What's fascinating is the fact that good science – not food puritanism masquerading as science – validates traditional wisdom, "recounts Sally Fallon in her recent *Wise Traditions President's Message* editorial, "An Open Letter to Michael Pollan."

Good science, as she continues, has discovered that vital nutrients in the fats and organs of animals, like Vitamin A, D and K, are critical to normal growth and reproduction. The "nasty" cholesterol and saturated fat that the real "fat cat" vegetable snake oil salesmen have managed to cast wholesale aspersions upon are in the final analysis, key and unavoidable imperatives for normal functioning of our brains, lungs, kidneys, immune and reproductive systems. This has already witnessed by all too many of us nutritional counselors in the past few years confronted with the sad sappy pallor of too many vegan vegetarians who've literally stripped out their body's fertility with their disciplined, and arrogant insistence on low fat, no fat or vegetable-oil-is-superior-to-animal-fat dogmatics.

"The nutrients lost when we move animals from grass to Concentrated Animal Feedlot Operations, are the very nutrients that protect the arteries from calcification, prevent arthritis, cure cancer and confer that greatest gift of gifts – children who are healthy, strong and happy," Sally Fallon emphasizes.

LOW CARB AND PALEO DIETS

Of course, as discussed before, Paleolithic man, up until only 10,000 years ago, for the most part feasted on whatever he could find close to him on his nomadic travels to access food and water. Loren Cordain, widely acknowledged as one of the leading experts on the natural human diet of our Stone Age ancestors, has discussed this thoroughly in his book *The Paleo Diet*, showing that early man was eating meats (raw) vegetables (cooked) shoots, nuts, seeds, fruits and whatever other mobile creatures he learned he could rely on to sustain his life. And while he might be pushing it, stretching it to think that ancient caveman stripped off the skin and threw away the bulbous fat to eat skinless, boneless chicken breast, his points are well-taken. Grains and dairy products simply weren't a part of the picture, either digestible or sustainable enough, for that matter, to be eaten over the long haul. Unless, of course, as we have discussed, they were subjected to transformation. Yet, this alone does not get them out of the proverbial dietary woods.

Today, this is reflected in dietary principles and practices such as the Atkins Diet, The South Beach Diet and Metabolic Typing, the basis of the no-grain *Dr Mercola's TOTAL HEALTH Program* book which I co-authored with Dr. Joseph Mercola, recommending and verifying diets low on the Glycemic Index.

Glycemic Index is a ranking of foods based on their rate of carbohydrate conversion to sugar. High glycemic foods, like processed sugars and starches, rapidly break down and release energy into the blood stream, wheras low glycemic foods such as higher protein meats and fats, release energy more slowly, preventing the abrupt spikes in blood sugar and insulin release that are known to exacerbate or facilitate insulin resistance, diabetes, weight control and cardiovascular problems. Foods that stimulate insulin surges such as white bread, commercial cereals, etc. can cause people to eat 60 - 70% more calories at the following meal, creating sugar cravings, causing hyperactivity and mood swings, cortisol production, fat storage, weight gain and other more insidious problems. Notice again that it's primarily the processed carbohydrates that are largely the culprits here.

Keeping blood sugars more stable through emphasis on low glycemic diets featuring natural foods helps to reduce hunger, increase satiety and endurance, and regulate hormonal levels, lower blood lipids, promoting well-being. Low glycemic food plans have been proven to reduce incidence of Type II diabetes and to help control Type I and II diabetes, hypoglycemia and hypertension. Low glycemic foods, the kinds that have been traditionally consumed over thousands of years, do not stimulate food-craving hormones and thus help people to keep their energy on a more even keel.

This is a major factor in today's inexhorable, insatiable sweet tooth and the generation of a multi-million dollar grain –based caloric and non-nutritive

artificial sweetener industry, contributing to an unprecedented incidence of Diabesity®, diabetes and obesity, our number one healthcare problem.

Commonsense, once again, could shortcut the debate. Usually when I ask the question, "And what do they use to fatten cattle?" the quiet answer is, "Oh yes……..grain."

But while the medical and healthcare industry has, for the most part, remained in denial, refusing to fully acknowledge the impact of our out-of-control sweet tooth, the rampant blood sugar control problem and the impact of such sweeteners as high fructose corn syrup on the situation, at least some consumers themselves are getting the picture and starting to reduce their consumption, leading natural foods industry marketing research firms like the Hartman Group to counsel food manufacturer's "to get the HFCS out of your foods and do it quickly." This is not the only area where consumers are taking things into their own hands when it comes to their dietary habits.

VEGAN VEGETARIANS VERSUS AAJONUS'S CARNIVORES

One of the more passionate and vociferous debates involving some of the most popular trends in contemporary dietary cultures is that of the raw food vegan vegetarians versus raw meat eaters. Like stalwart gladiators in the dietary coliseum arena, they appear as staunchly opposed enemies, locked in the battle over nutritional superiority.

The raw food vegan vegetarians have largely been inspired by the work of Ann Wigmore, Hippocrates Health Institute, in the 1970's, when she cured herself of a cancer death sentence by eating grass from her front yard. Her program, which has been developed and spread to a number of retreat centers throughout North America, involves adoption of a natural program of body purification, nutrition and rejuvenation through the use of fresh raw fruits, vegetables, juices, nuts, sprouted seeds, grains, beans, chlorophyll rich greens and wheatgrass juice. And thousands of sick and highly toxic people who have undertaken similar detoxification programs for days, weeks or even months, most assuredly see an improvement in their overall health and vitality, often emerging with a renewed sense of optimism, feeling perhaps better than they have felt in years.

As a short term detoxification program, —- often accompanied, incidentally, by fermented foods such as rejuvelac or sprouted and fermented vegetables, to help clean out, break through and dissolve the buildup of toxic waste products that are an unfortunate, but natural consequence of eating a S.A.D. (Standard American Diet) – they are unbeatable.

Yet, ironically, this is the same result that others report from following rejuvenation programs which are based upon eating animal products, including, yes… raw and fermented meat products. Spearheaded by the albeit eclectic, but well researched Aajonus Vonderplanitz, (purportedly a name he created for himself) these programs utilize raw foods, including vegetables, but rely on a much higher percentage of raw animal products such as raw milk, cream, raw and cultured muscle and organ meats.

Some comments from individuals after months or a year on this raw meat "Primal Diet." "I moved from a 100% raw vegan diet to the primal diet. So when I first ate raw meat it actually tasted good. Raw fish was even better. I found that the more fat content in the raw meat, the better tasting it is…. Also, I would eat the raw meat with raw butter mixed in with it. I like the natural taste of it. I believe because the raw animal foods are nutrient-dense, I am nourishing every cell in my body. On the raw vegan diet, I was always hungry. With adding the raw animal foods in my diet, my belly is always content."

The warning signs and problems with the exclusively vegan vegetarian raw food regimens start to appear when 1) the relieved and renewed patients, having successfully pursued a fasting or modified fasting program, extrapolate that this should be their permanent, longterm dietary regimen and that no matter what, this is the healthiest and — as we shall see — most holy way to eat. and 2) when the new converts become zealots, embracing their new dietary regimes with a religious fervor that shifts rapidly into "raw food fundamentalism," as they become dedicated to converting the whole world, beating and boring everyone they know with their newly found dietary philosophy, which they transfer into the moral and spiritual realm, all too frequently and unfortunately acquiring an air of superiority and an attitude of judgemental disdain for anyone who doesn't fully agree, embrace their regimen or "see the light."

Don't get me wrong, it is my belief as a food and nutrition professional that we all need to get into the habit of eating a balanced diet that contains a high percentage of fresh, healthy, organic, local, raw and, of course, cultured food. But I also know, personally and professionally, that what's best for me or anyone to eat, at any particular time, depends upon a variety of factors. Metabolism, weather and climate, just for a couple of examples. In the summer, for example, when it's hot and muggy, my body is just naturally drawn to and hungers for a fresh, raw diet. And so in the hot weather in the midwest, I eat an almost exclusively uncooked or fermented food diet such as yogurt, nuts, fruit, salads and vegetables.

Yet, at the same time, I personally have what is called a high oxidative metabolic rate, and burn up calories fast, characteristic of what we call a "protein type." While my Blood Type A, according to *Eat Right For Your Type* guru Peter D'Adamo, should make me the perfect vegetarian – especially because Blood Type A individuals produce less stomach acid and therefore should theoretically do better on plant-based foods, I have already been there, done that, and have proven to myself again and again, that I don't do well on a strict vegetarian diet.

In the past, through the long foray into exploring every single imaginable contemporary and spiritual eating philosophy going, I discovered that I don't get enough protein on a vegetarian diet. I'm always craving protein and fat, because my body has a higher natural requirement for these nutrients, and I do not tolerate unfermented soy products, such as tofu or soymilk. So I supplement my diet with at least a small amount of animal products, even in the summer. The reality is that my own father's Blood Type O, characteristically "omnivore" which I must have somehow integrated into my own system, has a greater impact on my system than might appear to be operating. I have an Blood Type A, yet it's all

Do Vegetarians Eat Animal Crackers?
- unknown

relative. And I'm the only one who can determine this, based on my own bodily yearnings, hungers, reactions, performance.

I'm using myself as an example here, because it's important to understand that each of us is unique, with distinct and specific nutritional and energy requirements that can change and vary depending upon the circumstances. And no matter what my theoretical "type", the fact is, I have to keep reasessing my own food needs, based upon what's happening in my life at the moment. We are each in this situation, and as we say in Metabolic Typing, "You are unique." You may not think so, but you are the expert when it comes to your own body and knowing what it needs at any particular time. No expert, no matter how knowledgeable or trained, can do this for you. You and only you are in the best position to determine what your body needs foodwise. Of course, being honest and listening to the deeper calls, versus, say, a craving for sugar or chocolate, is a prerequisite for this. Oops, sorry. Scratch chocolate there, we all know that everyone has their own minimum requirement for the chocolate food group. But once again, you alone can determine this.

Just a little aside insight here, inordinate cravings for such strong foods as chocolate, alcohol, coffee, etc. are being fingered as a reflection of neurotransmitter and hormonal imbalances. And with the newly discovered information about stress and digestion, and the not so surprising incidence of poor digestion and metabolism of proteins being a bigger problem in our current dietary dilemma than is widely recognized, it's actually no wonder that food cravings of this type are such a common occurrence. Dr. Brice E. Vickery tested over 2,300 clients, discovering that over 90 percent of them eating a Standard American Diet (S.A.D) were not digesting proteins properly. Nutritional researcher R. Neil Voss and associates also confirmed this.

Up until recently, science had identified 22 known amino acids. Recently two more were discovered. In addition to the 10 essential amino acids that must be acquired from food, the human body is known to be able to produce six amino acids itself.

However, these new findings, according to Voss, indicate that the purpose for producing these amino acids is to ensure that proteins are utilized as proteins instead of being changed into fat or carbohydrates only when the body is functioning normally, that is, not when the body is under stress. (Who is not under stress in this modern world?) This is a definite reason for consuming more raw, enzyme-active food every day, a live insurance policy to assist and support proper digestion.

Please know that not every vegan vegetarian raw foodist is radical and judgmental. Many people do acknowledge and embrace the wisdom of being flexible. For example, Donald Haughey, founder of Michigan's Creative Health Institute that teaches Ann Wigmore's raw food philosophy, follows the Wigmore diet. However, he shares that he does consume up to four or so eggs per week. And increasingly conscious, evolved individuals are recognizing the reality that all of us are different and that we all are unique, with individual metabolic, physiologic, social, cultural and philosophical differences that shape and determine our dietary needs at any particular time. No one diet is right for everyone, for all of us, or for anyone of us all of the time.

Furthermore, as a Metabolic Typing specialist, I know and have witnessed that people change and that their metabolisms change at different points in their life based on a wide variety of factors, from cultural to physiological, philosophical to spiritual, including age, level of activity, climate, location, environment and degree of conscious evolution. People's metabolisms can change, based simply on their tuning into and following their own body promptings of what they need, to say nothing of the concurrent changes in physiology that mirror even a simple shift in belief. This is, in itself, the subject of a whole other book.

If you would like more insight and understanding about the basics of Metabolic Typing, discovering and fulfilling your individual dietary needs, I suggest reading *Dr. Mercola's TOTAL HEALTH Program* and *The Metabolic Typing Diet* by William Wolcott.

Just an aside… I've often wondered:
Do vegetarians eat animal crackers?
　　-Author Unknown

RAW VERSUS COOKED

Another corollary, and at times violent, or at least vehement, debate among alternative food gurus and contemporary dietary authorities is the debate of "raw versus cooked." The raw food vegan vegetarians, including a subgroup who identify themselves as Natural Hygienists, are often unequivocally pitted against the cooked food macrobiotics. Following the contemporary teachings of Michio Kushi, based on the earlier work of George Ohsawa, these cooked food devotees embrace a peaceful lifestyle, a way of life called "macrobiotics." Ironically, a term ostensibly credited to Hippocrates, macrobiotics includes a contemporary dietary philosophy incorporating a simple diet of lightly cooked or fermented traditional foods such as brown rice, miso soup and vegetables.

The raw food fervorists are not the only ones who have succumbed to "should-ing." The macrobiotic devotees are not exempt from their own brand of nutritional elitism. Nor are they alone. Myriad dietary dialects and mini philosophies zoom in to attach and focus on a particular set of beliefs in regard to prudent eating.

In my own search for the causative "bottom line" of health, I have researched and explored many scientific, holistic and naturally-based principles, and noted that pH, the measurement of relative acidity and alkalinity in the body, was a basic premise of the relationship with food.

The *Alkalinize-or-Die* crowd, led by such luminaries as Dr. Robert O. Young, Naturopath, and doominaries, Dr. M. Ted Morter, Jr., MA, fixate on pH (the balanced measurement of acid and base in the body) as the benchmark and foundation for pursuing and maintaining proper health. The pH sect has devised complicated charts geared to strict consumption of foods based on pH reading, in an attempt to control and keep the body's pH level at a perfectly balanced 7 on the acid/base scale. They are certainly right about pH. It is an

indicator of health. The problem is just that it is only one indicator of health.

And trying to control and keep pH at a constant under the assumption that it is an assurance of no health problems is …shallow. This modality does not recognize normal everyday variations in pH of body fluids, saliva, urine, blood, nor the fact that everyone is different and that certain physiological and metabolic types are just naturally more acidic than some others.

So, some philosophies pigeonhole concepts and extrapolate them out to apply to everyone as if we are all alike. This is hardly different from the quantitative medical model that assumes everyone in a certain sex, weight and age range is going to have the same needs and requirements, and that we can reduce solutions down to the least common denominator in order to efficient-ize healthcare.

Others, in denial, mixing apples and oranges rationalizations, boast "Oh I can eat anything. I just transmute." Believable from as enlightened holy man, less so from someone who's obese.

ORTHOREXIA NERVOSA AND THE HEALTH FOOD JUNKIES

Sometimes with hysteria, most often with a lot of passion and emotion, the factions and debates rage on over the "right" diet and the "right" or "correct" way to eat, flashing on health magazines covers like lightning in a blinding storm.

Orthorexia Nervosa is a term coined by Steven Bratman, MD, who shares with me the reformed status of being a cook and an organic gardener in a rather large community in upstate New York.

His book, *Health Food Junkies*, does a lot to elucidate a balanced viewpoint on a long overdue subject, radicalism within the healthful food movement.

"A sense of admirable idealism is often a motivating factor encouraging people to take responsibility for their own health and to explore different diets.

However, the development of emotional attachments to philosophies underlying such diets can often end up becoming far more important for some individuals than the results they obtain or fail to. One result has been widespread refusal in the alternative diet community to face health and behavioral problems that may arise on these diets. A common thread is a kind of subjective "blinded naturalism" that has become more or less endemic in the vegetarian, raw-food, and alternative diet movements, which can lead to serious health troubles." Bratman insights.

Someone personally delivered to me a recent first hand account of one very prominent and well-known, then green-haired, raw food chef who was bodily removed from a total health show for throwing insults and styrofoam cups at the Hari Khrishna devotees serving their overcooked and soggy, but brimming with "chi" or prasad, holy blessed vegetables. "Holier than thou" attitudes about food are sometimes more toxic and acid producing than a whole plateful of commercial plastic cheese and synthetic snacks. This well known raw celebrity chef might be enhanced by heeding the words of Charles Eisenstein in *The Yoga of Eating*: "So please do not turn your reverence for food into an obsession that diminishes the sacredness of any other part of life."

"There are people who strictly deprive themselves of each and every eatable, drinkable, and smokable which has in any way

Entropy
Life and Fossil Fuels

Entropy is a measure of the dispersal of energy. It measures how much energy is spread out in a particular process, or how widely spread out it becomes. When energy is diffused, it is unavailable to do useful work. So, the higher the entropy the less energy is available to do useful work.

All physical systems move from a state of low entropy to a state of high entropy. The amount of energy available in a system is always less than the total energy of the system. Whenever energy changes forms or is used, a portion of it is lost to entropy.

It is important to understand that the total amount of energy in the universe is always growing, and can never be diminished. We can maintain the appearance of reducing entropy in a subsystem only by bringing in energy from outside of that subsystem and exporting entropy. But the total entropy of the universe will only increase.

Living things engage in a sort of shell game with regard to entropy, by hiding their entropy production outside of their subsystem. But in the end, they are really performing a balancing act because they have not reduced entropy, only shifted it elsewhere. Life requires low entropy and cannot exist in a high entropy environment. Let us look at the brewing process to illustrate the relationship between life and entropy.

A brewer's vat full of mash is a low entropy environment rich in carbohydrates and sugars. When we introduce yeast to this vat, they will begin eating and multiplying. The growing population of yeast produces high entropy in the form of carbon dioxide and ethanol. When the vat exceeds some critical level of entropy, the yeast will die off. Some yeast will remain to feed on the little remaining low entropy, but the vat will never return to its low entropy state without being emptied and refilled.

Human beings have taken the creation of entropy to new levels. It would seem that the one thing our socio-economic system does exceedingly well is to produce entropy. The human brewing vat (and our civilization) is currently subsidized by abundant, cheap fossil fuels. Human beings grow on this mash just as did the yeast in our example, multiplying our numbers and producing an abundance of consumer goods. In addition, we have produced high entropy in the form of environmental degradation, garbage, pollution and global warming. Now we are approaching the critical level of entropy that will result in a die-off.

Eating Fossil Fuels: Oil, Food and the Coming Crisis in Agriculture. Dale Allen Pfeiffer

acquired a shady reputation. They pay this price for health. And health is all they get for it. How strange it is. It is like paying out your whole fortune for a cow that has gone dry." Mark Twain

Socrates in his wisdom said it well: "*Thou shouldst eat to live, not live to eat.*"

BALANCING OUT THE DEBATE

With all the preaching and proselytizing about nutritional superiority I've witnessed from many of these dietary sects, I have found few food experts or nutritional experts, for that matter, who've attempted to approach this debate with a rational or balanced perspective, without an axe to grind about being "right."

Which is why I wrote the article "What Type of Raw Diet is Best for You" that can be found on www.mercola.com's website. Submitted under the title "Balancing out the Debate between Raw and Cooked Foods," I systematically point out the pro's and con's of both dietary approaches, and then propose some balanced conclusions. The age-old debate still rages, peppered with a wide diversity of opinions and philosophies across the contemporary "rainbow" of healthy diets. In the final analysis, what, is really the best, most healthful diet for us to consume – a predominantly raw, or a cooked food diet? This is a dynamic subject, and the evidence may surprise you.

To shed some light on this debate, we can take a look at some common food facts from history. While there is a growing consensus today that eating raw food is healthier, the fact is, throughout history all cultures have modified, "cooked" or altered the energy field of their foods in some way. This is one of the 11 fundamental Characteristics of Traditional

> "There are people who strictly deprive themselves of each and every eatable, drinkable, and smokable which has in any way acquired a shady reputation. They pay this price for health. And health is all they get for it. How strange it is. It is like paying out your whole fortune for a cow that has gone dry."
>
> -Mark Twain

Diets, based on extensive research on so-called primitive cultures throughout the world by Dr. Weston Price in the 1930s. Even the most primitive tribe discovered in our time, the Tasaday of the Philippines, who had not wheel nor weapon, but did have fire, started with wooden sticks and used to roast wild yams and other foods.

This makes sense from a functional standpoint. Warmth, moisture, darkness, time these are the elements of cooking. Whether through the application of heat (boiling, baking, frying, etc.), microorganisms (fermenting or pickling), mechanics (juicing, chopping), activation (sprouting) or preservation (canning, freezing, salting or drying, milling or other processing), "cooking" or altering foods is invariably a form of pre-digestion. This applies, as well, to the human body itself. For whether it's accomplished outside the body by chopping or processing before eating, or through the body's own warmth, moisture, darkness and digestive processes after eating, the fact is we have to break down and "cook" or process our food in some way in order to be able to absorb and assimilate it.

Cooking contracts vegetable foods, concentrating more nutrients with less bulk. Bitter greens, such as turnip greens and collards, traditionally prepared by lengthy stewing, are generally more edible when cooked. Cooking also eliminates the oxalic acid, which binds and interferes with calcium absorption.

METABOLIC AND PSYCHO-SPIRITUAL EFFECTS OF COOKING

Beyond simple preservation, cooking has a variety of profound metabolic, as well as psycho-spiritual, effects on humans. Fire equals warmth for survival, protection, community, socializing, togetherness, as well as for making foods more ready for digestion. Its application depends on a host of factors, including season, locality, heritage, genetics and customs.

In *Food and Healing*, Anne Marie Colbin points out that for most people, cooking supports mental concentration better than expansive salads with many different ingredients by saying, "The advantage of fire may have resulted in the development of civilization by mental focus and concentration." Cooking food for eating obviously has a long history in the annals of human existence.

There is no question that cooking deactivates some vital nutrients, including enzymes, but cooking also makes digestion less stressful. Many people with poor digestion don't handle raw foods or beans very well, which is in part why macrobiotic diets may have worked for some people recovering from various maladies. The higher proportion of nutrients in raw food is useless if the food can't be digested, absorbed and assimilated.

On the other side of the debate, live foods contain essential nutrition. Whole, live foods not only contain whole nutrition, but are also a source of the metabolic, digestive food enzymes and other factors needed to digest and effectively utilize our foods. Enzymes are delicate proteins, catalysts responsible not only for breaking down food, but for a host of other day-to-day processes, including transforming minerals into alkaline detoxifiers that neutralize the acid of our highly acidic diet. Enzymes are critically necessary for achieving our balanced pH, as well as our balanced diet. Enzymes are deactivated or destroyed by heat, mechanical and chemical reactions, not only the high heat of cooking, but the high temperatures involved in food processing and manufacture, handling and storage of food.

Unfortunately, in our predominantly processed, synthesized, cooked, micro-waved, convenience food selection today, too many enzymes, as well as other vital nutrients have either been destroyed or rendered unavailable. All too unfortunately, we are also not consuming enough of the traditionally lacto-fermented foods such as the healthful kefir that can easily help our body replenish its supply of valuable enzymes.

Enzymes in raw foods are destabilized at temperatures as low as 72 degrees, not the 115 degrees reported in some case studies, according to Dr. Gustavo Bounous and Dr. Allan Somersall in *Breakthrough in Cell-Defense*. Today, however, with over 90 percent of our foods cooked and/or processed, about the closest many people get to eating raw food is a 'side salad', the small lump of iceberg lettuce with a slice of hothouse tomato.

Cooked food increases white blood cell count. Swiss researchers in the 1930s found that eating unaltered raw food or food heated at low temperatures did not cause a reaction in the blood, whereas food heated beyond a certain temperature, or refined, chemically-treated or processed food always caused a rise in the white blood cell counts. This phenomenon was named pathological leukocytosis. The worst offenders, not surprisingly, were the high heat processed foods, including beer, refined carbohydrates such as white flour and rice, and homogenized, pasteurized or preserved foods.

BENEFITS OF RAW PLANT FOODS

Raw plant foods are rich in oxidizing, alkalinizing chlorophyll. They also just naturally have more vitality, more of the "life force" energy that researchers are discovering is responsible for "recharging" our cellular batteries, as well as enabling an acceleration of individual frequencies to allow more access to higher spiritual energies and information. This also provides insight, moving us closer toward a scientific understanding of the meaning of the term "the spiritualization of matter."

Taking supplements of isolated nutrients combined in a pill or capsule is not the same as getting nutrition from whole, natural, live foods. Even if the essential nutrients are included, nutritional supplements are almost always acidic, whereas live foods, especially greens, are alkalinizing.

Live foods contain a specific balance of natural forces that are programmed to affect the body in a particular way. That is, plant foods like vegetables have a wholeness and integrity that is more than just a collection of proteins, minerals, and vitamins found within them. Once again, the whole is greater than the sum of its parts.

There are many health promoting compounds and factors in whole, unbroken raw foods that we do not perfectly nor fully understand, even given all our scientific and technical advances. Dr. Price demonstrated this when he showed that butter from cows grazing on fast growing grasses during a specific time period in the spring of the year contained a compound, not present at other times, that, when consumed, improved health, bone density and healing much more effectively than cod liver oil alone. The compound, labeled Activator X, has still not been isolated, but recent studies are pointing to a form of Vitamin K.

Of course, with few exceptions, most raw food enthusiasts exclusively promote the virtues of a 100 percent totally raw, vegetarian or vegan diet. However, many fast oxidizers or "Protein" metabolic types, as discussed in *Dr. Mercola's TOTAL HEALTH Program*, do not really do well on exclusively vegan diets.

> All known cultures ate raw and all cultures ate cooked. All known cultures ate vegetables and all cultures ate meat. To say that one of these approaches is superior, the ultimate protocol, as it were, flies in the face of history and common sense.

GOOD NUTRITION IS A MATTER OF BALANCE

There are tradeoffs in each case. Ultimately, it comes down to the individual situation... and Balance.

This is ostensibly why dieticians have been telling us to eat a "balanced" diet with a variety of foods. Yet this is only a partial truth (too often typical of standard scientific fact). It is not only the total quantity of the food, but also the quality that is critically important, along with how the food is produced, treated, processed and handled; how it's stored and packaged, prepared, cooked, overcooked or denatured; and how our own bodies individually process and utilize it.

As Dr. Gabriel Cousens says, "There is so much we do not understand about the subtleties of nutrition that we are essentially shooting in the dark when we start to alter and process our foods."

It's actually ironic that we should even have to engage in an intellectual debate about this subject, since ostensibly we should KNOW, without having to think about it, what the optimum fuel for our personal vehicle, our body, is. This just shows us HOW FAR OFF we are, how out of tune and out of touch we are with our own bodies. Animals, for example, don't read articles or have to study about what to eat. They are instinctually attuned to their own needs without having the "gift" of being able to intellectualize about it. They eat only when hungry. When they're sick, they don't eat, or eat only grasses, even if they are omnivores like dogs, while we "smart" humans who "know so much" each usually end up being forced to listen to our body only when it screams in pain or groans with discomfort.

Everything in nature strives toward balance. The body is made so when given the right nutrients, body systems places them where needed and the body heals itself, affirms Dr. William B. Ferril, M.D. The body possesses an innate healing mechanism that constantly nudges us back to a state of equilibrium, a state of health. We are not machines that need repairmen. We can heal ourselves, if we pay attention and become aware; if we give ourselves the chance, if we listen to our bodies and that deeper part of ourselves.

Hippocrates' 'HEAL THYSELF' doesn't apply only to physicians. Each of us has a healer within. Thy food shall be thy medicine and thy medicine shall be thy food.

Or a more contemporary version from Dr. Gabriel Cousens: "With the proper diet, no doctor is necessary. With the improper diet, no doctor can help."

Instead of thinking "raw foods versus cooked foods," this diet or that philosophy is better, it's probably closer to the truth to focus on getting a BALANCE of raw and cooked foods, depending upon the season, the climate, your health, your level of spiritual evolution, etc. In the final analysis, the truth of the "raw versus cooked" debate lies somewhere in the balance.

> Thy food shall be thy medicine and thy medicine shall be thy food.
> - Hippocrates
>
> With the proper diet, no doctor is necessary. With the improper diet, no doctor can help.
> - Dr. Gabriel Cousens

MORE ABOUT BALANCE

Balancing inner and outer ecology is clearly a message we need to heed now if we want to continue living the good life on this planet. Clearly, from a metabolic and philosophical, as well as a practical standpoint, achieving balance is one of our biggest underlying concerns now, a concern that in the final

analysis, fermentation, and perhaps only fermentation with wisdom, can adequately and fundamentally address.

CAN WE REDUCE OUR CONSUMPTION PATTERNS?

We've talked a lot about both sides of the spectrum, our inner and outer ecology being out of whack. The fact is: they are clearly interdependent, so we can hardly "fix" one without addressing the other.

From the larger, macro perspective, the food energy, inputs and population ratio is yet another factor in the total equation of health and longevity on this planet. The sheer numbers of our human population inhabiting this globe has mushroomed, inching up toward maximum carrying capacity, as agriculture and later, the Green Revolution, increased available foodstuffs, pushing population growth even higher. The Green Revolution alone increased world grain production by 250% between 1950 and 1984.

While early civilizations were built on the energy of humans, especially slave labor – our current mass of humanity has become possible only through an abundance of cheap energy, primarily from hydrocarbons, fossil fuel-based fertilizers, pesticides, and hydrocarbon-fueled irrigation, to say nothing of petrochemical inputs for processing, storing, warehousing, transporting and marketing goods to support our current food system. It clearly has been the energy from coal, oil and natural gas that enabled the technological revolution of the last century.

To understand more of this picture, read Dale Alan Pfeiffer's *Eating Fossil Fuels*. His book puts into perspective that since the 1950's, modern agriculture has increased energy usage by an average of 50 times more than what was used by traditional agriculture. And in the most extreme cases, energy for agriculture has increased 100 fold or more. "Today, in the United States, the equivalent of 400 gallons of oil are used annually to feed each American, in what amounts roughly to a barrel of oil for a bushel of corn. "In a very real sense, we are quite literally eating fossil fuels," Pfeiffer poignantly reveals.

The ecology of our food system, as well as our land, is definitely out of balance, and is unquestionably unsustainable. Right now, the amount and flow of energy required to supply our current daily diet is achieved in only 20 minutes of labor. And unfortunately, if fossil fuels are removed from the equation, the daily diet will require over 111 hours of labor per person; in other words, the current U.S. daily diet would require nearly three weeks of labor per person to produce. The average "food miles", the distance food travels (energy again from fossil fuels), has risen dramatically since the 1980's. By 1996, almost 93% of fresh produce was moved by truck. One study found that produce grown in California destined for consumers in Toronto, Canada, traveled an average of 3,333 miles. Quite plainly, as fossil fuel production begins to decline within the next decade, there will be less energy available for the production and distribution of food.

Even now, while we enjoy the appearance of a super, ney, "uber" abundant food supply, things are not as lavish or as rosy as they appear on supermarket shelves or on your TV screen. To put this more into perspective, in total, there is only a two-to-three day supply of food available in all the warehouses in any one metropolitan area. And our illustrious U.S. food surpluses of the 1950's have now dwindled down to less than a 30-day supply.

Because of our reliance on non-renewable fossil fuels, the U.S. food system consumes ten times more energy than it produces in food energy. Studies suggest that without fossil fuel-based agriculture, the US could only sustain about two thirds of its present population. For the planet as a whole, the sustainable number is estimated to be about two billion.

At present, nearly 40 percent of all land has been captured by human beings for photosynthesis: the production of food. In the United States, agriculture consumes more than half of the energy made available by plants through conversion of solar energy by photosynthesis. And we in the western world, especially, continue to consume at a rate that amounts to our being classified as "energy hogs."

As Dale Alan Pfeiffer says, "We have taken over all the prime real estate on the planet. The rest of the biota is forced to make due with what is left. Plainly this is one of the major factors in species extinctions and ecosystems stress."

In *Eating Fossil Fuels*, Pfeiffer concludes that the energy depletion we are now only beginning to experience will be disastrous without a transition to a sustainable, re-localized agriculture, urging strong grass roots activism for sustainable, localized community-based agriculture and a natural shrinking of the world's population.

According to these calculations,"…to achieve a sustainable economy and avert disaster, the United States must reduce its population by at least one-third. And, for sustainability, global population will have to be reduced from the current 6.32 billion people to 2 billion, a reduction of 68% or over two-thirds. The end of this decade could see upwardly spiraling food prices without relief. And the coming decade could see massive starvation on a global level such as never experienced before by the human race."

> Events in the future are closer than they appear.
> -Unknown

This is nearly incomprehensible to most of us who are just trying to "make a living and get by." Once again, I am sorry to bring this up, but don't shoot the messenger.

To avoid reaching this critical level of entropy, we need to slow the production of entropy below the level of insipient solar energy. To do this, we must abandon the dominant socio-economic system based on constant growth and consumption. If we exceed the critical level of entropy, we will experience a die-off just as the yeast did. Furthermore, as there is no way to reduce entropy, we will never recover from this die-off.

There are things we can do. According to these experts, we have three choices. 1) we can voluntarily reduce our population and our inordinate consumption of resources. 2) we can impose governmental regulations that would force us to do this. 3) we can suffer the consequences. Should we fail to acknowledge this coming crisis and determine to deal with it, we will be faced with a die-off from which civilization may very possibly never revive.

But as Pfeiffer and others studying the situation aptly pose: "The questions we must ask ourselves now are, how can we allow this to happen, and what can we do to prevent it? Does our present lifestyle mean so much to us that we would subject ourselves and our children to this fast-approaching tragedy simply for a few more years of conspicuous consumption?

So now, finally, the mass consciousness has knee-jerked into a realization that we must go Green. The reality of the population scenarios we have just discussed have definitely not as yet seeped into the average person's awareness. Yet now, at the last minute, there is a slow dawning, an accelerating buzz and busyness, translated as "business," to get environmentally hip. Whether it will be enough or fast enough is another question.

Biomass, bio-fuels and carbon footprint have become new buzzwords in our vocabulary. And the rush to find alternative sources of energy and produce more fuel through growing crops for ethanol, albeit about 25 to 35 years too late, is mostly definitely on, at least if you believe TV commercials.

BUT CAN WE GROW ENERGY FOR FUEL AND FOR CROPS, TOO?

However, this brings up an important dilemma. And some additional information that may not be immediately apparent from all the advertising about "growing corn for running cars."

Given our continued burgeoning population, can we possibly hope to be able to achieve enough fuel through hybrids, or grow enough in the form of corn or other forms of biomass to meet our guzzling energy habits?

The answer, as experts like David Blume and Dale Alan Pfeiffer affirm is quite frankly, no. Studies of many different models of cars show that for the entire life of the vehicle (including its construction) hybrids consistently rank as among the most energy-hungry of vehicles — more so than some SUVs. And bio-fuels will at best hasten environmental deterioration and drive up the price of food while doing little to control energy prices, Pfeiffer points out in a recent interview. At the rate we are consuming fossil fuels, there is no way that we will be able to replace our current level of consumption with alternative energy. Some say we will be lucky if we can produce 10% of what we need through these sources.

Additionally, as David Blume, author of *Alcohol Can Be A Gas*, illustrates, the energy required to produce one gallon of biodiesel is equivalent to three-fourths of a gallon; there is little net gain through this approach, even if it looks and sounds good in advertising copy.

First, when discussing the subject of diverting field corn into ethanol production, it's important to understand that the bulk of all of America's corn crop is currently fed to animals. So, depending upon corn for biomass would require producing many more acres of corn than we do currently. Which means more mono-culturing, less of the biodiversity we need to reestablish ecological balance in our soil and, more than likely, the use of more biotechnology (read "genetically modified corn"). Good for corn producers, but not necessarily good for anyone else, or for the environment.

Second, the cattle to which this corn is fed are not evolved enough to eat it. The fact is 80% of the raw corn fed to livestock is not digested. This fact leads to some very interesting and astute conclusions from a couple of experts who've been viewing the subject with some very pragmatic, hardnosed and heartfelt common sense.

FERMENTATION TO THE RESCUE... AGAIN?

Listen to alcohol expert David Blume's suggestion: "If feed corn is first fermented to alcohol fuel, the concentrated spent grain can still be fed to cattle resulting in a more digestible product and greater weight gain than if the cattle were fed the original undigested corn grain. The byproduct of this highly improved animal feed is pollution-free alcohol fuel! The American farming community has the potential ability to revolutionize the way Americans produce their food and fuel their vehicles, moving away from mono-culture gene modified crops, while releasing our nation from dependence on foreign oil imports.

This makes infinite, practical dollars and ecological sense. And what's more, it's doable. There is no question that we need to reduce our population and our insane, off the charts consumption patterns.

But right now, farmers across the country are presently expanding the fuel alcohol industry, thereby invigorating depressed farm communities nationwide while creating pollution-free, inexpensive fuel.

In fact, American farmers produced more alcohol in 2002 than the amount of oil the U.S. imports from Iraq, according to David Blume. In the Midwest, 300 independent gas pumps already provide alcohol for vehicles. Did you know that in the 1990s, 95% of all cars in Brazil ran on alcohol?

So why isn't America running on alcohol fuel? Since World War II, oil companies have been a major part of the power elite that run this country. Witness our current administration run by former oil company executives. Follow the money and read the book. *Alcohol Can Be A Gas!* was originally written to accompany David Blume's 10 part television series that was produced by PBS station KQED, and aired in 1983. The series was so powerful that oil companies threatened to pull out all their funding if the series was distributed nationally through PBS as scheduled. As a result the series was never seen outside of San Francisco and the printing of the book was stopped at the press, even though KQED received thousands of orders. David Blume personally shared some of the heartbreak and the hardships that he has personally suffered as a result of this devastating power grab by oil barons with me this summer as I gave him a ride back to the Chicago airport after this June's Midwest Renewable Energy Association Fair in Stevens Point, Wisconsin.

Alcohol Can Be a Gas is not only a "how to" book, it is the story of why oil companies have reason to fear a change in public thinking, nationalism, environmentalism and a renewable industry of alcohol production. Buying it from David's website at www.permaculture.com or bringing David to your local community for an all day workshop on alcohol fuel production or joining his Alcoholics Unanimous organiation, will not only assist him to retrieve some of the debts that he has incurred from his ordeal, but also enable a grassroots initiative that can help us all get the word and the way out of a big mess out to the public.

David Blume is not alone. And there are others beside Nancy Lee Bentley who realistically see fermentation as a very practical, fundamental and inexpensive way to address a wide variety and number of related inner and outer ecological issues plaguing us today. These include, among others, *Body Ecology's Diets* Donna Gates, *Eating Fossil Fuels*

Dale Alan Pfeiffer, and Chris O'Brien, author of *Fermenting Revolution*.

And Chris O'Brien's approach is not only practical and realistic, it's lighthearted, fun and delicious, too.

Chris literally sees the revival of an ancient modern revolution in bringing back the earliest of fermentations. The answer is Beerology, and Chris quite literally sees us "Saving the World a Beer at a time. But NOT just any beer, and definitely not the mass produced bland tasting, consistently the same every time corporate type.

Chris is quick to revisit early history and how the fermentation of beer has consistently been an integral part of shaping different cultures around the world, bringing us up through our development and current agrindustrial, environmental, consumptive and health issues that are in part due to casting a jaudiced eye, ignoring fermentation – denying culture.

He, like myself and others, sees that sustainable microbreweries and other local fermentation activities and enterprises are not just a nice idea, they are a necessary part of rebuilding local economies and reseeding sustainable community that we must now undertake to survive. The mother beer, like the hearty sourdough and the sharp local stilton, will help nurture and suckle us back to health.

Pointing out that brewing beer, especially, has traditionally been a distinctly feminine pursuit — including the derivation of the associated word "bridal" whose translation is "bride's ale," a very important drink in the economics and negotiations of matrimony throughout the ages. "Beer has inspired mystical transcedence while also unlocking the secrets of natures bounty and for millenia has empowerd women while nourishing the human body as well as spirit." O'Brien muses.

On the other hand, he points out, the masculinization of beer – as with agriculture – is part of globalization, the mass produced, mechanized and dehumanized manufacturing of standardized, pasteurized, characterless belly wash that has us all in the throws of conformity and the herd me ntality.

Microbreweries, like local, artisan bakeries, regional wineries and grassfed specialty cheese crafters are all examples of the groundswell of fermentation microenterprises that are injecting a new lifeblood of activity and economy, flavor and eating enjoyment into life at the local level.

They are also part and parcel of new type of food community which I call a food circle.

One example of such a local, fermentation-based business is Cleveland's Great Lakes Brewing Co. You can read about this sustainable community seed on page 40, one of the prime examples of what I call "a local food circle." Not only is Great Lakes Brewing a wildly popular and successful local hot spot, a thriving business that's helping people to repatronize the older downtown area of the city, it is local fermentation project that has literally created its own local food community. It is one of the many sustainable "food circle" models I've profiled throughout this book – a wide variety of large and small examples of projects fermenting new life, economic and ecologic health, back into the local landscape. Find these in Fermentation at Work.

Ecologist and Economist Stacy Mitchell's 2006 E. F. Schumacher Lecture ends with the encouraging news that the decline of local enterprise we've been witnessing with globalization is by no means inevitable. Implemented broadly, the initiatives supporting locally owned businesses springing up all over the country have the capability of ushering out the handful of global corporations that have colonized our communities and replacing them with thriving local economies and vibrant self-reliant communities.

Even with these changes taking place, we are still "so hypnotized by the notion that the chain [stores] are somehow a superior and more advanced form of business," says Mitchell, "that we are blind to how much we lose when locally owned businesses disappear."

From an economic standpoint, most people do not realize that acquiring cheap products from wally world actually, in the long term, undermines the very economy of the local community in which they live. Many people do recognize that once the giant megaretailer Walmart has established its tentacles into a community, the mom and pop businesses around the square in the downtown area drop off like flies, but they don't often connect this with their own purchasing actions. Most people do not realize that this retailer now accounts for over 20% of our Gross National Product. With its global supply chain and megamuscle economic bullying power, the act of

buying from Walmart almost appears like sawing off the limb that we're standing on.

Economists talk about the local multiplier effect. The Local Multiplier Effect (LME) is a very valuable, hidden feature of our economies. The term refers to how many times dollars are recirculated within a local economy before leaving through the purchase of an import. Famed economist John Maynard Keynes first coined the term "Local Multiplier Effect" in his 1936 book *The General Theory of Employment, Interest and Money*. Each dollar that is generated within a local area and stays recirculating within the community increases the value of business activity and the local economy by a factor of as much as 10.

Imagine a hypothetical influx of money, say one million dollars, entering a local economy. Now imagine these dollars are spent on local goods and services. Imagine that each of the local vendors who earned those dollars then re-spends that money on more local goods and services. Envision this cycle happening several times before this money is finally spent on imports – goods or services from outside the region.

In this case, those one million dollars recirculating eight times would act much like eight million dollars by increasing revenue and income opportunities for local producers. Picture that same amount of money being spent immediately at stores (or online) with businesses headquartered in other regions on imported goods. These transactions add very little or no value to the local economy; one million dollars would act just like one million dollars instead of several million dollars.

In today's global economy, our local economies are like buckets with holes in them. The money may be generated in the local community, but if it's spent on goods and services generated by large corporations, the money flows to the place where that business is headquartered.

Local business activity and local currencies are actually signs and signals of a healthy economy. Bernard Liptauer, one of the economic consultants who helped to design the Euro, himself a proponent of developing local currencies, points out that federal economies are not truly healthy unless they are accompanied and supported by a diverse variety of local currencies in communities throughout the land.

The First IFOAM International Conference on

the marketing of organic and regional values, held August 30, 2007, stressed the critical importance of strengthening local and regional development bringing back value in local and regional economies that are increasingly getting lost in our globalized world.

Small scale fermentation projects are prime examples of low input, sustainable entrepreneurial and cooperative business ventures that are healthy seeds for redeveloping and reenergizing local community and local economies.

Fertilizing sustainable local community with enterprises fueled by fermentation not only repopulates and reinvigorates our own digestion and immunity — our inner ecology – it also helps to rejuvenate our outer ecology – the land, the livelihood and the very lifeblood of local community to which we all belong. Who knows, maybe it will help us get us out from under our fast food, internet isolation addiction and back into the flow of enjoying real taste, real food and real living again.

And what's more, small scale fermentation projects –whether they are a cooperative "Circle Of Three"™ or a competitive new business model are prime examples of ways for us to be able to manage and enjoy the benefits of healthy lacto-fermented foods and beverages. They naturally lend themselves to being done in groups, spreading the work, seeding a new sense of hope, fellowship, and fulfillment, as well as breathing life back into local community…. helping us once again, become Truly Cultured.

This is my vision and my mission, not just with this book, but with my life.

CLOSING THE CIRCLE

If this book has inspired you to begin to embrace the mysteries and masteries of fermenting true culture, you will want to read Sandor Ellix Katz's newest book: *The Revolution Will Not be Microwaved*.

You will definitely also want to visit the TrulyCultured.com website for more in-depth information about culturing and being truly cultured; including assistance in different formats such as e-courses and teleclasses for easier learning. On its sister website, TheFoodCircle.com, you'll find complete explanations and model templates for creating complete functioning local communities around food

and other common local interests. And check back regularly as well for the development of the exciting, The **Full Circles Community**™ network which is being developed to help us connect, communicate and cooperate with each other as we go into what could be some very interesting, if not unprecedented, times. See more details on the website.

Like those of us who have also been instinctively drawn into the depths, the darkside and the light of understanding this archetype, into the other realms of fermentation: Sandor Katz notes, with keen observation "that the word ferment also denotes and defines social ferment. The word ferment along with the words fervor and fervent, comes from the Latin verb fervere, to boil. Just as fermenting liquids exhibit a bubbling action similar to boiling, so do excited people. Filled with passion and unrestrained. Revolutionary ideas, as they spread and mutate, ferment the culture. Agitation of fermenting liquids stimulates the process and quickens fermentation, as evidenced by increased bubbling action. Agitation similarly stimulates social ferment."

It's time now for us to get reenergized, excited, effervescent…and "get a round to it."

We have a new key.

As I have been journeying down the long path to healing and the road to wisdom, considering where we are as a species are and the current nature of our planetary dilemmas, I have been investigating, intuiting and integrating, striving to discern the most plausible, practical and painless way for us to shift our sights and retrieve us from out of our looming sad future and synthesize a new practical do-able approach to achieving health and prosperity. What can we do to regain and preserve our health, freedom and sovereignty, not only survive, but thrive and flourish as individuals, together on the planet?

My conclusions: Wake up out of our complacency, take more responsibility for our own food, nutrition and health, and work together in small groups, in food and other circles, right where we are, to seed new projects, products, and community communion, as it were around food creating a new bouquet of options, new hope, a new flower of life for ourselves.

Toward Wholeness:

"The Renewal of Society will come when we can imagine it differently and when we are ready, like artists, to take on the actual work of creating new forms. The renewal of art will come when we can experience in our bodies the crystals of cosmic milk."

MC Richard

REMEMBERING CULTURE

The Beginning and the Ending; Ending with the Beginning

We as clever humans, the penultimate adapters and inventors, somehow still see ourselves as superior, the most evolved of all known species. The fact is that we live in a world dominated by microbes, the real agents responsible for this miraculous process of fermentation we've been talking about from so many angles. Despite the burgeoning retail displays of anti-bacterial soaps and cleaning agents, we do not live in a sterile environment, and neither did our ancestors. Our predecessors, like the organisms themselves, likely ingested, fought with, danced with, and finally partnered with a variety of microorganisms found naturally in their foods. Some were beneficial, while others produced infection and disease.

"Somewhere along the way in their struggle for survival, our ancestors allied themselves with certain species of microbes. Over time, our intestines, our digestive systems have evolved into a perfect microbial farm. We provide these microbes with furnished home and plenty of food, in return, they produce beneficial nutrients and help defend us from pathogens." This simple yet eloquent truth from *The Wisdom of The Healing Crow* is ample and ongoing proof that we have more in common than we have differences with the microbial world. We are, undeniably, interdependently linked.

Once our ancestors began experimenting with beneficial strains of bacteria to prevent spoilage, fight infections, and increase absorption of nutrients, our bodies became even further allied with the microbial world. This really was the origin of culture. As experts on the subject, including *Nourishing Traditions* author, Sally Fallon, have noted, there can be no true culture without culturing of food. For only through the discovery of fermentation and its ability to preserve food was man able to start moving about, carrying his sustenance with him. Cultured, fermented foods enabled us to evolve as a species. After all, where do you think our word culture comes from?

As microbiologist Lynn Margulis points out in her book *Symbiosis*, living beings defy neat definition. And they are never static. At the base of the creativity of all large, familiar forms of life, the phenomenon of symbiosis generates novelty, bringing together different life forms, always for a reason. The tendency of independent life is to bind together and reemerge in a new wholeness at a higher, larger level of organization.

Where man and microorganisms merged, in the culturing and transformation of novel foods, a new, more complex kind of relationship sprang forth: the birth of new community. The lessons of this merger are ones we need to remember and respect in order to continue to grow and survive on this planet. Not just alone and in usury as a dominant "superior" species, but in humility, harmony, and cooperation with the community of all life.

The End or The Beginning?
Everything Circles in Season and
Bears Fruit in its Time.

SO IT'S TIME TO ASK AND ACT:

When are we going to "Get A ROUND TO IT?"

What can we do?

Understand that You are Responsible for Your Own Health.

Take back control over your own health.

Listen to your body and learn what it says and needs. Then follow it.

Study and learn from others who are writing about the subject.

Check out resources and references at the end of this book.

Take more responsibility for the quality, nutrition and safety of the food you eat.

Get more connected to the source of your food.

Support local producers and processors who care about the quality and integrity of the food they produce.

Eat less processed and more whole, natural, organic, local and fermented foods.

Change your perspective about what is edible and the cosmetic appearance of food versus the nutrients in it.

Understand that your dollars count. What you and others buy stays on the market. What you and others refuse or do not buy cannot stay on the market. Vote with your dollars.

Grow at least some of your own food.

Try permaculture solutions. Plant vegetables with your flowers, herbs in pots on your patio, recycle your wastes.

Create a Circle-Of-Three™ –even you and two of your friends–to seed out any sustainable project. For more information, visit www.TheFoodCircle.com.

Participate in food cooperatives.

Create a cultured foods coop. Organize a circle to create several months supply of cultured and fermented vegetables together.

Find others to create a circle for making and sharing kombucha tea. Work out a system for sharing your baby mushrooms and for encouraging others to try and make their own fermented beverages and other foods.

Form your own food circle.

Help to support or organize a family, neighborhood or local food circle.

Think of all the circles of people you already know. Bring the circle idea to others.

Bring two or more circles with common goals together; for example, your spiritual or dreaming circle with your CSA or your cultured foods circle.

Join with others in local food circles or groups to begin to be more involved with acquiring your own food.

Locate and contact others who are of like mind and help create a neighborhood or municipal food circle community and help plug in the network of healthy food producers and consumers where you live.

Reexamine your notions about how you think life should be...

Don't assume that life is always going to be the way it is now.

Remember that gratitude for what you have is a key to manifesting more of what you want.

Be open to new possibilities.

REMEMBER Yourself.

Now that you have read about the history, benefits and significance of fermented and cultured foods, it's time to create some of them! We have entitled this second part of Truly Cultured "The How-To's of Fermented Foods" because this is where you get your hands into the practical side of making these healthful dishes in your home and with friends. One correction here: I should say "practical side of 'controlling the conditions' for making these healthful dishes." Once you get the ingredients together under the right conditions, the fermentation happens spontaneously. You don't actually do much, usually, except wait.

Because culturing is a skill and an art that can only truly be learned by doing it, your grasping this section will more likely be something that happens within you than because of anyone's explaining it. Taking the plunge to start is a huge step that can only lead to surprising revelations about how easily the process can actually be achieved. In the process, it is very likely you could be learning a lot more about yourself, as well as picking up a set of new skills.

The information here is not exhaustive; however, this section will give you a good start on the foundations and fundamentals of what is involved in mastering successful culturing and embarking on a process that could save your digestion and health, and your life, as well.

And for some of you, the learning that will ensue will be about learning patience, and reaping the rewards from patience, a commodity that seems to be in short supply in this contemporary culture. This alone may be one of the more valuable fruits of your labors.

HOW PART II IS ORGANIZED

We have organized Part II to make it easy for you to produce your favorite cultured foods in your own kitchen. "The How-To's of Fermented Foods" is laid out with practical supporting information, helpful notes about equipment, ingredients and approaches followed by recipes, sequenced from simple to complex.

In Part II, Chapter 1, you first will find background facts about culturing, including some historical and technical information, plus tips, guidelines and shortcuts that may help reduce your learning curve to producing these foods. The section includes associated techniques such as on sprouting that will prove valuable.

Part II, Chapter 2 is a set of recipes for delicious, healthful fermented foods, starting with 40 of the most basic formulas for favorite fermented foods. Then, an additional 80 plus recipes for making everything from appetizers to desserts using fermented foods, including some of the basics you may have already created with the basic formulas in the front of the section.

In addition to ingredients and step-by-step instructions, recipes also include basic nutritional content, as well as helpful tips, substitutions, resource efficient hints or other valuable information, including recipe categories and types such as raw, gluten-free, vegan or vegetarian.

THE RECIPE SECTION IS DESIGNED TO:

1) demystify the process of making fermented foods at home
2) show you how easy it is to do this in your own kitchen
3) provide techniques and approaches that are geared toward your busy lives
4) give you simple, step-by-step instructions to enable you to make theses foods, even the first time
5) help you to move beyond the basics to create and to increase your confidence even in making some more sophisticated "gourmet" type foods without fear, and
6) give you the inspiration and the education to advance your knowledge and skills — enough that you feel comfortable and capable of producing these foods for yourself, if not on a regular basis — which would certainly benefit you in many ways — but also in the not-out-of-the-realm-of-possible scenario in which you may need to depend on creating fermented foods in order to ensure that you can eat. Period.

SPOILED OR NOT SPOILED?

"Spoiled" is actually a subjective term, influenced by cultural and social perceptions, as well as individual tastes. Generally, spoilage is a term used to describe the deterioration of a food's texture, color, odor or flavor to the point it is unappetizing or unsuitable for human consumption.

Microbial spoilage of food often involves the degradation of protein, carbohydrates and fats by these microorganisms or their enzymes. Ironically and factually, the degradation or transformation of the nutrients during the process of fermentation is exactly and precisely what develops some of your favorite flavor, taste and textural characteristics. But whether some food is perceived as spoiled or delicious depends upon the individual doing the perceiving. Some people think Limburger cheese is disgusting, whereas the obviously overripe, raunchy flavor of St. Albans cheese is highly prized by many Frenchmen.

> Old Par, an English peasant, age 152 years and 9 months, is presented as existing—even 'thriving'—on a diet of "sub-rancid cheese and milk in every form, coarse and hard bread and small drink, generally sour whey."
> —Terence McLaughlin, *A Diet of Tripe*

When it comes to fermenting and culturing, the knowledge of what is good and what is not, most assuredly comes with experience of and working with these foods. There is no need for paranoia. Take heart; even the most bungled home fermented food is unlikely to harm you. The fact is, in this regard, your nose is your best ally. If the food is so disgusting that you can't bear to eat it, it's probably not worthy of being eaten.

Still unsure if something is "spoiled" or not, unfit to eat? We include the astute and very appropriate recommendations to the 19th century housewife by author Marion Harland in her *Common Sense in the Household, a Manual of Practical Housewifery*. This profound and practical advice, quoted by the esteemed food writer, MFK Fisher, contains worthy guidance as applied to most fermented foods: at the end of recipe for Preserved Green Corn, Ms. Harland, with the determined optimism of a good hausfrau, wrote, "Green corn is difficult to can, but I know it will keep if put up this way… Should the top layer be musty, dig lower still, and you will probably be rewarded for the search." —MFK Fisher, *The Art of Eating*.

We also like this humorous tongue-in-cheek spoilage test for dairy products:

Food Spoilage Tests For Dairy Products:
Milk is spoiled when it starts to look like yogurt. Yogurt is spoiled when it starts to look like cottage cheese. Cottage cheese is spoiled when it starts to look like regular cheese. Regular cheese is nothing but spoiled milk anyway and can't get any more spoiled than it is already. Cheddar cheese is spoiled when you think it is blue cheese, but you realize you've never purchased that kind.

The bottom line: Your nose knows.

SAFE OR NOT SAFE?

In our terror-dominated society, many of us are almost phobic about germs. Needlessly so, for this is one of the key points that we are making in this book. We have come to fear and loathe bacteria, instead of embracing them with gratitude and co-existing with them. People have existed for centuries without either the sanitary antiseptics or the benefits of anti-microbial soaps that dominate the market today. And as we've said, this may be contributing to the inner (and possibly outer) ecological imbalances we're experiencing in our world today. Just think about how much impact all the antiseptics and anti-microbial soaps are having after they go down the drain.

In the ongoing battle against menacing microbes, some scientists are raising a new concern that the widespread use of anti-microbial soaps may cause problems worse than the ones they aim to cure. A 1998 report from Tufts University School of Medicine says a substance used in these soaps, and in plastic toys and other "antibacterial" products, behaves a lot like an antibiotic — and could possibly encourage bacteria to mutate in ways that make them impervious to anti-bacterials, including antibiotics. "Spraying antibiotics around in the environment, whether as soaps, additives to animal feeds or given to children, are behaviors that are going to come back to haunt us," says pediatrician Phillip Landrigan, chair of the Department of Community and Preventive Medicine at Mount Sinai School of Medicine in New York. "They will create selection pressures to force the rapid evolution of bacteria into superbugs." We've discussed how very adaptive they are, and this is just one additional example.

It's true, of course, that there are pathogenic bacteria around that can kill us. Often though, the problem is exacerbated or made worse in mono-culturing environments such as factory farms or large industrial agriculture fields raising one crop, such as corn or soy. The natural protection provided by the biodiversity or ecological balance of many species is absent, and so certain strains win out and take over.

 Salmonella and E. coli, for example, are naturally present in and around us, but can also be deadly in processed foods. It all depends upon the environment and conditions. But the fact that properly sanitizing hands, utensils and surfaces in food production situations almost always results in safe foods is actually dismissed or minimized by government and industry with sweeping so-called remedies such as *irradiation pasteurization* that come in behind to "take care of anything" that could possibly cause problems. This process also carries the dubious label of "cold Pasteurization": rather than a heat treatment, irradiation pasteurization uses ionizing radiation from cobalt-60, cesium 137 and other radioactive waste to eliminate all bacteria and pathogens. Precautionary, good old-fashioned plain soap and water can do a lot to forestall problems without nuking our food or unbalancing the ambient environment. Having clean utensils is important, but usually, sterilization is not required.

ARE PASTEURIZED FOODS SAFE?

The standard line is that we need pasteurization to be safe. Yet, you might have been surprised to learn that bacteria, even pathogens, can grow in pasteurized milk! Germs do grow in pasteurized milk, especially when critical temperatures are not maintained. In the 1938 pathology studies, it was shown that killing all bacteria in the milk actually allowed bad bacteria to grow. Raw milk, however, retains all bacteria, and this helps to control the bad bacterial growth.

There is a natural, proactive, protective mechanism in some foods, such as mayonnaise/citric acid/eggs, including raw, fermented or cultured products and other foods that needs to be recognized as a real operant factor and basis for reestablishing reliance on the natural protection of ecological diversity and balance. We need to retire our blind allegiance to the theory of pasteurization, which was based on information that Pasteur himself admitted was erroneously incomplete, and taken out of context. We need to replace the germ theory with the Gaia theory and start looking to proactive solutions for safeguarding our health through boosting digestive and immune health with naturally fermented foods.

The final 1999 report of the BgVV Working Group, a German subcommittee of the Federal Institute for Health Protection of Consumers and Veterinary Medicine reviewing the use of adding lacto-bacteria to food, noted and concluded that there has not been a single case of infection that could be traced back to the ingestion of food produced using lactic acid bacteria. They also noted that epidemiological studies show that the incidence of individual strains of lactic acid bacteria in healthy people is high, whereas in sick people, it is extremely low. They concluded that the use of these microorganisms as production cultures for food products over a period of more than 100 years is sufficient proof of the fact that they are safe.

CATEGORIES OF FERMENTED AND CULTURED FOODS

Now, we will take a look at the main types of cultured foods by categories. This won't include every single type of fermented or cultured food known to man. If you're interested in finding more about gari, fufu or idli, for instance, you can consult any number of reference texts or do a search on the Internet.

We've organized this section by categories of the major types of fermented foods you may be inclined to produce in your own home or with your neighbors and friends in your own food circle. The first recipes in this section give you step-by-step instructions for making basic fermented foods; however, this section will give you some valuable general information about specific food groups to help you as you begin or continue to work with them. And, as mentioned before, with the exception of a couple of examples, fermented alcoholic beverages such as beer and wine are beyond the scope of this book. In short, this section will enhance your knowledge and your skills in making fermented foods yourself.

CULTURED DAIRY PRODUCTS: SOURED MILKS

Yogurt, kefirs and buttermilks are some of the most traditionally cultured milk products that have long been known for their beneficial effect on gastrointestinal, respiratory and urinary tracts and are still gaining increasing popularity for their role as ideal carriers or sources for additional fortification with these probiotics. Milk products, with their balance of carbohydrates, proteins and vitamins, are ideal media for the growth of the complex lacto-bacteria that make these products so healthful.

You will find recipes for yogurt, buttermilk and kefir in Basic Fermented Formulas. All of them require some kind of a starter: powder, liquid or a small amount of the finished product to clabber or thicken the milk. Yogurt is primarily produced by lactobacillus bacteria, whereas kefir is produced by a unique symbiotic blend of bacteria and yeast that developed a working relationship over many years. They yield similar results, except that kefir usually has a more tartly acidic bite.

Producing these lacto-fermented foods in your own home is simple, requiring almost no special equipment other than a thermometer. In *Nourishing Traditions*, Sally Fallon mentions using a Finnish culture called piima, derived from milk of cows that have fed on the butterwort plant, as a foolproof aid to fermenting dairy products. However, piima requires a constant temperature of 72 to 75°F., so it's best to find a place like a closet or cupboard with a light bulb, where the temperature is constant, if you are going to use piima. You can make piima cream as a starter at home that will keep for several weeks.

Sour milk products made from raw milk will be the most nutritious, with higher active proteins and enzymes that digest lactose (milk sugar), and casein (milk protein), in the intestines. You also can make them from pasteurized milk, although you may need to add additional calcium chloride to make up for the loss that occurs in the heat treatment process. Do not use ultra-pasteurized or homogenized dairy products, since these do not have the nutrients or the structure necessary to support the culture.

You can obtain buttermilk when making your own cultured butter at home, or by following the recipe in Basic Formulas. The whey, or liquid part of the cultured milk products that separates out can be saved and used to initiate the fermentation process in other products such as sauerkraut, naturally fermented soft drinks, even homemade baby food.

Note: Be aware that whey contains a higher percentage of lactose (milk sugar), to which some people are intolerant.

You will find most success storing these products in your refrigerator after making them, although traditional cultures have stored them in a cool place such as a stream or cellar. How long they will keep depends upon many factors, including storage conditions. These milk products may separate, which is okay, but if they smell really foul, as opposed to just funky, or taste bitter or rancid, start over.

CULTURED DAIRY PRODUCTS: CHEESE

As Clifton Fadiman once said, "Cheese is milk's leap toward immortality."

> As Clifton Fadiman once said, "Cheese is milk's leap toward immortality."

Cheese is undeniably one of our favorite fermented foods. And with about 17 million different kinds of cheeses in the world, cheese is also one of the largest categories of cultured foods.

There are three basic types of cheese categories, which all cheeses fall under —- whey cheeses, un-ripened casein cheeses and ripened casein cheeses.

Whey cheeses, similar to ricotta, are not as common in the US as in other parts of the world. Highest in lactose, whey cheeses are generally un-ripened, young cheeses that are usually soft and creamy with a higher percentage of water, thus more susceptible to spoilage than some others. The earliest cheese, discovered by the nomadic Bedouins was this type, much like cottage cheese or curds and whey.

Un-ripened casein cheeses are cheeses in which the cheese making process is stopped just after the curd separates, giving us familiar soft cheeses such as cream cheese, cottage cheese, pot cheese and farmer's cheese.

Ripened casein cheeses are the most familiar types of cheeses, from the familiar brick, blue and brie to provolone and Swiss. During the production process, the liquid, watery whey is removed after the cheese curds have formed, concentrating the nutrients and reducing the water, thus more of the potential for spoilage. These cheeses are then aged after inoculation with unique molds that give them their characteristic color, flavor, aroma and texture. They can be stored the longest.

Processed cheeses are manufactured. Not technically included in the three major categories (although according to federal standards, they 'start' with cheese), these "cheese" products, whether "process cheese food or spread" or "imitation process cheese food product" are basically created by combining minced cheese (usually scraps leftover from the production process) with an emulsifying agent and blending until the mixture forms a homogeneous plastic mass. (Are you thinking "yuck" yet?)

Cheeses, especially the simple type, can be easily made at home. See recipes for cream cheese and yogurt cheese that can be made in your own kitchen using equipment you already have on hand. The aged cheeses can be much more involved to tackle at home, although they are more labor intensive than difficult to produce.

The basic process in cheesemaking does amount to a considerable amount of steps, but each one is not necessarily difficult to accomplish.

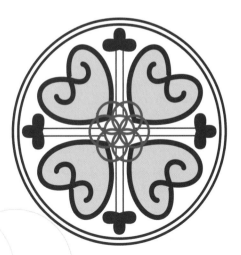

Pasteurizing:	sterilizing milk by indirectly heating to 161°F
Ripening:	acidifying the milk by using a starter culture
Renneting:	adding a rennet enzyme which coagulates the protein to form a curd
Cutting:	breaking up the curd mass to release the liquid whey
Cooking:	heating the cut curd to force moisture out and firm it up
Draining:	removing the whey by hanging the cheese in cheesecloth bag
Salting:	adding specialty grade salt to season, aid drying and preserve the cheese
Pressing:	removing whey by mechanical pressure in a cheese press
Drying:	allowing air to dry the cheese and protective rind to develop
Waxing:	sealing the cheese in melted wax to protect from air during aging
Aging:	resting the cheese while the cheese's unique character and flavor develop

Notes about pasteurized milk: The bulk of domestic cheeses start with pasteurized milk to standardize and sterilize the product, insuring that other competing bacteria will not become dominant. Raw milk can be used to make these foods at home without fear, as long as you know that it comes from a clean and preferably organic source. Cheeses of this type, made with raw milk, are recommended to be aged from 60 to 90 days. Many European cheeses are raw.

If you are going to attempt making aged cheeses at home you may want to visit a cheese making store or website to acquire some necessary equipment and ingredients. There are many commercial cheese-making kits available. You can also make your own homemade cheese press from common utensils around the home, an easy process thanks to the instructions from David Fankhauser, PhD, University of Cincinnati Clermont College on his web site: http://biology.clc.uc.edu/Fankhauser/cheese/cheese.html.

The type of cheese determines storage requirements. The moist cheeses with the most water are the least stable, designed to be refrigerated and consumed, once opened, within a few days. With the exception of cottage cheese, all cultured dairy products have a low pH, which discourages growth of some spoilage bacteria but promotes growth of yeasts and molds that are more acid tolerant. So yeasts and molds are what usually limit keeping quality in most cultured products.

Starter cultures are basically the microorganisms used in culturing dairy products such as yogurt and especially cheese. The milk's natural micro flora are usually either inefficient, uncontrollable, and unpredictable, or, in the case of commercial dairy products, destroyed altogether by the high heat treatments. Use of starter cultures, particularly lactic starters, give you more control and predictability. And starter cultures also impart the various unique flavors, aroma, textures and character of cheese, and also to determine enzymatic activity and to inhibit undesirable microorganisms.

There are two main types of lactic starter cultures for making most hard cheeses. Essentially, they contain either single strain or mixed bacterial strains and are characterized as mesophilic or thermophilic cultures. Mixtures of mesophilic and thermophilic microorganisms can also be used as in the production of some cheeses. You can get these through visiting cheesemaking stores or websites you'll find in the Resources section.

FERMENTED VEGETABLES

Almost any kind of vegetable or fruit can be, and has been fermented. This means that you can likely substitute almost any reasonable vegetable in a standard fermented vegetable recipe. The general guideline for vegetables is that 10 pounds of cabbage, for instance, will fit into a 2-gallon crock, or 15 pounds of cabbage for a 5-gallon crock. Roughly 3 tablespoons of salt is enough to ferment 5 pounds cabbage.

One of the keys to remember about fermentation is that it is an anaerobic process (without air) so it's important to keep fermenting vegetables and fruits submerged in the liquid brining solution. This can be accomplished by placing cabbage or other leaves over the solution and weighing down with a plate and rocks or gallon jugs filled with water. As mentioned in the equipment section, you can purchase expensive German fermentation crocks that have built in weights, or you can improvise with things around the house.

The best sauerkraut is made slowly at temperatures of about 60°F. or under, taking as much as a month to ferment. Fermentation will take place faster at higher temperatures. One way to check on the progress of the ferment is to rap on the side of the crock with your hand, then remove the top layer of scum. If no bubbles rise to the surface, fermentation is completed. Store the kraut at 40°F. or less (refrigeration is good).

PICKLES, OLIVES

Speaking scientifically, a pickle is any perishable ingredient that has been preserved in brine. But pickling isn't strictly about science, it's about tradition, community economy responsibility and family. Our ancestors, no matter what part of the globe they hailed from ? pickled to preserve fruits, vegetables, meat and fish. They pickled to save money. They pickled together with family and friends, to assure the safety of, and to make the most of their food. Harsh winters, humid tropical climates, short growing seasons, poor soil, fast spoiling staples (fish), even summer abundance and gardening pride all have spawned the arts of pickling and food preservation. Pickles and olives are archetypal foods that illustrate our unique history here in the states.

It is important to use the best quality organic vegetables, sea salt and filtered or pure water for lacto-fermentation. Lactobacilli need plenty of nutrients to do their work; and, if the vegetables are deficient, the process of fermentation will not proceed. Likewise if your salt or water contains impurities, the quality of the final product will be jeopardized. See Salt Sidebar or Resources.

As lacto-fermentation specialist, Charles Eisenstein, author of *Yoga of Eating* says, "Lacto-fermentation is an artisanal craft that does not lend itself to industrialization. Results are not always predictable." For this reason, he notes, when the pickling process became industrialized, many changes were made that rendered the final product more uniform and more saleable, but not necessarily more nutritious. Mainly this involved the use of vinegar added to the brine, which results in a product that is more acidic and definitely not beneficial when eaten in large quantities. The final insult is subjecting most pickles to pasteurization, effectively killing all the lactic-acid-producing bacteria and robbing us of their beneficial effect on digestion.

There are still a few lacto-fermented pickle products available on the market, but these are usually the fresh pack or quick process pickles, and refrigerated pickles.

FERMENTED FRUITS

When most people think of fermenting fruits, their thoughts usually go to alcoholic beverages. That's because fruits are the most quickly transformed by the fermentation process. Their simple sugars are readily available and quickly to turn into alcohol under the right conditions. As anyone who has bought fresh apple cider knows, you literally don't have to do anything but let it sit out in the open to get spontaneous hard cider. Ciders, wines, and that jailhouse-favorite hooch, now called "pruno", are all produced through fermenting fruits.

> "A fruit is a vegetable with looks and money. Besides, if you let fruit rot, in turns into wine; something no Brussels sprout will ever do."
>
> PJ O'Rourke

Much of the fermentation that involves fruits transforms them into alcoholic beverages, but there are many other traditional foods from all over the globe made with or by fermenting fruit that do not. This includes fruit preserves, kimchis, chutneys and of course, vinegars. You'll find recipes for all of these in the recipe section under Basic Formulas or Condiments. Generally, these are designed to be eaten fresh, stored in the refrigerator and consumed within a few weeks.

Vinegars, of course, are the exception. This is the end of the fermentation line; as far as you can go with the fermentation process. Although the least healthy, with the exception of apple cider vinegar which is often used as a medicinal tonic or elixir with maple syrup, they are the most stable, requiring virtually no additional storage care. A jug of raw apple cider vinegar with its rubbery 'mother' intact can sit in a cool dark place through the ages…

A note about wines, beers and alcoholic beverages: the world of fermented alcoholic beverages is literally it's own wide-wide world, not our main focus here.

FERMENTED MEATS

Meat is very susceptible to spoilage by microbes, so it is no surprise that through the centuries without refrigeration, many meats were subjected to the processes of drying, brining and fermentation in order to preserve them after the hunt.

Production of dried and cured meats can be traced back to prehistoric times. First mentioned in Homer's Iliad, sausages were being consumed early in history, although it's difficult to determine exactly when fermentation became part of the process. The first documentation of sausage making as a craft dates back over 2000 years to China. We know with accuracy that in the Western world, fermented sausages can be traced back to 1730 when they were first mentioned in Italy. From here the art spread to Hungary and Germany, which boasts around 330 types of fermented sausages alone. The fact that so many of these processed meats are mentioned is testimony to their long tradition as a form of meat that is safe to eat.

The major types of fermented meats are divided into two categories: chopped or ground meats such as sausages, wursts and salamis, and whole meat products such as hams and bacons.

SAUSAGES

For thousands of years, butchers have chopped up meat (a broad term which includes everything from lips to openings to the intestines), mixed it with fat and seasonings and stuffed it into casings made from who-knows-what.

Today, the United States is home to over 21,000 sausage makers, producing over 6.3 billion pounds of sausage a year, according to the *Dictionary of American Food and Drink*.

All sausages share a basic technology, starting with

50-70% lean meat, to which are added binding agents, fat, salt, curing and flavoring agents. Casings can be natural pig, sheep or cow intestines or manufactured from cellulose, edible collagen and plastic.

Major types of sausages include semi-dry fermented sausages, such as thuringer and summer sausage, and the dry fermented sausages, including pepperoni and salami.

Regardless of type, the added salt lowers the water activity, makes the proteins in the meat more soluble, and forms a stable emulsion with fat, inhibiting oxidation and food spoilage microorganisms. Percentage of water is the most important variable in spoilage, but this is usually in a carefully controlled range of 2 - 5%. However, too little water in cured meat products can actually accelerate rancidity.

That's why most commercial processed meat products contain nitrates and nitrites, especially as required by law for interstate transport, which stabilize finished product, especially semi-dry sausages with higher water content. However, at home it is up to you whether you add them or not. Nitrates in meats are controversial, because of the formation of carcinogenic nitrosamines, enhanced during high heat processes such as frying and grilling. The levels commonly used by manufacturers have gone down five fold over a 20-year period, according to the Council for Agricultural Science and Technology, but many consumers are still suspect.

Ascorbates and erthrobates are compounds that are beginning to replace nitrates in commercial sausage making, along with increased levels of Vitamin C, along with antioxidants such as TBHQ and BHA, and herbs like rosemary and thyme, which are natural oxidation inhibitors.

Fermented sausages are inoculated with fermentation organisms and allowed to ferment under controlled, low 10% humidity while the meat dries and the flavors, colors and aromas develop. Sausages are often smoked, as well, which adds to their flavor, color, bite or texture and keeping qualities. Smoking also hastens the drying process, tightening casings, and enhancing keeping quality.

Ready-to-eat meats like bolognas and luncheon meats are the most problematic in terms of concern over bacterial contamination from certain strains of microorganisms such as Listeria moncytogenes, which can proliferate sitting in a refrigerator case. But this may be more of reflection of modern meat quality and production practices, since these types of meats have been reliably produced for centuries. Regardless, while the meat industry routinely addresses the issue of safety of meat products, even they maintain that totally eliminating potentially harmful food products is impractical and costly.

Once again, a healthy immune system can handle and protect your body from minor pathogens, which, as opposed to causing serious illness by compromising the immune system, are simply inactivated. Having lots of "good" friendly bacteria in the digestive system from eating lacto-fermented foods is getting more and more essential to survive in this out of balance world.

BRINED MEATS

Larger or whole pieces of meat such as hams and bacons are generally brined, marinated or soaked in a brining solution to cure them. The ratios are roughly 8 pounds of salt and 2 lbs. of sugar in 4-1/2 to 6 gallons water for 100 lbs. of meat.

Refrigerated meat can be brined in a solution with only 6 lb salt, but just make sure the meat is thoroughly submerged under the brine, and then turned periodically. The meat is generally cured in the sugar/salt brine for 2 to 3 days before smoking at 38°F. Below 36°F., the meat won't absorb the brine, and above 42°F. spoilage organisms get activated.

If you're making sausages, the optimum temperatures for smoking are between 90°-150°F., preferably the former. As with most fermented foods, there are no hard and fast rules for the length of time meats should be smoked. The required amount of time depends generally upon the size of the piece. Bacon for example, can take 48 hours, while hams may need about 60 hours. Try smoking the meats for 2/3 of the expected time, and then sample some. Continue with the smoking if it isn't as highly flavored as you'd like.

OTHER CURED AND DRIED MEATS

Dried meats: In addition to fermented meats like sausages, hams and bacons, there are a variety of other traditionally cured and dried meats that can be preserved simply at home. Drying is one of these, an ancient process. Often cured meats are processed with a combination of one or all of brining, fermenting drying and smoking techniques. Like most ferments, often there isn't strictly one microbe or process involved.

While not all dried meats like jerky are actually fermented, the technique is an allied and valuable one to know for home preservation. The drying process preserves the food by removing most of the water, since microorganisms can't thrive without moisture, or at a low pH, made possible by the concentrated sugar or salt environment. FYI, bacteria need only 18 percent moisture, yeasts need 20 percent and molds need only 13 to 16 percent moisture to survive. Foods like meat that are dried or dehydrated will shrink to 1/6th to 1/3rd their normal size.

The Native American Pemmican, which starts with meat that has been jerkied or dried with salt and seasonings and pulverized, was traditionally fermented in animal skins after being mixed with fat and fruits or vegetables. Kept away from air, the meat was then stable for long journeys, which is why it has traditionally been known at the first trail food.

BREADS AND GRAINS

Bread, with all of its meanings and connotations, and in all of its forms from thick, liquid-y beer mixtures that was its first form, to round flatbreads and mounds to oblong loaves —- has been a central fixture of our eating for about 7,000 years. While grains were never part of our original Paleolithic diet, which we discussed in Chapter 2, most people still think we've been eating bread for eons. The fact is we had to learn how to get rid of their anti-nutrients by sprouting or fermenting or both, before grains could rise beyond a benign place in our daily diet to a mainstay.

The simplest breads contain only four ingredients, Flour, water, salt and starter. Today the starter is usually yeast; a fungus that was first standardized and produced commercially by Charles Fleischmann in 1868. But the growth in artisan micro-bakeries, along with local microbreweries has reawakened the proofing and the health of modern grains with some old-fashioned techniques and wonderful additional ingredients: olives, nuts, fruits and seeds. Before commercial yeast was available,

virtually all bread was developed from leaven, what we now think of as sourdough starter. Water and potatoes, wheat or rye grains were mixed and left to naturally ferment with the aid of natural wild yeasts, which are present on the surface of the grains and in the air. Beer was also used to accelerate and develop leaven for bread, just as bread has been used to hasten the leaven for beer.

Sourdough breads, made from starters that can and have literally lasted for hundreds of years, are not only more delicious, with more character and chewier texture than the bland, neutral experience of eating yeast raised, refined flour white breads, they are more healthful. Fortunately, there's been an upsurge in the availability of really hearty and nutritious artisan breads made with organic grains and good old-fashioned sourdough starter.

But they're easy and infinitely more exciting to make at home, restoring the magic and mystery of fresh-baked bread's seductive, tantalizing aroma wafting from your kitchen. But once again, as with most fermented foods, you do have to wait for the fermenting and proofing for them to produce those mystical images and aromas in your brain and in your nose. And really good sourdoughs and other homemade breads doughs often need 6 to 7 hours of proofing.

This is slow food, but the wait is worth it.

SOYFOODS

While soyfoods have been around for centuries, most notably utilized by the Chinese since the Zhou Dynasty in 664 BC, as we've discussed in Part I, Chapter 1, the Oriental populations, when they did, primarily consumed soy products in their fermented form. That is, in the form of foods such as soy sauce, miso, tempeh and natto---not, as many people believe, in the health food industry's proliferation of so many industrial nonfermented soy products -- soymilks, tofus, soy powders and processed textured vegetable proteins on the market today. You will find recipes for making some basic fermented soybean products in the Basic Fermented Formulas Section, but we are purposely omitting lengthy discussion on the subject. Even though there are soybeans that are marketed as "certified organic," the only kind you should consider using, due to soybean's questionable status as a "health food" and the fact that with the recent run away explosion of genetic engineering practices, close to 99% of soybean products are either genetically altered or inadvertently contaminated with these by-products, we do not generally recommend consumption of soy products.

SPROUTING

Sprouting is another basic new culture technique that will be valuable to you as you become more familiar and at ease with transforming grains into more nutritious food forms like the bread we adore.

Sprouting not only increases the nutrients in the spouted grain or seed, it also decreases the anti-nutrients such as the phytates and oxalates that bind up calcium and throw a monkey wrench into our digestive processes. Sprouting also helps to deactivate and digest the wheat protein gluten, which many people (besides outright celiacs, or celiac sprue sufferers), do not tolerate, and it is another related energy efficient food processing technique worth mastering.

Easily accomplished at home, it is a very inexpensive and flexible method for producing fresh, live foods in your own kitchen anytime of year. And sprouts in paper toweling and a plastic bag or sprouting bag can even grow while they're traveling with you on a trip. They literally qualify as a survival food; if you had to do it, you could technically survive on 2 ounces of sprouts per day.

An allied technique and an integral part of the fermentation process for many foods, sprouting is one the first steps in beer making, as well as for producing more digestible basic Essene-type breads at home. And in the home, rejuvelac, the fermented soak water from grains, can provide a tangy beverage source of microorganisms that can help rebalance gut flora. See Recipes in Basic Fermented Formulas.

SPENT GRAINS

As we are becoming more conscious of resources, energy efficiency and ecological balance, the practice of using "spent" grains, the sprouted, fermented barley and other grains used in the beer making process, for other food related purposes is an increasing reality in environmentally responsible businesses.

Based in Paul Hawken's *Ecology of Commerce*, this philosophy translates into a simple "Take, Make, Waste" business equation, is a new barometer of sustainable practices now gaining acceptance as part of just plain good business practices. So ecologically aware business owners like Dan and Pat Conway, owners of Great Lakes Brewing Co. in Cleveland, are closing the circle, so to speak, by utilizing their spent grains in a variety of ways, such as for their restaurant's spent beer breads and pretzels, as feed converted into the organic beef and pork they serve, and as a base for locally growing organic mushrooms. You can view a profile about their business practices in the Community Fermentation projects on page 40, Their spent grains are just a signal of the coming times when we will all become more resourceful and create our own food circles.

If you sprout wheat or other grains in your home, you can use them several times, over and over, to produce more rejuvelac. See the recipes in Basic Fermented Formulas. Sprouted grains are also the nutritious chief ingredient in making nubbly, flourless or modified Essene Bread, which you can also learn how to make on page _. If you decide to get into making beer, you can also mirror the industry's recycling practice by incorporating your leftover mash into recipes such as cookies, breads and other goodies. A few recipes using "spent grains" are included in the Recipe Section.

Permaculturist David Blume suggests going a step further. In the wake of all the new buzz and activity about biofuels, the author of "Alcohol Can be a Gas," says it makes much more sense to ferment grains for alcohol, either in the brewery or in small scale ethanol production plants, then feed the fermented grain to cattle or poultry.

Fermentation at Work
Naturally Fermented Sodas

David Plante is a mechanical engineer who says he didn't know anything about healthy eating for most of his life. Then to deal with developing health concerns in his 40s, he started studying nutrition and exploring different ways to improve his health through food. When he discovered the Weston A. Price Foundation and started feeling better from eating traditional foods, he became fascinated with the phenomenon of ferrmentation. Now he is a Maine Chapter president for the Foundation and is becoming known for his delicious, naturally fermented sodas.

He joins a small, but growing number of local, traditional food advocates who are replacing sugary, addictive carbonated commercial sodas with healthier, naturally brewed, effervescent beverages that are not only delicious, but also full of active, beneficial lactobacteria that promote good digestion and health. And in the process, zhe says, he's not only healthier and happier, he is really enthralled with his his new avocation: Microfarming. It's like having your own farm in a bottle, says David.

David who is resourceful and believes in doing things simply, makes about 3-4 gallons of natural, lacto-fermented sodas per week for his wife and five kids and 3 or 4 other families in his neighborhood. In return, his neighbors provide him with homemade sourdough bread, raw milk and vegetables in an informal barter system they keep track of on a kitchen clipboard.

The process of making natural sodas is very much like brewing beer, but the drinks are non-alcoholic, essentially a young fermentation, much healthier and more delicious than commercial sodas. "While sodas aren't necessary foods, in the midst of exploring the process, you develop a relationship with these critters, and learn a lot about them and yourself," says David Plante.

David Plante, Southern Maine/York County
(207) 676-7946,
dplant@maine.rr.com

When it comes to making instead of buying your own fermented foods, there are two key words you should keep in mind: containers and community.

In this author's humble opinion, both these ideas are keys to incorporating this easy process into your new healthy life. Sandor Katz, fellow fermentation ferverist, champion and author of *Wild Fermentation* who has of the most friendly and home-style attitudes about the subject, points out that a simple, empowering and earthy approach to creating your own cultured foods in your own kitchen can be done without having a lot of special equipment or ingredients.

And making these foods cooperatively in the company of good friends, with some good eats and conversation, is right in line with Sandor's recommendations and my own. Quite frankly, fermentation is superbly and ideally accomplished through a group approach. With everyone being so busy nowadays, it just makes sense to pool time and resources, to split up the work and the spoils…ahem…so to speak…well…sorry. Fermentation projects are among the finest and most productive activities for creating community around food.

Containers. Containers or vessels are the main equipment needed for simple fermenting. Generally you will be able to do most simple fermentations with things such as quart or gallon glass jars you already have around your home or can easily obtain at hardware or other retailers. Glass and ceramic are really optimal, but truthfully, any type of non-metal container, even food grade plastic buckets, can be used for fermentation containers.

CAUTION: DO NOT USE plastic that formerly contained paint or chemicals.

For larger quantities of fermented vegetables or dairy products, you might want to acquire ceramic pottery crocks. They are still available new from limited sources, like cast ironware, which you can find in the Resources section. The classic German Harsch fermentation crocks, complete with lids and weights are like culturing 'Cadillacs,' including their price, but you can also be creative and find your own. And remember, you'll probably have to lift your container, so obviously don't ferment in something the size of a horse watering trough or bathtub, although you could do this if you needed to. "If you're going to make 6 gallons of natural sodas, says soda maker John Plante, it makes more sense to make smaller batches in 2 or 3-gallon vessels."

Old crocks. These are a rare find. Most often you're likely to find them at yard sales or flea markets, the most inexpensive source, although they are often available in antique stores, usually at a heftier price. The old style crocks may be duo-colored with numbers like 1, 2, 3, denoting the number of gallons they can hold.

If purchasing old crockery for culturing, look for straight-sided, cylindrically shaped crocks having smooth, unbroken surfaces without cracks. Crackless is required, at least on the inside, which otherwise may be a source of contamination that can affect your final results. There's a huge 120 stuffed with flowers in the corner of an antique mall stall nearby that I'm hoping no one spies before I can retrieve it. On the whole, though, you'll most commonly find the 1, 2 and 3-gallon crocks. Clean them thoroughly and test for leaks. They can still make marvelous fermentation caches.

Cheese press. Some other types of cultured foods such as aged cheeses that are a little more involved to make, and may require having some special equipment. Even so, these still need not be expensive, or involve unusual or hard-to-find materials. You can actually construct a cheese press yourself, at home. See instructions on Professor David Fankhauser's helpful website: http://biology.clc.uc.edu/Fankhauser/Cheese/Cheese.html.

The world of beer and wine is literally it's own universe. If you want to start getting into some of these larger scale fermentation projects with more complicated processes, you will likely want to acquire special equipment such as carboys or fermentation vessels with locks, presses, and other types of distillation apparatus. All fermentation projects are a learning experience.

This author is still a student, not an expert in this oenophile and microbrewery realm, so this book focuses primarily on fermented foods versus beverages. You will find recipes for beverages in this section, but, as a rule, these are "young" fermentation drinks, like kvass, kombucha, etc. that have no or almost no alcohol and are really nourishing "liquid foods" in their own right. All naturally fermented beverages ARE undeniably some of the most nourishing quaffables you can get your hand around, especially for nourishing fun and entertainment…and community.

You probably won't need large fermentation vessels like carboys, used for brewing beers, unless you start making products like naturally fermented sodas, (which would actually be a very good thing, since with these delicious beverages you can wean your kids or spouse or partner off and away from devastatingly bad, addictive commercial soft drinks.) Then you will get a taste of the whole world of brewology. There are a wealth of excellent sources for equipment and supplies for making beers and wines, including many websites, mail order sources, trade magazines and catalogs.

For a great overall introduction to the subject of beer, including its rich heritage, I suggest you acquire a copy of Chris O'Brien's *Fermenting Revolution, New Society Publishers*, 2007.

Hand shredders, graters, mandolins. These are the very inexpensive, very common and very necessary, basic tools in the fermentation kitchen. And they will ensure that you can create simple fermented sauerkrauts or other vegetable ferments anytime.

Grinder. Other pieces of equipment you could use in the home fermentation process include: grinders, like the old style hand cranked meat grinders with different plates that can be used for a variety of tasks. Champion juicers, with the right plates, can also work well. As Food Network food guru, Alton Brown says, "No uni-taskers!" If you dig out or pick up a manual model, then you have extra benefits. You can use it if/when (note the hint) the electricity goes off, and you will get some extra exercise from hand cranking. By the way, you won't be judged if you happen to have and use an electric-powered piece of equipment.

Food processor. One of the most indispensable–albeit is electric–appliances in the contemporary kitchen is the food processor. With its many blades and capabilities, it is one of the most

valuable tools any culinarian can have. Food processors are a godsend for incorporating past-their-prime yet still-edible leftovers: marginal but unattractive, fibrous peelings or other refuse, nutritious but yucky "green" things your kids won't touch, even cheese you'd never serve a rat, even if he tries to convince you he's a chef… (What? A movie script!!)

However, don't make the shortsighted miscalculation that any cheap, wimpy, counter-walking model will do. At yard sale or in appliance mart, look for and insist upon a heavy-duty version, 300 watts or more, that will be able to handle the grueling work of grinding and pureeing tough, hard, whole foods like nuts, seeds, carrots and other tubers. I have a hand-crank version in my emergency closet just in case I can't plug in the electric one. That's how important this wonder tool is to my cooking.

Long ago and far away, during the early days when I was working my way through the legions of macrobiotic, hygienic and vegan vegetarian raw food kitchens I've managed and cooked in on my way to the perfectly balanced, healthy eating attitude and approach, I had an answer for the disdaining pronouncements from my purist cohorts who absolutely shunned and judged anything electrical in contact or vicinity of food.

"If I'm making hummus for 300 people, I'm not going to be using my feet to do it. And besides, if my energy and frequency is not higher than an electric blender's, I'm really in trouble," I have been heard to say, more than once. Consciousness transmutes a lot, including the negative "vibes" from electrically powered kitchen appliances. Frequency rules, but so do I when it comes to elevating the energy of food in my hands.

Strainers and colanders. Once you start making fermented foods, you'll find that these little (and bigger) babies come in mighty handy. Even though we hate plastic, I find that synthetic, non-metal fine sieves with long handles and larger-holed colanders with double handles, from a few cups to gigantic 4 gallon ones are invaluable utensils for rinsing, draining, and straining, for washing large whole fruit or berries, or lined with natural coffee filters or cheesecloth for making yogurt or kefir cheese.

Cheesecloth. This is really loose, almost holey cotton fabric that is designed to be layered and used for many related applications including covering containers, keeping bugs and other crawlies out, while permitting air and breathing of container contents. Great for covering upturned gallon jars filled and draining rinsed sprouts. Wild yeasts can fall in, that's ok. Flies…no, not in my kitchen. You can also improvise, creating loose pouches for spices or other steeping ingredients, quick and pliable strainers, on-the-road sprouting bags, and such. Find cheesecloth in fabric or hardware stores, canning sections, through mail order, or in Truly Cultured™ Starter Kits you can order through www.TrulyCultured.com. Find a coupon for a discount off your first order at the back of the book.

Rubber bands. Great for a multitude of tasks, most especially securing cheesecloth or other fabric over the top of fermenting jars or containers, fastening tea bags or even creating your own little fabric pouches for loose tea or brewing spices. You can, of course, always use string or twine.

Gallon glass jars with wide mouths. I'm mentioning these again because they are a blessing to any cultured foods aficionado, for anything from brewing your KT to larger batches of pickled vegetables. So if you can, find any jars that formerly housed pickles or olives from your favorite restaurant or bar dumpster, or better yet, work out a deal with the chef, cook or barkeep, promising that you'll recycle them with love and affection.

Quart glass jars with wide mouths, needless to say, are indispensable. And the best for fermenting the small quantities consumed by most families of modest size, especially when you're just starting to learn and introducing these nutritious nuggets into your family's meals.

Making sauerkraut or yogurt in quart jars also minimizes the risk of contamination from other airborne microbes that usually mess up your final result.

Grolsch-type bale-top bottles, the dark brown or green glass beer (and sometimes soda) bottles with wire bales and ceramic stoppers are very desirable items around the fermenter's domain. You can use them to neatly hold and seal many a ferment, including young beer, and beverages like kvass or natural sodas you might try to make (delicious, by the way). But so is the Grolsch ale treat you'll have a reason to buy and enjoy now for the containers!

Thermometer. While much of your early fermentation learning curve will involve becoming acquainted with the critters and the criteria for successful ferments, in getting to know and becoming comfortable with the processes, the looks, the sights, sounds and smells, an actual feel for the subject at the various stages of this transformative process, you will find that a kitchen thermometer is a very helpful instrument for reading and righting your experiments. It will help you immensely, expedite your learning, and be essential, in certain cases.

All microorganisms involved in the fermentation process are sensitive to specific ranges of temperature and pH, but some cultures demand a very precise range. Piima culture, for example, for making kefir, demands to be maintained in a tight temperature range of 18 to 28°C. (65 to 82°F.) is good; about 22°C. (71°F.) is optimal.

pH paper. This can be helpful for testing the pH or relative acidity or alkalinity of your products, both in your learning and in your ongoing practical everyday making of them. Fermentation reactions, dependent upon what type, usually lower the pH or acidity of a food mixture down to about 3 or 4 on the pH scale. As you work with these foods, you'll become more familiar with the changes in pH that happen at various stages of the process. You can get pH paper, what you probably remember as litmus paper in your high school chemistry class from a pharmacy or through mail order. If you are a diabetic, you are familiar with test strips that tell the pH of body fluids. Same thing.

Household scale. You don't need to own an expensive one, but having even a common manual scale is valuable when it comes to fermentation projects. This way you can weigh your produce before its processed, called a.p. or "as purchased" weight in the culinary world, after its cut up, to see how much unusable peelings or trimmings you average, and then how much finished product you yield. You should be able to find a manual 22 lb (10 kg) scale for $17 to 25 in a hardware or kitchen store, or online.

Bathroom scales can be used in a pinch, although they're not that accurate for measuring small weights, plus it is a bit difficult to balance a 5-gallon bucket on them and see the reading at the same time. Of course, you can always weigh yourself holding an empty container first, and then weigh yourself and a full container, subtracting to get the difference or the net weight of product.

Weights. Any kind of heavy object, even a clean rock, can be used as a weight to hold down the contents of your container while it's going through its fizzing process. Lacto-fermentation depends upon the vegetables or whatever you are transforming being submerged in liquid, so weights are used, usually on top of a space plate or lid, to keep product down in the brine. The Cadillac of German fermentation crocks come with built in lid weights, but you can also simply use a 1-gallon jug filled with water.

Corral your equipment. You would be smart and wise to create a closet or corner of your pantry devoted to housing your fermentation tools and equipment. This will cut down on time lost running around collecting what you need from all over, and will make it easier for yourself to be motivated and get into the habit and flow of producing fermentables on a regular basis for you and your household, even if it's yourself or only two people. This way, you can always count on having a clean, serviceable colander, for example, right where you need it and you'll see that you're running low on cheesecloth or salt. You can also store your clean jars and vessels in this area, as well as product going through its bubbling process or resting and waiting for you to consume it.

Make a note. Tack up a small note pad with a pencil on a string to your shelf or cupboard so you can quickly jot down items you're running low on. Then as you grow in knowledge and confidence, as well as frequency in making these goodies, you'll find yourself more willing and more able to regularly incorporate scheduled sessions when you create new batches of kombucha or yogurt, easy ones to start with, as well as multi-tasking in preparing other dishes or ingredients for meals for the week or for the freezer.

Choose quality ingredients. Whether it's high trace mineral Celtic sea salt or organic evaporated cane juice, you are creating a superior, high quality food product and for what it's worth, for all the time, energy and money (albeit less than you think) you invest in this process, you might as well use the best ingredients available. See Resources and www.TrulyCultured.com.

Water, salt and cabbage. What could be simpler. These are the only ingredients necessary for simple fermentation of vegetables such as sauerkraut. But the fact is fermentable ingredients can be vegetables, fruits, meats, nuts, seeds, grains, legumes, dairy products, virtually any kind of food can be fermented.

Water. Fermentation takes place in the presence of water, whether it is in a brine or in a piece of fruit. So it is the most common ingredient called for in the fermentation process. The best advice about water is to use the best water available, but avoid distilled or chlorinated water, because it destroys microorganisms. If your tap water is chlorinated or you can smell it, it's a good practice to boil the water briefly to evaporate the chlorine before using it in fermenting.

Salt. Salt is a common, universal ingredient. Salt draws water out of vegetables, helping to create the brine that is the medium for fermentation to occur. Salt in the brine preserves food by reducing bacterial growth, reducing the pH or acid/base balance to inhibit the growth of putrefying microbes, promoting the growth of the "good" lactobacteria. However, all salt is not equal. It's created equal, as in found naturally in the earth, but differs tremendously in its consumable form. Refined commercial salt contains many additives, including iodine and anti-caking ingredients, that can interfere or affect the fermentation process. The best salt to use for fermenting is Celtic sea salt, sea salt, or kosher salt. See Resources, salt sidebar, next page.

Sugar. While most foods contain adequate sugars or starches that can be converted to sugars to create the fermentation substrate, some recipes require addition of supplemental sugars to initiate or accelerate the process. Kombucha tea, for example, and fermentations producing alcohol such as cider, are examples. You certainly can use white sugar or

Salt

Salt, an essential mineral for proper body function, has been one of the most highly prized commodities known to man, long held as sacred by many civilizations, including the Greeks and Romans, who even used it as currency. So precious it was almost a sin to waste, spilling salt was a travesty, at least remediated by the practice of throwing salt over the left shoulder, supposedly to blind the devil.

TYPES OF SALT

Celtic Sea Salt: Sea salt and Celtic Sea Salt® Brand are unrefined salt crystals remaining after salt water is dried by the sun. High in macro and micro nutrients, especially minerals calcium, potassium, magnesium, it is by far the best type of salt to use for instigating fermentation at home. www.TrulyCultured.com

Table Salt: Resident of most salt shakers, common table salt is sodium chloride. Mined from inland salt deposits, heated and refined, it usually contains anti-cakiing ingredients and sometimes even sugar, so it is not a good salt for creating fermented foods.

Iodized Salt: Iodine in the form of Sodium or Potassium Iodide, is added to regular table salt to prevent iodine deficiency or goiter. But the iodine will kill the lacto-bacteria, so it is not a good salt to using in fermentation.

Kosher or Coarse Salt: Used primarily in commercial kitchens, kosher salt is basically the same as table salt but milled to a larger granule size. Okay for fermentation.

Light Salt or Salt Replacements: Lower sodium salt substitutes made with varying amounts of potassium chloride.

Industrial Ingredient Salts: Potassium Bromides and Sodium Nitrates are examples of other industrial salts used in food processing by manufacturers.

LOW SALT OR LOW SODIUM

Fermented vegetables such as sauerkraut can be made without salt or with other types of salts, but the result will not be as crispy or probably as tasty.

NUTRITIONAL NEEDS

A beautiful material that's literally available in a rainbow of colors, salt is an essential mineral for the human body. Ironically it is made up of two deadly poisons, sodium and chlorine. When combined in chemical reaction, they form a stable salt that is essential for life. Natural sea salt or celtic sea salt contains valuable, easily absorbable minerals that refined salt does not, which some professionals feel is part of the problem. Too much salt, of course, can lead to dehydration, imbalances in minerals.

SALT IN FERMENTATION

Salt, water and vegetable or fruit, grain or dairy are the primary ingredients normally treated by fermentation. The salt lowers the acidity of the mixture, promoting the development of the good lactic acid bacteria which does the job of breaking down the sugars in the food and producing and preserving the produce.

Find high quality Celtic Sea Salt Brand by The Grain and Salt Society,® exclusively used in our Truly Cultured™ Starter Kits, www.TrulyCultured.com.

brown sugar (although you may not want the molasses), however, many of us now prefer to substitute organic equivalents, evaporated cane juice, organic sugar, demerara or Rapadura, maple syrup.

Honey may be too high in microbials that can imbalance your fermentation, although obviously it is the main sugar in the ancient beverage mead. Avoid corn syrup or high fructose corn syrup.

Whey. The illustrious "curds and whey" of nursery rhymes, whey is the liquidy portion from milk, either still in liquid or in dried form, that is full of the lactose which our friendly lactobacteria feast upon. It can be used in non-dairy fermentations, such as vegetable fermentations like sauerkraut, to accelerate and enhance the growth and conversion of the active bacteria, assuring more potential success with your fermentations. You can either collect and save it yourself when making a young cheese like kefir or yogurt cheese, or you can purchase it in bulk or dry packets to add to your experiments. Body-builders know that it is a high quality, digestible protein that can enhance their performance and muscle-building, and often purchase it either plain or in formulas available in health and natural food stores, or Truly Cultured™ Starter Kits.

Organic ingredients. Buy the healthiest, most nutrient dense ingredients you can find. That doesn't mean they have to be organic, but at this point in our evolution, organic foods at least have some standards. Certified organically grown foods are required to be grown albeit that many forces are continually working to dilute and destroy these standards. "Natural", on the other hand, is a meaningless term that has no standards or definitions. So don't buy into the marketing hype. Just because it says natural doesn't mean it's healthy.

If organic farming is the natural way, shouldn't organic produce just be called "produce" and make the pesticide-laden stuff take the burden of an adjective? ~ Ymber Delecto

Local foods. It just makes sense that foods grown and produced within 100 miles of where you live are going to be the freshest and most nutritious. Broccoli grown a thousand miles away must be harvested before it is ready to use, must be transported, often thousands of miles using many calories of energy, is handled many

times before you buy it plus, you do not know just where it was grown, who tended the crop, or the condition of the region.

One related note: We have truly become spoiled and fooled by the appearance of produce available to us. We have been marketed into an expectation that all fruits and vegetables should be picture perfect, huge and brightly colored, and that less than this is unfit or unworthy to eat. Regardless of how nutritious it is. Here's a tip. Examine and reevaluate this assumption, because the reality is likely that you could be forced to eat a lot of possibly inferior looking produce in the future, and very possibly food that you would never consider eating under any circumstances. Just remember, cosmetic appearance is like labels, it's not reliable indicator of nutrient value. Hint: produce in the market doesn't just naturally grow this way without some serious producer or processor assistance.

By favoring locally grown food, you will be rewarded with the best flavor and nutrition, and the vitality of fresher produce or groceries. Inferior ingredients produce inferior results—acknowledging, of course, that the process of fermentation is about the only treatment that can actually IMPROVE the quality of marginal and/or less than prime foodstuffs. You can ferment older or satellite parts of food, like root ends or tops, etc. or parts that you wouldn't serve "as is". Just as chefs all over the world can do magic with seconds, (still usable but less than beautiful food), you can include those ugly, not-ready-for-prime-time ingredients into your fermentation projects and come out smelling…well not like a rose, exactly, but you get my drift. You will be eating very well.

This is something you may want to take note of and file somewhere in your cranium for the future. You might just need to take advantage of this fact to feed yourself and your family sometime. Again, no fear; just information. Fact is, you can always count on fermentation. Regardless of what else you don't have, you'll always have the benefit of this naturally occurring spontaneous process as a nutrient-enhancing, food processing and preservation technique that doesn't even require any energy inputs like electricity.

It's always a good idea to start with as clean and vital food as you can meaning if there are obvious rotting spots or growths or bruises on produce, cut them out, not so much because they are "yucky" and disgusting, but only because they may inject other microorganisms into the mix that will interfere with a good lacto-fermentation.

Conditions or environment. So, to reiterate, fermentation and culturing reactions are highly dependent upon time, temperature and other environmental conditions such as pH. Heat enhances fermentation; cold slows it. Therefore, your fermentation reactions will skyrocket during summer and slag along during the colder winter months. But these are the principles. To reawaken a sleeping sourdough, give it some more fresh flour and warmth by the stove or a fire. To slow down a fermentation reaction, put it in a cool or cold place, like a closet, cellar or the refrigerator. Sauerkraut and other fermenting vegetables do just fine in the back of a closet by themselves on the shelf, usually when they are active and then as they proceed to their more stable resting phase.

Batch sessions for many of us are the smartest and most efficient way to incorporate and manage preparing homemade foods, fermented or otherwise, into busy schedules. I'm not denying that we're all busy. I'm very busy myself. But it's actually not the amount of time devoted to scheduling food prep sessions that seems to trip us up. It's getting our minds around the idea and overcoming the inertia that seems to be the big obstacle.

You can do an amazing amount of basic and supplemental food preparation, including fermented foods, on a regular basis in a few-hour blocks on a weekend or even some evenings. For example, on Saturday or Sunday, you could prepare and roast two or three chickens, one of which you can serve for Sunday dinner. While they're roasting, you can be cooking up a batch of beans and making a pot of rice. While they're on the fire, you can boil water for a new batch of kombucha tea, start a new batch of yogurt, soak nuts or wheatberries for sprouts. Clean and cut up some vegetables and bone some chicken once it's cooled and you've got a jumpstart on creating your femented and regular foods for the week, just one example. Look for other tips like this on www.TrulyCultured.com.

And once you try this approach and start doing it,

you're going to wonder why you let yourself get hung up on the idea that you couldn't handle making healthy foods at home. It's mostly about rearranging your mind.

Vincent Van Gogh: "If you hear a voice within you say, 'You cannot paint,' then by all means paint and that voice will be silenced."

Make it easier for yourself. In the end, it may come down simply to using the factor of habit?built in to all of us?to get yourself in the swing, so to speak of using a batch session approach to fermentation, and for regular family meals, for that matter. Our subconscious is very obedient and literal. It will invariably take what we say and put it into motion, taking the burden of routine matters away from our conscious minds. So we are constantly using this phenomenon, whether we realize it or not, theoretically to make our lives simpler. And it works, of course, depending upon the quality of choices we make. It works for both "good" and "bad" habits. But regardless, it takes 21 days to firmly form a new habit.

Once you've moved through this phase, and are working hand-in-hand with the companion of habit, inertia, you are on your way! A body at rest tends to stay at rest; a body in motion tends to stay in motion. So become conscious of, if you aren't already, the power of your wonderful subconscious and inertia. So, why not use these to your advantage, instead of being used by them, to help make it easier for yourself to get into a healthy lifestyle choices mode.

Work with others. One of the main points I keep coming back to in this book. This is true: another incentive and source of labor for getting these projects done is to co-create with your friends and family members. Fermented foods are absolutely the best excuse for getting people together for a fun, productive, social gathering. It can start small, with as few as two or three – you and two of your friends, a Circle-of-Three™ an idea we'll be sharing more about as we continue to develop patterns and practical solutions for using foods, especially high quality, nutritious, fermented, local, organic foods, and activities around these foods as a seed for forming local community food circles on www.thefoodcircle.com and www.fullcirclescommunity.com.

Table of Contents

Basic
Fermented
Formulas

Ceviche

Ceviche is a delicious, traditional South American "raw" fish dish. Tecnhnically raw, it's "cooked" or transformed from pale pink to opaque white only by the acids in the lemon or lime juice.

2	lb firm, fresh, deboned, red snapper fillets, cut into ½-inch pieces
¾	cup parsley or cilantro, chopped finely
½	med vidalia onion, finely diced
1	cup fresh tomatoes, peeled, seeded, and chopped
1	serrano chili, seeded and finely diced
2	tsp Celtic or sea salt
1	cup freshly squeezed lemon and/or lime juice

Into a glass or ceramic dish or jar, place fish, onion, green herbs, tomatoes, chiles and salt.

Add Tabasco sauce, if desired. Pour the lemon and/or lime juice over the top, mixing the ingredients well.

Let set in refrigerator. Each hour stir to assure fish is evenly coated with juices. Marinate for 4-6 hours.

Serve as part of an appetizer or main dish along with avocados or leafy green mesclun salad mix.

Recipe Type:
Appetizer or snack, basic fermented formula, dairy-free main dish, gluten-free, raw, seafood

Yield: 8 servings
Prep time: 15 min.
Inactive prep time: 4-6 hrs.

COOKING TIPS

Firm cod or other firm fish can also be substituted for red snapper.

NUTRITION FACTS

Nutrition (per serving):
16.5 calories; 3% calories from fat; 0.1g total fat; 0.0mg cholesterol; 473.9mg sodium; 121.2mg potassium; 4.6g carbohydrates; 0.6g fiber; 1.7g sugar; 0.5g protein.

Coconut Kefir

Real kefir grains can be used to culture the juice of fresh, young green coconuts, producing a refreshing and healthful probiotic drink.

Recipe Type:
Basic fermented formula, beverage, dairy-free, gluten-free, raw, vegan, vegetarian

Yield: 12 servings
Prep time: 60 min.
Inactive prep time: 24 hrs.

COOKING TIPS

*Once kefir grains have been used to ferment a water-based liquid such as coconut or fruit juice, they are known as 'water kefir grains.' They should then not be used to culture milk.

4 young fresh green coconuts
1 Tbsp water kefir grains*

Cut off the top of the coconut with a hacksaw. Or use a cleaver and a rubber mallet, hammering the cleaver through the tough wall. Pour the juice into a blender. Each fresh young green coconut will yield approximately 1-1/2 cups liquid.

Scrape or cut out the coconut meat with a large metal spoon or knife. Add to blender.

Blend coconut juice and meat together on high into a milk. Put coconut liquid into a clean, quart-size glass jar.

Gather one tablespoon of real kefir grains that have NOT been used to culture milk into a piece of cheesecloth that has been doubled. Twist to close. Wash them by swishing the cheesecloth back and forth in a small jar of filtered water.

Dump the kefir grains into the coconut liquid, screw on the lid and leave at 68-77°F. to ferment for 24 hours. Transfer to refrigerator and keep for as long as 3 weeks.

Drink the kefired coconut juice straight or diluted with water. Reuse the water kefir grains to culture more coconut juice or another type of fruit juice.

NUTRITION FACTS

Nutrition (per serving):
468.5 calories;
79% calories from fat;
44.3g total fat;
0.0mg cholesterol;
26.5mg sodium;
471.1mg potassium;
20.2g carbohydrates;
11.9g fiber; 8.2g sugar;
4.4g protein.

Recipe Source:
www.bodyecology.com

Crème Frâiche

Pronounced "fresh," this delightful cultured cream will add French flair to your favorite dishes.

2 cups fresh, whole, raw cream, if possible
¼ cup cultured buttermilk

Measure cream and buttermilk into medium bowl.

Whisk the mixture together about 20 strokes.

Place covered bowl in a warm place for about 12 hours.

Final product will be thick like stiff sour cream.

Recipe Type:
Basic fermented formula, gluten-free, raw, vegetarian

Yield: about 2 cups
Prep time: 5 min.
Inactive prep time: 12 hrs.

COOKING TIPS

Store Crème Frâiche in tightly covered container in refrigerator for up to 2 weeks.

NUTRITION FACTS

Nutrition (per serving):
31.8 calories;
84% calories from fat;
3.1g total fat;
6.5mg cholesterol;
9.3mg sodium;
24.1mg potassium;
0.7g carbohydrates;
0.0g fiber; 0.1g sugar;
0.5g protein.

Crispy Nuts

The original recipe for these tasty, easier-to-digest crispy nuts comes from Sally Fallon's Nourishing Traditions.

Recipe Type:
Appetizer or snack,
Basic fermented
formula, gluten-free
holiday, sprouted,
vegan, vegetarian

Yield: 4 cups,
serves 16

Prep time: 18 hrs.

**Inactive prep
time:** 7-8 hrs.

4 cups whole raw nuts, such as pecans, walnuts, macadamia nuts,
   or almonds
1 Tbsp Celtic or sea salt
Filtered water to cover

Mix nuts with salt in a glass, ceramic or stainless steel container. Cover with purified water. Leave in a warm place for 7-8 hours.

Drain in a colander.

Spread nuts on a stainless steel baking sheet and place in a warm oven, no more than 150°F. for 12-24 hours, turning occasionally, until completely dry and crisp. Or dehydrate in dehydrator at 105°F. for 24-30 hours.

Store in an airtight container at room temperature. Note: walnuts should be stored in the refrigerator.

COOKING TIPS

"Raw" cashews aren't actually raw, so they require a slightly different process. Soak for 6 hours maximum. Cook at 200°-250°F. for 8-12 hrs..

Try a delicious variation on Crispy Nuts: Rosemary Walnuts on page 166.

NUTRITION FACTS

Nutrition (per serving):
203.4 calories;
72% calories from fat;
17.6g total fat;
0.0mg cholesterol;
427.1mg sodium;
204.5mg potassium;
8.7g carbohydrates;
3.1g fiber; 0.0g sugar;
5.9g protein.

Recipe Source
Sally Fallon
Nourishing Traditions

Elderberry Wine

A classic, tasty, tangy elderberry wine that will boost festivities!

5 lb fresh whole elderberries, black or red raspberries
1 gal cold water
3½ lb granulated sugar
½ oz yeast
6 whole cloves
1½-inch piece fresh ginger root, sliced

Rinse berries. Place in large non-aluminum kettle or stockpot with water and simmer over med low heat until fruit is tender. Remove from heat and let cool to room temperature.

Strain juice into crock.

Add sugar and spices, stir thoroughly and when cooled to lukewarm, add yeast.

Cover crock, store in cool place for 10 days, then strain and bottle. Patiently wait 6 months for the finished product.

Recipe Type:
Basic fermented formula, beverage with alcohol, gluten-free, vegan, vegetarian

Yield: 1½ gal, serves 24

Prep time: 30 min.

Inactive prep time: 10 days

Recipe Source:
Phyllis Hughes, ed.
Pueblo Indian Cooking

130

NUTRITION FACTS

Nutrition (per serving):
377.7 calories;
0% calories from fat;
0.0g total fat;
0.0mg cholesterol;
21.2mg sodium;
217.2mg potassium;
32.3g carbohydrates;
0.0g fiber; 18.4g sugar;
0.5g protein.

Essene Bread

This moist, dense and chewy bread is easily made from sprouted grains in your own kitchen, and is much tastier and healthier than the commercial, pale white spongy stuff.

3-4 cups grain, sprouted (see page 154)
water

Select the grain you've decided to use for your recipe. Grain must be raw, organic whole grain berries that are suitable for becoming alive! Hard wheat berries and rye become sweet when sprouted. Follow the recipe for Sprouted Grains.

Sprouts are ready to use when sprout hairs are about twice as long as the berries.

Let grain sprouts drain and dry 3-6 hours prior to grinding.

Grind sprouts in a food processor, Champion juicer, wheat grass juicer or meat grinder. End product will be a smooth paste, may be a light and dark variegated sticky dough.

Oil your clean hands with your favorite cooking oil and knead the dough, folding the dough over itself and kneading more. Knead for 5 minutes.

Form the dough into 3-inch balls or flatten to fill a ten-inch pan.

Place on unoiled cooking sheet. Flatten ball to 10-inch diameter, about 1-inch thick.

Bake in a cool oven at 150°F. for 12-24 hours. Bread is done when the top of the loaf is firm. Bread will be moist in center.

Recipe Type:
Basic fermented formula, dairy-free, sprouted, vegan, vegetarian

Yield: 1-2 small loaves, serves 18

Prep time: 48 hrs.

Cooking time: up to 24 hrs.

COOKING TIP

Add grated carrots, coconuts, raisins, or nuts, as desired, before forming dough into balls.

NUTRITION FACTS

Nutrition (per serving):
140.4 calories;
4% calories from fat;
0.8g total fat;
0.0mg cholesterol;
0.9mg sodium;
145.1mg potassium;
29.0g carbohydrates;
5.2g fiber; 0.2g sugar;
6.6g protein.

Recipe Source:
Willow Alderson
Uprisings: The Whole Grain Baker's Book

Farmer's Cheese

Also known as soft farmer's cheese or "chèvre," the French term for the creamy soft goat cheese prized as a delicacy the world over.

Recipe Type:
Basic fermented
formula, gluten-free,
raw, vegetarian

Yield: 1 round,
serves 15

Prep time: 20-60 min.

**Inactive prep
time:** up to 11 days

1 gal fresh, whole, raw cow's or goat's milk
2 Tbsp cultured buttermilk
¼ tablet rennet dissolved in ¼ cup lukewarm water OR
1 drop liquid rennet
½ tsp Celtic or sea salt

Pour milk into gallon jar or glass or ceramic container. Allow to reach room temperature.

Mix rennet mixture into the buttermilk and cream mixture. Stir in buttermilk, mix well.

Cover. Put in a warm place for 24 hours. The curd should be firm enough to cut into ½-inch cubes.

Line a strainer with 2-3 layers of cheesecloth. Place a container underneath to catch and save the whey for other recipes.

Move the curds into the strainer in large chunks by using two spatulas or a ladle. Cover and let the whey drain for 2 hours in a cool place.

Salt to taste. Press together and mold into round shape. Wrap in cheesecloth. Store in covered container in refrigerator for up to 10 days.

NUTRITION FACTS

Nutrition (per serving):
150.3 calories;
52% calories from fat;
9.0g total fat;
23.9mg cholesterol;
162.5mg sodium;
445.0mg potassium;
9.7g carbohydrates;
0.0g fiber; 9.7g sugar;
7.8g protein.

Recipe Source
©David B. Fankhauser, Ph.D., Professor of Biology and Chemistry, University of Cincinnati, Clermont College, Batavia, OH 45103, http:biology.dc.uc.educ/fankhauser/cheese.htm

Ginger Ale

Recipe Type:
Basic fermented
formula, gluten-free,
raw, vegan, vegetarian
yeast or alcoholic
ferment

Yield: 1 gal, serves 16

Prep time: 30 min.

**Inactive prep
time:** 10 hrs.

COOKING TIP

This recipe will make
8-16 ounce bottles.

*For this incomprable homemade soft drink, baking yeast will work,
but for better flavor, pick up some ale yeast at a brewery store.*

2-3 oz fresh ginger root
3 Tbsp lemon juice
3 Tbsp orange juice
¾ cup organic, evaporated cane juice or natural cane sugar
4½ qt water
1 oz yeast, preferably brewer's or champagne

Chop or grate the 2-3 oz ginger root, using more for a very strong ginger ale. Juice the lemon and orange.

Simmer ginger, juices, sugar and 1½ quarts of water in large pan for 30 minutes to 1 hour. The longer it simmers, the stronger it will be.

Remove from heat and strain through a kitchen strainer. Compost the plant material.

Mix the strained brew with the other 3 quarts of water in large container, like a gallon glass jar. Let cool till lukewarm.

In a small jar or cup, stir in ⅛ tsp yeast into ¼ cup warm water. After 15 minutes, add yeast solution to lukewarm brew.

Cover jar with several layers of cheesecloth secured with rubber band. Let the brew set for 10 hours in a warm place.

Bottle it up! Chill and serve. Will keep up to 2 months.

NUTRITION FACTS

Nutrition (per serving):
46.7 calories; 0% calories
from fat; 0.0g total fat;
0.0mg cholesterol;
6.0mg sodium;
47.5mg potassium;
11.9g carbohydrates;
0.1g fiber; 11.1g sugar;
0.2g protein.

Jerky

Homemade jerky from beef, turkey, buffalo or venison or even wild game makes a handy, healthier snack.

5 lb organic or grass-fed steak or roast
2/3 cup wheat-free tamari soy sauce
1 Tbsp garlic powder
1 Tbsp ginger powder
2 tsp Celtic or sea salt
2 tsp black pepper

Slice meat diagonally across the grain into as thin slices as possible.

For basic marinade, combine soy sauce, garlic and ginger powder, salt, and black pepper. Or use one of the variations below.

Marinate meat overnight in rectangular baking dish or pan, covered with the marinade prepared in step 2.

Drain excess marinade. Place meat on cookie racks to allow excess marinade to drain, repositioning pieces to drain thoroughly.

Place individual pieces of meat directly on rack in oven at 140°F. to 160°F. for 7-12 hours, or in dehydrator at 140°F. until meat is dry throughout. Oven door can be left slightly ajar to allow for the free movement of air.

Store finished jerky in an airtight container. Keeps indefinitely.

Variations:

Easy Style: 1½ cups soy sauce, 1 cup red wine vinegar, ¼ cup brown sugar

Yankee: ⅓ cup MSG free Worcestershire Sauce, 1 finely chopped med onion, 5 tsp black pepper

Baja Style: 3 tsp salt, 2 Tbsp ground coriander, 1½ tsp chili powder, 1½ tsp ground ginger, ground turmeric, 1½ tsp ground cumin

Oriental Style: 5 tsp salt, 5 tsp black pepper, 1 large minced onion, 5 cloves pressed garlic, 1 cup brown sugar, ⅓ cup soy sauce, 1¼ cup red wine, 1½ cup pineapple juice

Taj Mahal: 5 tsp salt, 3 tsp curry powder, 5 tsp black pepper, 4 cloves pressed garlic, ½ tsp cinnamon, 3 tsp ground ginger, ¼ tsp ground cloves, 1 cup cream sherry, ½ tsp ground cumin

Valley Style: 1½ cups soy sauce, 1 tsp nutmeg, 5 Tbsp Worcestershire sauce, 1 tsp ginger, 5 tsp black pepper, 10 tsp liquid smoke, 4 cloves pressed garlic, 5 tsp dried crushed peppers, ¼ tsp powdered onion

Recipe Source
bowhunting.net

Recipe Type:
Basic fermented formula, barbeque, meat

Yield: 25 servings
Prep time: 60 min.
Inactive prep time: 7-12 hrs.

COOKING TIP

Jerky can also be skewered with a toothpick through one end. Place toothpick on oven rack, rotating so that jerky hangs down.

Lean tender cuts of meat will make the best jerky, even with wild game like deer, antelope, moose and bison. High fat and high tallow content will increase chances of off-flavors and rancidity.

NUTRITION FACTS

Nutrition (per serving):
125.7 calories;
29% calories from fat;
4.1g total fat;
35.4mg cholesterol;
431.0mg sodium;
305.0mg potassium;
1.1g carbohydrates;
0.2g fiber; 0.2g sugar;
19.8g protein.

Recipe Type:
Basic fermented formula, beverage, gluten-free, raw

Kefir and Kefir Cream

Kefir is thicker than buttermilk and has a wonderful tart flavor.

2 cups fresh whole milk, room temperature
½ cup cream, raw organic, if possible
1 Tbsp kefir granules or kefir powder

Yield: about 2 cups, serves 4

Prep time: 10 min.

Inactive prep time: 1/2 to 2-3 days

If starting with new kefir grains, rinse them with milk in a fine strainer.

In a clean wide-mouth quart jar, place milk and cream, and kefir grains. Stir well and cover loosely with a cloth.

Place in warm place 65°-70°F. such as an oven with pilot light, top of the refrigerator, or wrapped with a towel on the counter, for 12 hours to 2 days, stirring 2-3 times during the process.

Each time the kefir is stirred, taste it. When it tastes pleasantly tart to your liking, and/or becomes thick with a pungent bite, it is ready. Remove kefir grains with a fork prior to serving.

Cover quart jar and store in refrigerator for up to 2 weeks.

COOKING TIP

If the milk is cold, you can bring it up to room temperature quickly by placing jar in a pan of hot water for a few minutes.

Kefir Cream:

Mix ½ cup of kefir with 1½ cups of raw double weight cream and leave to culture for 12-24 hours. Refrigerate the kefir cream until ready for use.

NUTRITION FACTS

Nutrition (per serving):
187.3 calories;
72% calories from fat;
15.5g total fat;
58.0mg cholesterol;
91.3mg sodium;
245.5mg potassium;
7.9g carbohydrates;
0.0g fiber; 1.4g sugar;
4.9g protein.

Recipe Source

Sally Fallon, *Nourishing Traditions*

If you are new to culturing kefir you may wish to visit www.rejoiceinlife.com/kefir/riln14.php to get more detailed instructions.

137

Kombucha

Kombuchu tea is a fermented mushroom beverage that has been used in the Far East for over 2000 years.

Recipe Type:
Basic fermented formula, beverage, dairy-free, gluten-free, raw, vegan, vegetarian

Yield: 3½ qt, serves 26

Inactive prep time: 10-15 days or longer

3½ qt	filtered water
2	cups organic evaporated cane juice or granulated sugar
10	regular pekoe tea bags or ½ c. loose tea
1	starter kombucha mushroom

COOKING TIPS

Use clean hands when handling the mushroom. Preferably use wooden or glass utensils and jars. Purified water is better, because chlorine will kill the mushroom. If using tap water, boil, uncovered, for 10 minutes to evaporate chlorine.

Kombucha is soothing and detoxifying. If you are very toxic begin with 2 oz per day. You can work up to 1 quart a day as your body gets healthier. It will tell you.

Bring water to a boil. Remove from heat. Stir in sugar and then add tea. If using bulk tea, put in tea ball or wrap in cheesecloth. Allow to steep until lukewarm.

Remove the tea bags and pour the cooled tea into a larger, very wide mouthed container.

Put the mushroom gently into the container. Sometimes it will float on top, sometimes it will sink to the bottom and sometimes it will position itself at a 45 degree angle. The position it takes is not reflective of its viability.

Cover with several layers of cheesecloth, or a single layer of linen secured with a rubber band. The mushroom needs oxygen to flow through the weave of the fabric, but the weave must also be tight enough to keep fruit flies out.

Keep at 70-85°F (23-30°C) for 7-10 days. After 7 days, taste daily by gently pushing mushroom down.. If you like the taste and wish to halt the progress, either drink the beverage or refrigerate.

Longer fermentation times produce a fizzier product that can be tart, almost vinegary tasting. Use obviously sour kombucha as a vinegar substitute.

NUTRITION FACTS

Nutrition (per serving):
59.5 calories; 0% calories from fat; 0.0g total fat; 0.0mg cholesterol; 0.0mg sodium; 0.3mg potassium; 15.4g carbohydrates; 0.0g fiber; 15.4g sugar; 0.0g protein.

Kimchi

This spicy kimchi is the Korean's fiery national dish; but may share the table with up to 10 of these small condiment-sized traditional "salads" - some hot, some not.

- 1 head Chinese or Nappa cabbage
- 1½ Tbsp Celtic or sea salt
- 1-2 tsp crushed red peppers
- 3 cloves fresh garlic, peeled and chopped
- 1 Tbsp fresh ginger root, grated
- 2 fresh green onions, finely chopped

Select cabbage that is pale green in color with no visible mold. Cut cabbage in half. Then cut each half into thirds. Compost core. Cut into two-inch chunks.

In a large ceramic or glass container, spread a layer of cabbage chunks. Sprinkle with salt and continue layering until all ingredients are in the container. Stir well.

Let set at room temperature for 8 hours. Rinse cabbage thoroughly with water.

Drain cabbage well. Gently squeeze out excess liquid with your hands.

Place the drained cabbage in a large bowl and add the remaining ingredients including a tsp of salt.

Press cabbage into glass jars and cover. Let stand at room temperature for 24 hours. When kimchi tastes to your liking, transfer to refrigerator.

Recipe Source

www.angelfire.com/journal/ adoptionhelp/kimchi.html

Recipe Type: Basic fermented formula, condiment, dairy-free, gluten-free, raw, salad, vegan, vegetarian

Yield: 5 cups, serves 20

Prep time: 30 min.

Inactive prep time: 32 hrs.

COOKING TIPS

"Kimchee" will get hotter the longer it ferments. Introduce your family to mild Kimchi and increase the spiciness as they are ready.

NUTRITION FACTS

Nutrition (per serving): 4.8 calories; 8% calories from fat; 0.0g total fat; 0.0mg cholesterol; 509.8mg sodium; 55.2mg potassium; 1.0g carbohydrates; 0.3g fiber; 0.3g sugar; 0.3g protein.

Sidebar (Kvass)

Recipe Type:
Basic fermented formula, appetizer, gluten-free, raw, vegetarian, yeast or alcoholic ferment

COOKING TIPS

See other variations for making Kvass in Beverage Section.

Yield: serves 24

Prep time: 20 min.

Inactive prep time: 5 days

NUTRITION FACTS

Nutrition (per serving):
109.6 calories; 0% calories from fat; 0.1g total fat; 0.0mg cholesterol; 2.3mg sodium; 85.6mg potassium; 29.4g carbohydrates; 0.5g fiber; 27.4g sugar; 0.6g protein.

Yields: 16 servings

Prep time: 30 min.

Cooking Time: 30 min.

Inactive prep time: 26 days

COOKING TIPS

Ideal temperature for fermentation is 65°-75°F.

NUTRITION FACTS

Nutrition (per serving):
2.6 calories; 14% calories from fat; 0.0g total fat; 0.0mg cholesterol; 0.3mg sodium; 13.6mg potassium; 0.5g carbohydrates; 0.1g fiber; 0.1g sugar; 0.2g protein.

Kvass, Honey

Kvass is a basic fermented beverage originating in Russia that can be made from a variety of starters, including fruit and bread.

2 cups raw honey, preferably dark
5 qt purified water
4 tsp baking yeast
1 cup organic raisins
2 med lemons, juiced

Boil water in large ceramic or stainless kettle or stock pot. Remove from heat. Stir honey into hot, boiled water until dispersed. Let cool to room temperature.

Add yeast and stir to distribute. Set aside to ferment for 24 hours in a warm place. The liquid will begin to foam.

Skim scum from the top of liquid. Discard.

Put 10 raisins and 1 Tbsp lemon juice into each bottle.

Pour liquid into bottles, cap and store in cool place. Honey kvass tastes best after 5 days of cold storage.

Mead, Honey

Mead, considered the very first fermented food, is a delightfully refreshing beverage that happens naturally when honey and water are left to ferment.

1 gal purified water
2½ lb honey
1 med lemon, juiced
½ tsp nutmeg
1 pkg ale or champagne yeast

Heat water. Add honey, lemon juice and nutmeg. Bring to a boil.

Skim the foam from the top. Continue boiling and skimming the foam from the top until the foaming process has stopped.

Cool to room temperature. Add yeast. Put in a warm spot for 12 days.

Bottle and let it age 14 days. Store in refrigerator. Contents can be explosive.

Variations:

Vanilla Mead: Add 2 whole vanilla beans. Remove prior to bottling.

Orange Mead: Add 2 Tbsp orange zest. You may wish to omit nutmeg.

Miso | Fermented Bean Paste

A basic fermented paste that you will want to use as a flavoring and nutritional boost for lots of menu items.

1 med onion, peeled and coarsely chopped
3 cloves garlic, peeled
3 cups cooked beans
1 Tbsp Celtic or sea salt
¼ cup whey

Place onions and garlic in food processor process until fully chopped.

Add remaining ingredients and process until smooth.

Place in a quart-sized, wide-mouthed quart jar, leaving 1-inch of space between the top of the beans and the top of the jar.

Cover tightly and leave at room temperature for 7 days.

Store in refrigerator for up to three months.

Recipe Type:
Basic fermented formula, condiment, protein, raw, vegan, vegetarian

Yield: 3 cups, serves 48

Prep time: 15 min.

Inactive prep time: 7 days

NUTRITION FACTS

Nutrition (per serving):
8.8 calories; 25% calories from fat; 0.3g total fat; 0.0mg cholesterol; 163.7mg sodium; 41.0mg potassium; 1.3g carbohydrates; 0.1g fiber; 0.7g sugar; 0.6g protein.

Recipe Source

Sally Fallon
Nourishing Traditions

142

Natto

Recipe Type:
Basic fermented
formula, condiment,
dairy-free, gluten-free,
protein, raw, vegan,
vegetarian

Yield: 25 servings
Prep time: 30 min.
**Inactive prep
time:** 12-30 hrs.

COOKING TIPS

Natto can be frozen up
to 2 months by placing
in suitable freezer
container. Natto can be
used to inoculate the
next batch of cooked
soybeans, by using 10%
natto to cooked
soybeans. For inoculating,
use frozen natto prior to
2 months.

NUTRITION FACTS

Nutrition (per serving):
74.4 calories;
43% calories from fat;
3.9g total fat;
0.0mg cholesterol;
0.4mg sodium;
221.4mg potassium;
4.3g carbohydrates;
2.6g fiber; 1.3g sugar;
7.2g protein.

*Natto is another type of fermented bean paste, like miso.
It is often, but not always sweet.*

2 cups small, organic soybeans
6 cups filtered water
1 tsp natto spore starter powder
2 Tbsp cooled, boiled water to dissolve natto

Gently wash beans, removing any damaged or discolored beans. Place beans in large enamel crockpot. Cover with water. Soak soybeans 12 hours or overnight in a warm place. Strain water off beans.

Add 6 cups water and cook soybeans, covered, for 8-9 hours in crockpot on high. Beans should be well cooked and soft. Set beans aside with lid on to cool for 1-2 hours.

Use very clean, sterile cooking techniques from this point on. Sterilize bowls and spoon by pouring boiling water over them. After 1-2 hours, with very clean hands, quickly stir in 1 tsp natto starter, using the sterilized spoon. Replace cover on pan.

Place pan with beans and natto starter into a large beverage or picnic cooler. Cover with a heating pad, optimally set at a temperature of 92°-104°F. Natto will be ready in 12-24 hours, depending on temperature of the heating pad.

Remove to clean covered container, refrigerate or freeze. Use like miso or as innoculant starter for more. Keeps several months.

Naturally Fermented Sodas

Yes! You can make your own delicious and healthy natural sodas right in your own home.

- 1 gal non-chlorinated water
- 3 cups sugar
- 1-2 2-inch pieces ginger root, sassafras or other roots
- 2 cups culture

To make syrup, bring 1 gal nonchlorinated purifed water to a boil. Add desired roots, such as ginger or sassafras and boil for 1/2 to 1 hour. Remove roots.

Dissolve 3 cups sugar in the hot water. The sweet, liquid you have now is called "syrup."

Pour the syrup and the remaining 1 gal water into fermentation vessel. The resulting diluted syrup is still too hot for the culture. You can either wait, or cool the syrup first by letting the pot sit in a sinkful of cold water before adding it to the vessel.

Add any other flavorings, such as lemon juice to the diluted syrup. Make sure the syrup has cooled to body temperature. Add about two cups of culture.

Cover the vessel (doesn't need to be completely airtight) and let it ferment. Fermentation rate is highly variable. Depending on how fast it is fermenting, 2-5 days is usually enough time to create carbonation. For a sweeter soda, four or five days might be sufficient. To ferment out most of the sugar, allow at least 10 days.

To bottle, siphon from carboy to bottles through siphon tube. if you are fermenting in a jar you can simply pour it into bottles or scoop it in with a glass measuring cup. Seal the bottles, either with a bottle capper or stoppered bottles (both available at brewing supply stores). Do not bottle the thick layer of sediment at the bottom of the fermentation vessel.

When carbonation is sufficient, stop fermentation by putting the bottles in the refrigerator. Not enough room? A cold basement will work too, slowing down fermentation but not quite stopping it. Usually soda will keep just fine in the basement for a month or more.

Recipe Source
Author: John & Charles Eisenstein
Source: Weston A. Price, *Wise Traditions Newsletter*, Spring 2003

Recipe Type: Basic fermented food, beverage, dairy-free, raw, vegan, vegetarian

Yield: 1 gal, serves 16
Prep time: 30 min.
Inactive prep time: 2-10 days

COOKING TIP
Some additives such as mint and honey tend to inhibit bacteria and drastically slow.

NUTRITION FACTS
Nutrition (per serving): 80 calories; 14g total fat; 61mg cholesterol; 16mg sodium; 26mg potassium; 19.6g carbohydrates; .02g fiber; 19.48g sugar; .52g protein.

Nut Milk, Cream and Nog

This unusual, creamy recipe can be the basis for a variety of quick and tasty drinks, toppings and creams, using just about any type of nut or seed except peanuts, a legume.

1 lb nuts or seeds, almonds are excellent
filtered water to cover

Soak one pound of nuts in filtered water. Keep container covered. Add water as needed to cover the nuts.

After 12 hours use a food processor or blender to grind the whole mixture including the soak water until creamy.

Put the mixture in a covered container that would accommodate twice the volume of the puréed mixture. Leave the mixture on the counter for another 12 hrs.

Variations:

Nut Milk: After step 1, blend 1 cup soaked nuts with 4 cups soak water in blender. Add sweetness and flavor by adding 1/2 banana, 1 Tbsp raw honey, or 2 Tbsp maple syrup or 2 Tbsp pitted dates and 1/2 tsp real vanilla extract, if desired. Blend at high speed until blended. Serve as is or as a base for smoothies.

Nut Cream: Follow main procedures above.

Nut Nog: For a delectable non-dairy holiday "egg nog", after step 1, blend 1 cup drained, soaked nuts with 3 cups fresh apple cider or juice. Strain through fine sieve to remove skins. Return to blender, add 1 tsp freshly grated nutmeg. Blend on high until light and creamy. Pour in glasses and sprinkle with nutmeg. Serve immediately.

Recipe Type:
Basic fermented formula, protein, sauce, raw, vegan, vegetarian

Yield: Milk: 4 cups

Cream: 3 cups

Nog: 4 cups

Prep time: 20 min.

Inactive prep time: 24 hrs.

COOKING TIPS

Use this delicacy as a base for salad dressings, soups, sauces or other cooked foods to add flavor or for thickening just before serving. Mixture can be forced through fine sieve to remove skins, if you prefer a better appearance. Store in the refrigerator for several days.

Ferment single types of nuts alone. Combining different types may result in one nut fermenting before another.

NUTRITION FACTS

Nut Milk

Nutrition (per serving):
328 calories; 28g total fat; 0.0mg cholesterol; 175mg sodium; 412.78mg potassium; 11.19g carbohydrates; 6.69g fiber; 2.72g sugar; 12.05g protein.

Recipe Source:
adapted http://pascaljalabert999.blogspot.com/2006/06/nutritional-tools.html

Nut Seed Cheese

This slightly fermented non-dairy cheese made from soaked, sprouted nuts/seeds has a pleasantly tangy flavor and creamy texture, very much like cream or yogurt cheese.

2 cups hulled sunflower seeds, preferably organic
1/2 cup cashews, preferably organic, water just to cover
purified water to cover
1/2 Tbsp vegetable seasoning salt such as Spike or Mrs. Dash
2 tsp Herbes de Provence or ground cumin (optional)

Sort and rinse seeds and nuts in colander. Place in glass container or stainless bowl. Cover with water and soak overnight, 6-12 hours, covered with toweling.

The next day, drain seeds. Reserve soak liquid in container. Rinse seeds thoroughly and drain again.

Sprout seeds 12-24 hours, rinsing and draining a couple of times, while soak water ferments at room temperature in uncovered container.

Combine sprouted seeds, soak water, vegetable salt and any desired herbs in blender container or food processor. Process until smooth.

Let this mixture stand again in uncovered container for 12-18 hours. Mixture will expand and thicken. Scrape off any unsightly dark surface (perfectly safe) and transfer to covered container. Refrigerate until ready to use.

Variations:

Cashew Nut Cheese

This variation uses cashew nuts and rejuvelac, or soak water from wheat sprouts, instead of the cashew soak water for fermenting. Follow the procedures above, but substitute the following ingredients: 2 cups raw cashews, 1 cup rejuvelac (See page 149) sea salt to taste, 2 Tbsp light miso, optional, and 1 Tbsp nutritional yeast, optional.

Recipe Type:
Basic fermented formula, dairy-free, gluten-free, protein, raw, sprouted, vegan, vegetarian

Yield: 1 gal, serves 16
Prep time: 15 min.
Inactive prep time: 48 hrs.

COOKING TIP

Serve this non-dairy cheese spread to your vegetarian friends or family members as a snack or spread for kudos and compliments.

NUTRITION FACTS

Nutrition (per serving):
114.4 calories;
70% calories from fat;
9.6g total fat;
0.0mg cholesterol;
130.5mg sodium;
137.9mg potassium;
5.1g carbohydrates;
1.1g fiber; 1.0g sugar;
3.9g protein.

Pemmican

Recipe Type: Basic fermented formula, appetizer or snack, dairy-free, gluten-free, meat, protein, raw

Yield: serves 24
Inactive prep time: 7-10 days

The original trail food, our Native American's nutrient-dense, meat and fruit or meat and vegetables convenience food is handy, delicious, and quite frankly could be a lifesaver.

1 recipe Jerky
1 cup dried cranberries
1 cup raisins
1 cup beef or turkey or coconut oil fat
1 Tbsp thyme leaves

Prepare jerky from recipe on page 136.

Grind or shred jerky in mortar and pestle, food processor or manual grinder.

Combine ground jerky, dried fruit, fat, and seasonings until mixed.

Pack into glass jar or traditionally into skins, pushing out air. Seal and let ferment for 7-10 days. Keep air out.

COOKING TIP

Pemmican would be an ideal food project to produce for yourself and your family or make available in a small or larger community food circle.

NUTRITION FACTS

Nutrition (per serving):
309.1 calories;
38% calories from fat;
13.6g total fat;
35.4mg cholesterol;
432.7mg sodium;
367.9mg potassium;
26.8g carbohydrates;
2.0g fiber; 4.3g sugar;
20.0g protein

Pickles | Lacto-Fermented

Live, lacto-fermented pickles are healthier, more delicious, with many more interesting flavors than the pasteurized store bought kind.

> 1 qt small cucumbers, cut in half
> 1⅓ Tbsp Celtic or sea salt
> purified water to cover

Put cucumbers, salt and other desired flavorings into a quart glass jar. Cover with water. Screw on lid.

Leave pickles at room temperature for 5 -7 days. Transfer to refrigerator or other cool area. Keeps several weeks.

Variations

Add any of the following for varied flavor:

½ tsp dill seed, 2 garlic cloves, ½ tsp chili powder, ½ tsp black pepper, ½ tsp fennel, 2 bay leaves, 1 wild grape leaf

Poi | Fermented Taro Root

Taro and related tubers found throughout the tropical world are traditionally eaten fermented, sometimes by being buried in the ground for several days to several months.

> 2 lb fresh whole taro root
> 1 Tbsp sea salt
> ¼ cup whey

Poke a few holes in the tubers and bake in an oven at 300°F, for about two hours or until soft.

Peel and mash with salt and whey. Place in a bowl, cover and leave at room temperature for 24 hours.

Place in an airtight container and store in the refrigerator. This may be spread on crackers like cream cheese. It makes an excellent baby food.

Recipe Source

Sally Fallon
Nourishing Traditions

Recipe Type:
Basic fermented formula, condiment, dairy-free, gluten-free, raw, snack, vegan, vegetarian

Yield: 10 servings

Prep time: 5 min.

Inactive prep time: 5-7 days

NUTRITION FACTS

Nutrition (per serving):
11.16 calories; 0.0g total fat; 0.0mg cholesterol; 900.0mg sodium; 71.92mg potassium; 2.55g carbohydrates; .74g fiber; 2.18g sugar; .38g protein.

Yield: 9 servings

Prep time: 20 mins.

Cooking time: 2 hrs.

Inactive prep time: 24 hrs.

COOKING TIPS

Use sweet potatoes instead of taro for loads of available beta-carotene.

Taro is a relatively bland fermented food. Serve it along with some spicy favorites for wonderful flavors.

NUTRITION FACTS

Nutrition (per serving):
14.2 calories; 2% calories from fat; 0.0g total fat; 0.2mg cholesterol; 795.4mg sodium; 83.8mg potassium; 3.0g carbohydrates; 0.0g fiber; 3.0g sugar; 0.5g protein

Recipe Type:
Basic fermented formula, beverage, dairy-free, raw, vegan, vegetarian

Yield: 1 gal, Serves 16

Prep time: 15-20 minutes

Inactive prep time: 4 days

Rejuvelac | Basic & Gluten-free

Attributed to Hippocrates Health Institute founder, Ann Wigmore, this simple, energizing drink is a versatile and healthful natural product of live food culturing.

2 cups organic wheat, spelt, rye or kamut berries
2 qt purified water

Place wheat berries in 1 gallon glass jar. Fill half full of purified water. Cover with cheesecloth or paper towel and let soak overnight.

To sprout the wheat berries for rejuvelac, drain. Rinse plumped wheat berries, cover with cheesecloth or paper towel, fasten with rubber band and invert to drain. Repeat 2-3 times over a 24 hour period.

Following the 24 hour period of rinsing and draining, cover sprouts with water and secure opening with cheesecloth or paper towel. Let sprouts soak for another 24 hours.

Drain off liquid, which will become your current batch of rejuvelac. Let the liquid ferment for about 48 hours at room temperature in jar lightly covered with cheesecloth to prevent contamination. Drink or refrigerate.

The wheat sprouts can be processed one to two more times for additional batch of rejuvelac before they are recycled, used in recipes as "spent" grains, for Essene breads or to create sourdough starter.

Variations:

Vegan and Gluten-free Rejuvelac

Substitute sproutable millet or buckwheat for wheat and follow directions as given.

Salsa

This fermented salsa recipe produces a tangy tomato sauce with strong flavor and probiotic goodness. No cooking is required.

2 lb fresh tomatoes, diced
1 large bell pepper, diced
3-6 fresh chiles, diced
1 med fresh red onion, peeled and diced
3-4 cloves fresh garlic, diced
1 bunch fresh cilantro, coriander leaf, or Chinese parsley, coarsely chopped
1 tsp Celtic or sea salt

Clean and dry a quart jar and a large bowl.

Mix all ingredients together in the bowl with salt and spices. Mix well!

Pack tightly into jar, leaving space at the top. Cover with cheesecloth. Leave to ferment 2-3 days.

Store in the refrigerator. Salsa will continue to slowly ferment in refrigerator, getting more sour as time progresses. Use within several days.

Recipe Source:
adapted from http://en.wikibooks.org/wiki/Cookbook:Salsa_(fermented)

Recipe Type:
Basic fermented formula, appetizer, sauce, condiment, dairy-free, gluten-free, raw, vegan, vegetarian

Yield: 4 cups, serves 16

Prep time: 15 min.

Inactive prep time: 2-3 days

COOKING TIPS

Iodized salt will inhibit fermentation.

The kid in you will love watching the fermentation taking place. Watch for bubbles rising from the bottom. Take care not to seal the jar tightly and have a fermentation explosion! Protect your counter surface from overflows by placing the jar on a flat tray or sheet.

NUTRITION FACTS

Nutrition (per serving):
21.9 calories; 8% calories from fat; 0.2g total fat; 0.0mg cholesterol; 124.1mg sodium; 213.8mg potassium; 4.8g carbohydrates; 1.3g fiber; 2.4g sugar; 1.0g protein

Sauerkraut

Recipe Type:
Basic fermented formula, condiment, dairy-free, gluten-free, raw, vegan, vegetarian

Yield: 2 qt

Prep time: 15 min.

Inactive prep time: 3-7 days

COOKING TIP

Iodized salt will kill the bacteria.

Traditional sauerkraut is made with shredded cabbage, salt and water, but you can create many varieties substituting other vegetables in the basic recipe.

1 med head fresh cabbage, shredded
2 Tbsp Celtic or sea salt
Purified water

Mix shredded cabbage and salt. Bruise thicker pieces of cabbage with a wooden mallet, potato masher or meat tenderizer.

Place bruised cabbage and juices in a quart jar. Use mallet or hands to pack cabbage, brusing it so juices start to release, until it is 2 inches from the top of jar.

Add purified water until cabbage is fully covered. Leave 1-inch of air between the top of the liquid and the top of the jar.

Cover the jar with manufacturers lid. Leave at room temperature 3-7 days. Taste each day, after 3 days, until the taste you desire is achieved. Store in the refrigerator. Will keep 2-3 months.

Variation:

Ruby Red Sauerkraut with Caraway

To shredded cabbage in step 1, add one 1 med peeled and shredded beet, 2 minced garlic cloves, and 1 tsp caraway seeds. Proceed with directions in basic recipe.

NUTRITION FACTS

Nutrition (per serving):
21.4 calories; 4% calories from fat; 0.1g total fat; 0.0mg cholesterol; 13550.2mg sodium; 218.9mg potassium; 5.0g carbohydrates; 2.0g fiber; 3.2g sugar; 1.3g protein

Sour Cream

Sour cream is made by the same procedures as buttermilk using cream instead of milk.

- 1 cup cultured buttermilk (see page 128)
- 3 cups fresh cream, raw, organic and/or grass-fed, if possible

Mix cream and fresh buttermillk in a clean quart jar. Any amount will work in the ratio of 1 part buttermilk, 3 parts cream. Cover with several layers of cheesecloth, and secure with rubberband.

Let the mixture set in a warm room for 12-24 hours.

Store in refrigerator in covered container for up to 2-3 weeks.

Recipe Type:
Basic fermented formula, condiment, gluten-free, raw

Yield: 38 servings

Prep time: 10 min.

Inactive prep time: 12-24 hrs.

NUTRITION FACTS

Nutrition (per serving):
42.9 calories; 88% calories from fat; 4.3g total fat; 16.0mg cholesterol; 10.8mg sodium; 22.2mg potassium; 0.7g carbohydrates; 0.0g fiber; 0.4g sugar; 0.5g protein.

Sourdough Bread Starter

With your own perpetual sourdough starter, which you can literally keep for years, you can make many delicious, healthier breads, including pizza, without yeast.

- 1 cup water
- 1 cup organic whole wheat flour
- 1 tsp yeast, optional

Combine equal amounts of flour and water in a quart jar. Cover with cheesecloth secured with a rubber band. Add the optional yeast, if desired.

Keep starter at 70°-80°F. Each day throw half of the starter away and feed it with 1/2 cup flour mixed with 1/2 cup water.

After 3-4 days the starter should be producing lots of bubbles. It may puff up and will have a pungent smell like beer. Sourdough starter is now ready to use.

If you don't use your starter daily, store in the refrigerator. Hammer a hole in the manufacturer lid with a clean nail. The nail hole will allow the starter to breath.

To keep your starter fresh, feed it every week. If you miss feeding, don't distress, just beging feeding again.

A dark watery liquid may form on top which smells much like beer. Stir it in or pour it out. It is safe and normal.

Recipe Source
www.io.com/~sjohn/sour.htm

Recipe Type:
Basic fermented formula, dairy-free, raw, vegan, vegetarian

Yield: 2 cups

Prep time: 10 min.

Inactive prep time: 3-4 days

COOKING TIP

Avoid using metal implements or materials for your starter.

Spent Grain Granola

This is a tasty, nutritious and resource-efficient way to use "spent" or soaked grains left over from your sprouting and brewing experiments.

Recipe Type:
Breakfast, brunch, snack, uses fermented foods, vegetarian

Yield: Approx 1 gal, serves 32

Prep time: 15 min.

9 cups	spent barley grains or soaked wheat, kamut or spelt grains
1 cup	spelt or whole wheat flour
½ cup	debittered nutritional yeast
½ cup	wheat germ
1 cup	unsweetened coconut
1 cup	raisins
1 cup	flax seeds
1-½ cups	sunflower seeds
1 tsp	Celtic or sea salt
2 tsp	nutmeg
1 cup	honey or maple syrup
½ cup	melted coconut oil or organic butter
1 cup	boiling water
2 tsp	vanilla

Preheat oven to 350°F.

Combine all dry ingredients in large bowl.

Blend water, syrup, melted oil or butter, and vanilla wet ingredients in blender. Add to dry ingredients and mix until well distributed.

Crumble the mixture and spread onto cookie sheet.

Start baking at 350°F. for 15 min., then lower heat to 200°F. and bake, stirring occasionally, until dry about 1 hour.

Remove from oven. Let cool. Store in covered jars.

NUTRITION FACTS

Nutrition (per serving):
274.8 calories;
43% calories from fat;
14.2g total fat;
7.6mg cholesterol;
250.9mg sodium;
371.1mg potassium;
34.0g carbohydrates;
6.6g fiber; 10.3g sugar;
27.3g net carbs;
6.1g protein

Recipe Source:
adapted from http://breworganic.com/recipes/Cooking-Recipes.html

Sprouting Grains

Whole grains like wheat, rye, triticale, and oats can be soaked, sprouted, then turned into a host of digestible and nutritious, live drinks, breads, salads and vegetables.

> 2 cups organic wheat, spelt or kamut berries
> 2 qt purified water

Place wheat berries in 1 gallon glass jar. Fill half full of purified water. Cover with cheesecloth and let soak overnight, or 12 to 24 hours in colder environment.

Drain liquid into half gallon jar or two quart jars. This becomes the first batch of rejuvelac.

Variations:

To make Rejuvelac: See recipe on page 149.

To make Sprouts: Rinse soaked and plumped wheat berries with water in original gallon glass jar. Drain. Cover with cheese cloth or paper towel, fasten with rubber band and invert to drain.

Repeat step 3 process 2-3 times over a 24 hour period.

Grains will start to develop sprout "tails." When tails are twice as long as kernels, they can be made into Essene Bread, at this point, if desired.

To make Essene Bread: When sprout tails are 3 - 4 or more times longer than kernels, they are ready to be eaten, by themselves or used in salads, spreads, soups or stews, like chili.

Steak Tartare

Traditional Steak Tartare is a classic seasoned raw meat entrée, using high quality beef or in some places, buffalo meat, purportedly invented by the nomadic Tartars.

Recipe Type:
Basic fermented formula, appetizer, main dish, meat, raw

Yield: 2 lb, serves 8
Prep time: 35 min.

2 lb sirloin steak or filet mignon, grass-fed
1 egg yolk
2 Tbsp extra virgin olive oil
Salt and pepper
1 Tbsp Worchestershire or tamari soy sauce

Trim and grind the meat twice in a meat grinder or food processor.

In a bowl large enough to hold all of the meat, mix the egg yolk and olive oil. Beat lightly for a few seconds with salt and pepper or sauce to taste.

To the bowl add your selection of spices using ingredients in variations listed below, if desired. Stir with a fork.

Add the meat and stir to blend. Refrigerate or serve immediately, formed into patties on a bed of lettuce, garnished.

Variations:

Classic French: 1 Tbsp finely chopped onions, 2 tsp Dijon mustard, 2 tsp capers, 1 Tbsp minced parsley.

Classic Spice: 1 Tbsp finely chopped onions, few drops of Tabasco sauce, 1 tsp Worcestershire sauce, 1 tsp minced parley, 2 tsp chopped pickles, 1 Tbsp brandy.

Nepalese Spice: 1 Tbsp grated fresh ginger root, 2 garlic cloves, minced, ½ seeded hot pepper, 1 tsp fenugreek seeds.

COOKING TIP

Steak Tartare is traditionally made from aged raw beef.

NUTRITION FACTS

Nutrition (per serving):
320.2 calories;
54% calories from fat;
18.9g total fat;
102.2mg cholesterol;
83.9mg sodium;
511.5mg potassium;
0.1g carbohydrates;
0.0g fiber; 0.0g sugar;
35.1g protein.

Tempeh

Recipe Type:
Basic fermented
formula, protein,
vegan, vegetarian

Tempeh is another basic fermented soy bean product, popular in Indonesia, with a nutty, meaty taste, good for vegetarian main dishes or Tempeh Reuben sandwiches.

Yield: 2 lb, serves 8
Prep time: 30 min.
Inactive prep time: 1½-2 days

2 lb organic soybeans, rinsed and soaked for 24 hr
½ oz Rhizopus oligosporus culture (tempeh yeast)

Put beans in a saucepan with water to cover. Soak overnight. Pop the outer shell from the beans.

Boil for 30 minutes. Strain water from the beans. Allow beans to cool before inoculation.

Put beans on a cookie sheet with lip around the edges. Sprinkle tempeh yeast evenly over beans and disperse well using a flat spatula. Cover with an inverted cookie sheet.

Ferment at 32°C (89°F.) 1½-2 days. Final product will have a slight ammonia smell. Color may have some black or gray spots.

Store covered in refrigerator or wrapped well in freezer. To use, cut into desired size pieces and use in your favorite recipe.

NUTRITION FACTS

Nutrition (per serving):
91 calories; 45% calories from fat; 5g total fat; 0mg cholesterol; 279mg; 402 mg potassium; 9.6 g protein; sodium; 7.4g carbohydrates; .9g fiber.

Recipe Type:
Basic fermented
formula, gluten-free,
raw, vegetarian

Yield: serves 10

Prep time: 5 min.

**Inactive prep
time:** 2½ hrs.

Yogurt Cheese

*Thick and creamy Yogurt Cheese is also amazingly simple to make.
Delicious as plain bagel spread or sparkled with fresh herbs for
veggie dippers or sourdough crackers.*

I qt fresh yogurt (see page 159)

Place colander, lined with cheesecloth. over stainless steel bowl or pan.

Pour yogurt into colander and cover with toweling. Or gather ends of cheesecloth together to form a ball, secure with rubber band and suspend over colander. Let drip for several hours.

Remove cheesecloth from thick yogurt cheese and place in bowl or covered container. Use plain as cream cheese spread or flavored by stirring in your choice of herbs. Add Celtic, sea or vegetable seasoning salt to taste, if desired.

Store in refrigerator for up to 10 days. Save liquidy whey, which separates from the yogurt, for other recipes.

NUTRITION FACTS

Nutrition (per serving):
59.8 calories; 48% calories from fat; 3.2g total fat; 12.7mg cholesterol; 45.1mg sodium; 4.6g carbohydrates; 0.0g fiber.

Yogurt

Homemade yogurt is extremely easy to make and keep in your own kitchen, gifting plenty of delicious uses and savings over store-bought.

Recipe Type:
Appetizer, Basic fermented food, gluten-free, raw, vegetarian

Yield: serves 8

Prep time: 15 min.

Inactive prep time: 8-18 hrs.

COOKING TIPS

Optimal temperature for yogurt formation is 105°-122°F. Since oven thermostats don't go low enough, keep track of temperature by placing a thermometer into a bowl of water in the oven.

A thin yellow liquid, or whey may form during fermentation or refrigeration. Pour it off for use in other recipes, or stir it back into the yogurt.

NUTRITION FACTS

Nutrition (per serving):
79.4 calories; 47% calories from fat; 4.2g total fat; 16.9mg cholesterol; 59.9mg sodium; 6.1g carbohydrates; 0.0g fiber.

1 qt whole milk, preferably organic, raw
¼ cup yogurt

Start with a clean, glass quart jar with lid. Preheat jar by filling with hot water. Pour off hot water.

Pour room temperature milk and starter into jar. Place lid on jar.

Place the filled jar in a very warm spot overnight. An oven set at 150°F. with the door slightly propped open, in a gas oven with a pilot light, (newer gas ovens don't have a pilot light and therefore can't be used), an insulated cooler, or a dehydrator set at 95°F. You may leave in the open in a warm place, wrapped in a terrycloth towel, which will work but will take longer.

Keep the liquid still during incubation. Movement will cause the process to take much longer. Yogurt will be done when it is the consistency of pudding. Longer fermentation times will produce a thicker, and tangier product. Yogurt will be done in 8-14 hours.

Keep in the the refrigerator 1-2 weeks. Use the yogurt as starter for a new batch of yogurt within 7 days so it will have maximum regeneration.

Notes

Appetizers and Snacks

needs spice

Black Bean Olive Paté with Walnuts

A chunky, hearty and delicious paté you can serve to family or guests.

½ cup dry black beans or 1¼ cups cooked
OR 1-15 oz can black beans, drained
1 Tbsp olive oil
¼ yellow onion, peeled and finely chopped
2 cloves fresh garlic, chopped
¼ lb fresh mushrooms, coarsely chopped
½ cup fresh walnut pieces
12 organic kalamata olives, pitted
2 tsp dried thyme
¼ tsp pepper
2 tsp wheat-free tamari soy sauce

Soak the beans in 2 cups water overnight. For rapid soak, combine beans with 2 cups of water in medium saucepan. Bring to a boil and boil for 2 minutes. Turn off heat. Cover and let stand 1 hour at room temperature. Cook in soaking water over medium heat until very tender, about 45 minutes to 1 hour. Drain.

Heat oil in small skillet over medium to medium-low heat. Add onions and garlic and sauté lightly until translucent, 2-3 minutes. Add mushrooms, and sauté, stirring frequently for 5 minutes. Remove from heat.

In dry food processor workbowl, place walnuts and pulse to grind to consistency of cornmeal. Add sautéed onions and garlic, cooked black beans, thyme, pepper and soy sauce and process until ingredients form a paste. Mixture should still be a little chunky, not smooth.

Spoon into small serving dish and chill. Garnish with pimento slices and serve with chips, vegetable crudite or your own homemade sourdough crackers.

Recipe Source

Lindsay Wagner and Arian Spade, *The High Road to Health*

Recipe Type:
Appetizer, snack, condiment, uses fermented foods, vegan, vegetarian

Yield: 2 cups, serves 32

Prep time: 15 min.

COOKING TIPS

If using dry beans, why not save energy and time by cooking a larger batch now, using some for another meal later in the week and freezing the rest for days when you need to put together a meal in a hurry.

NUTRITION FACTS

Nutrition (per serving):
30.2 calories;
57% calories from fat;
2.0g total fat;
0.0mg cholesterol;
59.5mg sodium;
46.9mg potassium;
2.3g carbohydrates;
0.8g fiber; 0.2g sugar;
1.1g protein.

Garlicky Tahini Dip

A creamy, garlicky Middle Eastern sesame seed sauce that is delectable as a vegetable dip, sauce or dressing.

Recipe Type:
Appetizer, condiment, dairy-free, sauce, uses fermented foods, snack, vegan, vegetarian

Yield: 1 cup,

serves 16

Prep time: 10 min.

3 cloves garlic, smashed
1/2 tsp Celtic or sea salt
2/3 cup organic tahini, sesame seed butter
1 heaping Tbsp golden barley or red miso
1/2 cup water
1 large lemon, juiced

Traditionally prepared in a mortar and pestle, but you can simply smash and chop the garlic and blend the mixture in a bowl, or use a food processor.

Pound garlic and salt to a paste, if using a mortar and pestle. Or in food processor, turn on motor and add garlic and salt.

Add tahini and miso, and then slowly add in 1/2 cup water, blending until smooth, or add more water, for a thinner consistency. Stir in lemon juice. Add more salt, if desired.

COOKING TIPS

Drizzle over steamed broccoli spears or turnips or other vegetable; add some fresh, chopped herbs and it becomes a dairy-free salad dressing.

NUTRITION FACTS

Nutrition (per serving):
1.8 calories; 1% calories from fat; 0.0g total fat; 0.0mg cholesterol; 59.0mg sodium; 6.8mg potassium; 0.5g carbohydrates; 0.0g fiber; 0.1g sugar; 0.0g protein.

Recipe Source
Rebecca Wood

Quicker Nut and Seed Cheese

A super quick and versatile version of the basic nut and seed cheese.

I cup whole, raw almonds, preferably organic
I Tbsp kefir or yogurt whey
1/2 cup purified water

Grind the almonds to a meal in a food processor or grain mill.

Mix whey and water. Add to ground almonds in food processor and process until smooth.

Spoon the mixture into a glass jar, only half full. Cover loosely with cheesecloth or paper towel fastened with rubber band or screw top lid.

Ferment in a warm place 77°F. for about 8-12 hours or until the mixture has doubled in size. Final product will smell cheesy. Store covered in refrigerator and use within 4-5 days.

Recipe Type:
Basic fermented appetizer, snack, food, protein, raw, sprouted, vegan, vegetarian

Yield: 2½-3 cups, serves 24

Prep time: 5 min.

COOKING TIPS

A half cup of Rejuvelak can substitute for the tablespoon of kefir whey and water.

Nuts and seeds are best stored in the refrigerator because of their volatile oils. Optimally they should be fresh, whole, organic, and free from mold.

What's not a nut?
1) Peanuts are a legume.
2) A coconut is a fruit.

NUTRITION FACTS

Nutrition (per serving):
34.4 calories;
73% calories from fat;
3.0g total fat;
0.0mg cholesterol;
0.2mg sodium;
43.4mg potassium;
1.2g carbohydrates;
0.7g fiber; 0.3g sugar;
1.3g protein.

Raw Hummus

A raw version of the classic Middle Eastern delicacy that can be a delicious dip, spread, sandwich filling, sauce or salad dressing everyone loves.

Recipe Type:
Basic fermented food, appetizer, condiment, dairy-free, gluten-free, protein, raw, sprouted, vegetarian

Yield: 3 cups, serves 12

Prep time: 10 min.

COOKING TIPS

Sprout chickpeas by placing in a container, covering with purified water and leaving in a warm place for 12 hours or overnight.

2 cups chick pea sprouts
2 whole lemons or limes, juiced
1/4 cup fresh orange juice
4 cloves fresh garlic
6 Tbsp raw organic sesame tahini, sesame seed butter
1 tsp Celtic or sea salt
2 tsp ground cumin
2 Tbsp finely chopped chives, optional
2 Tbsp extra virgin organic olive oil

In food processor workbowl, combine all ingredients. Process until smooth. Add additional water or olive oil and blend to desired consistency. Should be smooth, but stiff, not runny.

Place in serving dish or storage container. Refrigerate for an hour or so, or several hours to blend and improve flavors. Best next day. Serve with crackers, vegetable sticks or organic chips.

NUTRITION FACTS

Nutrition (per serving):
200.8 calories;
35% calories from fat;
8.3g total fat;
0.0mg cholesterol;
165.9mg sodium;
397.0mg potassium;
25.6g carbohydrates;
6.6g fiber; 6.6g sugar;
8.0g protein.

Recipe Source: Shayla Roop

Rosemary Walnuts

Recipe Type:
Appetizer or snack, condiment, gluten-free, vegetarian

Have an ample supply of Crispy Nuts on hand to prepare this savory warm and healthy snack.

- 4 cups crispy walnuts
- ¼ cup organic grass-fed butter
- ¼ cup dried rosemary
- 2 tsp Celtic or sea salt
- 1 tsp cayenne pepper

Yield: 4 cups, serves 32

Prep time: 20 min.

To prepare the walnuts, melt butter with rosemary, salt, and cayenne pepper. Toss the walnuts, spread on a parchment-lined cookie sheet, and bake at 350ºF. for 10 minutes.

Cool and store in an airtight container in the refrigerator until ready to serve.

NUTRITION FACTS

Nutrition (per serving):
81.9 calories;
83% calories from fat;
8.2g total fat;
0.0mg cholesterol;
117.8mg sodium;
56.3mg potassium;
1.7g carbohydrates;
0.9g fiber; 0.3g sugar;
1.9g protein.

Recipe Source

Sally Fallon, *Nourishing Traditions*

Nancy Lee's Sunsé™ Seed Mix

Nancy Lee's signature, award-winning, versatile and nutritious basic seed mix can be easily adapted to many recipes and regions, and she'll show you how to make it happen, for your family or your food circle.

2-½ cups sunflower seeds, organic
½ cup sesame seeds, organic
½ cup pumpkin seeds, (green pepitas)
½ cup flax seeds, organic

Combine seeds.

Store covered in refrigerator or freezer for up to two months.

Variations:

Super Healthiest Sunsé Seed Mix: Soak Basic Sunsé™ overnight in glass container in purified water. Drain. Let soaked seeds sprout for several hours, 8-12. Dry in the sun, in a food dehydrator or at lowest possible oven setting. Store in covered container and use as you would for Basic Sunsé.

Sweet Sunsé Seed Mix: To Basic or Super Sunsé Seed Mix, add 3/4 cup dry, unsweetened coconut, 1/2 cup dried currants or raisins, 1/2 cup dried cranberries or cherries, 1 tsp nutmeg and 1/2 tsp ground cinnamon. Store in tightly covered glass jar in refrigerator or freezer.

Savory Golden Sunsé Seed Mix: In heavy dry, cast iron skillet over medium heat, lightly toast Basic or Super Sunsé Seed Mix, stirring constantly, until pumpkin seeds start to pop and aroma of lightly toasted sesame appears. Remove from heat. Add 1/2 cup dry mixed vegetables or vegetable soup mix that has been whirred to powdery in blender, 2 Tbsp poultry seasoning, 1 Tbsp thyme leaves, 2 Tbsp debittered nutritional yeast, and 1-1/2 tsp Spike® vegetable seasoning or Celtic or sea salt. Stir, cool, and store in container with lid in refrigerator for up to six weeks.

Sunsé Seed Gomasio: Blend 1 recipe Savory Sunsé™ Seed Mix, above, in blender until it becomes a fine powder. Store in covered container in refrigerator. Use as a topping or seasoning for salads, vegetables, casseroles or baked potatoes.

Sprouted Sunsé Seed Mix: Follow directions for Super Sunsé Seed Mix. After sprouting, drain and rinse. Use right away as salad, snack, or base for Roll-Up or sandwich filling.

Recipe Type:
Appetizer or snack, dairy-free, gluten-free, protein, raw, vegan, vegetarian

Yield: 4 cups, serves 32
Prep time: 5 min.

NUTRITION FACTS

Nutrition (per serving):
57.0 calories;
69% calories from fat;
4.7g total fat;
0.0mg cholesterol;
1.6mg sodium;
69.2mg potassium;
2.4g carbohydrates;
1.4g fiber; 0.1g sugar;
1.0g net carbs;
2.2g protein

Sushi Nori Rolls

Recipe Type:
Basic fermented food, appetizer, dairy-free, gluten-free, raw, vegetarian

Raw, vegetarian and fermented, these delicious nori rolls boast color, flavor and power-packed nutrition.

- 1 med cucumber, peeled and seeded
- 3 sheets nori seaweed, dried not roasted
- 1 med carrot, grated
- 1 avocado, peeled, seed removed
- 1-2 Tbsp wheat-free tamari soy sauce
- 3 Tbsp nut seed cheese (see page 148)

Yield: approx. 3 med rounds, serves 12

Prep time: 20 min.

Inactive prep time: 4-5 weeks

Slice cucumber in half, then in thin lengths. Cut avocado into quarters, then sllice each piece into three slices.

Cut nori sheets into quarters with scissors.

To assemble nori rolls, place quarter sheet nori on cutting board or flat surface. Place 2-3 thin slices of cucumber, and 1 slice avocado on nori.

Add grated carrots. Sprinkle with a few drops of soy sauce and add a dollop of nut cheese.

Roll up diagonally and place with fold side down on decorative serving plate. Serve immediately.

NUTRITION FACTS

Nutrition (per serving):
49.3 calories;
70% calories from fat;
3.9g total fat;
0.0mg cholesterol;
205.2mg sodium;
120.8mg potassium;
3.0g carbohydrates;
1.6g fiber; 0.6g sugar;
0.8g protein

Beverages

Kvass

Recipe Type:
Basic fermented formula, beverage, condiments, dairy-free, raw, vegan, vegetarian, pot, yeast or alcoholic fermant

Yield: 1 gal
Prep time: 10 min.
Inactive prep time: 4-6 weeks

Bread Kvass

1 lb black rye bread, dried
5 qt purified water
4 tsp yeast
½ cup sugar
1 cup raisins

Cover bread with boiling water and let sit for 24 hours.

Strain.

Add yeast and sugar. Mix well.

Ferment for 1-2 days in a warm spot.

Pour fermented liquid into clean glass bottles. Add several raisins to each bottle. Close tightly. Return to warm spot for 1 day.

Kvass is ready to drink the next day.

Store in the refrigerator. Will keep for two months.

Yield: 24 servings

Beet Kvass

3 lb fresh beets
3 Tbsp coarse kosher rock salt
2 Tbsp brown sugar or molasses
2 qt purified water, up to 3 qt

Scrub beets, pare and cut into quarters.

Place in a clean jar or crock and sprinkle with the salt.

Cover the mixture with purified water. Add the sugar or molasses.

Cover with the cheesecloth and tie with the string. Set in a cool place (60°F.) to ferment for about 1 week. (Do not do this in hot humid weather; it will decompose, not sour.)

Flavor develops in 1 to 2 weeks. Taste. It should be sourish but mild, not brackish.

Pour into clean dry jars and cover. Will keep for several months.

Yield: 10 servings

Cranberry Kvass

2 lb cranberries
2 lb sugar
5 qt water
4 tsp yeast

Pour sugar and cranberries into a pot. Cover with water. Bring to a boil.

Cool untill the mixture is safe to work with. Blend the mixture in a blender or food processor.

After assuring the mix is slightly warm and not hot, add yeast and mix well.

Set in a warm spot to ferment, for 3 days.

Cranberry kvass can be consumed immediately.

Store in a cool place.

Yield: 24 servings

Caraway Seed Kvass

2 cups whole caraway seed
5 qt purified water
1 lb organic sugar
1 cup raisins
4 tsp baking yeast

Place caraway seeds in medium saucepan and add purified water to cover.

Turn heat to high. Bring to a boil. Reduce heat slightly and simmer for 15-20 minutes. Remove from heat.

Strain seeds from liquid through sieve into glass container. Cool down slightly to 105°F./40°C warm.

Add sugar, yeast and raisins and stir to blend. Set in a warm spot to ferment for 2 days.

Pour into clean bottles and cap tightly. Store in the refrigerator or other cool place. Ready to serve in 2-3 days.

Yield: 24 servings

Kvass is another ancient, fermented beverage that is traditionally made with stale bread, but can also be made from fruit, grain and seeds. Originating in Russia, it has been enjoyed by peasants and poor people the world over because it is a fermented drink simply made by recycling old bread or other ingredients. Kvass is energizing and nutritious, what might be considered a natural soft drink, although varieties of this drink range in taste from being extremely sour to extremely sweet and heavily carbonated.

Shrub

Recipe Type:
Basic fermented
formula, beverage
(alcohol), gluten-free

Yield: 2 gal, serves 16
Prep time: 30 min.
**Inactive prep
time:** 10 days

Shrub, an old Arabic word that means "drink" related to the word "sharba" for syrup, is a very, very early beverage, a basic punch the Colonists liked sweet, sweet, sweet...

1½ qt orange juice
8 lemons
4 qt rum
6 lb sugar
3 qt water

Before squeezing the lemons, peel off the rinds very thinly.

In a gallon jar, place 1 pint orange juice and the juice of 2 or 3 lemons. Add 2 quarts rum. Cover and let stand for three days.

Put 2 lb sugar into water and bring to boil. Add the sugared water to the remaining rum and fruit juice, cover, and let stand for two weeks.

Then strain and bottle. Product will be ready in 10 days.

Switchel

Recipe Type:
Beverage, uses
fermented foods, dairy
and gluten-free, raw,
vegetarian

Yield: 2 qt
Prep time: 10 min.
**Inactive prep
time:** 8 hours

NUTRITION FACTS

Nutrition (per serving):
54.7 calories; 1% calories
from fat; 0.1g total fat;
0.0mg cholesterol;
9.2mg sodium;
96.5mg potassium;
14.3g carbohydrates;
0.1g fiber; 12.0g sugar;
0.2g protein.

Originating in Nova Scotia, Switchel is a tangy, flavorful beverage rich in minerals and good for the digestion.

½ cup apple cider vinegar
¼ cup molasses
½ cup honey
1½ tsp ground ginger
½ cup oatmeal, optional
purified water to make 2 qt

Measure the vinegar, molasses, honey, ginger and oatmeal into a clean glass, 2 qt pitcher. Add purified water to fill.

Mix well. Place in refrigerator overnight.

Serve with ice.

Seasonal Fruit Smoothie

Recipe Type:
Appetizer, beverage, breakfast, gluten-free*, uses fermented foods, vegetarian

Yield: 1½ cups
Prep time: 5 min.

The basic fruit smoothie, made with fruit in season and loaded with nutrient boosters, is the fast and delicious answer to breakfast these busy days.

½ cup fruit, fresh or frozen (not pineapple)
1 cup yogurt (see page 159)
or kefir (see page 137)
or nutmilk (see page 145)
½ tsp nutmeg or cinnamon

Put the chopped fruit and other dry ingredients into the blender first. Add liquid or yogurt.

Place lid on securely and blend on high speed for about 20 to 30 seconds. Add several cubes of ice, if desired, and any optional nutrition boosters and blend. Serve and enjoy!

Variations:

Add one or more nutrition boosters

1 Tbsp lecithin or nutritional yeast
2 Tbsp wheat germ, oat bran, ground flax seed, or nut butter
1 free-range egg

COOKING TIPS

If using frozen fruit, can omit the ice and add water, if needed, to achieve desired consistency.

*Basic recipe is gluten free. The addition of wheat germ or brans will add gluten.

NUTRITION FACTS

Nutrition (per serving):
188.4 calories;
39% calories from fat;
8.6g total fat;
31.9mg cholesterol;
112.9mg sodium;
545.1mg potassium;
20.1g carbohydrates;
1.5g fiber; 18.9g sugar;
9.3g protein.

Left: Blueberry Fruit Smoothie

173

Tiswin

A festive, fall beverage much like spiced cider, fermented and enjoyed by the Pueblo Indians

2 lb dried white organic corn
1 gal purified water
1½ cups evaporated cane juice or maple syrup
2 Tbsp dried orange or lemon peel
3 cinnamon sticks
1 Tbsp whole cloves

Preheat oven to 300°F. Place shucked corn in a shallow pan and roast, stirring occasionally, until light brown.

Grind coarsely in food processor, grinder or small quantities at a time in blender.

Place coarsely ground corn in mixing bowl. Swirl the water and the hulls will rise to the top. Discard hulls.

Put washed corn in pottery crock, crock pot, ceramic or other non-metal container. Add water, stir in evaporated cane juice or maple syrup, orange peel, cinnamon and cloves.

Cover and let stand in a warm place for 5 or 6 days or until bubbly and fermented.

Strain through cheesecloth and serve.

Recipe Source

Phyllis Hughes, *Pueblo Indian Cookbook*

Recipe Type:
Basic fermented formula, beverage, dairy-free, vegan, vegetarian, pot, alcoholic ferment

Yield: 1 gal
Prep time: 1 hr.
Inactive prep time: 5-6 days

NUTRITION FACTS

Nutrition (per serving):
87.1 calories; 1% calories from fat; 0.2g total fat; 0.0mg cholesterol; 4.4mg sodium; 67.3mg potassium; 22.7g carbohydrates; 1.6g fiber; 18.0g sugar; 0.1g protein

Tor's Hard Cider

Special supplies needed for this recipe include party balloons and a second glass jug.

Recipe Type:
Basic fermented food, beverage (alcohol), dairy-free, gluten-free, vegetarian

Yield: 1 gal,
serves 24

Prep time: 15 min.

Inactive prep time: 2-3 hrs.

COOKING TIPS

Cider purchased in the store will almost always contain preservatives that will prevent the cider from undergoing the fermentation process. Instead, it will rot. Buy the freshest, local organic cider you can find.

Adding more sugar product yields a sweeter cider with a higher alcohol content.

NUTRITION FACTS

Nutrition (per serving):
214.9 calories; 0% calories from fat; 0.0g total fat; 0.0mg cholesterol; 2.9mg sodium; 38.4mg potassium; 58.2g carbohydrates; 0.2g fiber; 58.0g sugar; 0.2g protein.

1 gal unfiltered, organic apple juice or cider without preservatives
½ tsp baking yeast
5 cups raw honey
1 balloon

Pour off some apple cider into a glass or measuring cup. Reserve for later.

Pour off about 1/4 of the cider into a large saucepan. Add the honey. Heat over low heat, stirring occasionally, just until honey is dissolved. After honey is dissolved, remove from heat. Set aside to cool.

When the cider has cooled to a warm temperature, return to the original glass jug.

Put 1/2 tsp yeast into the jug of cider. Take the reserved cider from step 1 and top off the jug, leaving a couple of inches of air at the top of the bottle. Feed the rest of the yeast to your septic tank by sending it down the sink. The rest of the glass of cider that's left is a little refreshment for the cook.

Flush water into the balloon rinsing out the white powder inside. Place the balloon over the neck of the bottle, then prick a hole in the balloon with a pin. The small hole will allow air to escape while maintaining a barrier against bacteria.

Set the jug aside for 2-3 weeks.

After 2-3 weeks the hard cider is drinkable, but will continue to get better with age, just like you do! To remove the dregs or dead yeast in the bottom of the bottle which is no longer viable, carefully pour the hard cider from one bottle to another leaving behind as much of the dregs as possible. You can also siphon the cider off of the top leaving the dregs.

Replace the balloon on the neck of the jar. Set the jug aside for another 2-3 weeks. Every 2-3 weeks, once again remove the dead yeast from the cider.

Optimal hard cider is ready in 2-3 months, However, it can be maintained for longer periods if the dregs are regularly removed from the bottom of the brew.

Recipe Source
forevermore.net

Notes

Breads

Basil crackers

A surprisingly tasty and delicious treat that uses up your nutritious vegetable juicing leftovers.

- 1 cup soaked nuts
- 5 cups carrot or vegetable pulp from juicing
- 1 clove fresh garlic
- ½ cup fresh basil or cilantro, chopped
- 2 ripe tomatoes, chopped
- 1 tsp sea salt, dulse or soy sauce (or to taste)

Soak almonds sesame, sunflower seed or other nuts in water for 12 hours. (For more specific soaking times see recipe for Crispy Nuts page 127) Drain and grind in food processor or with grinder to coarse consistency.

In food processor workbowl or mixing bowl, combine nuts, vegetable pulp, herbs, garlic, tomatoes, and seasonings. Pulse lightly just to combine and fom and bind together.

Use spatula to spread over teflex sheet in dehydrator or onto cookie sheet. Dehydrate in oven on very low heat or in in dehydrator 110°F. for about 8 hours or until completely dry.

Remove from pan and store in dry, covered container. Wonderful with guacamole or other dips!

Recipe Type:
Basic fermented formula, appetizer or snack, bread, dairy-free, gluten-free, vegan, vegetarian

Yield: 18 servings
Prep time: 15 min.
Inactive prep time: 7-10 days

COOKING TIPS

Most ovens are only capable of going down to 170°F, really too high if you want to call these raw. You can rig up a make shift dryer in your oven with a light bulb, leaving oven door open 1 inch or so.

NUTRITION FACTS

Nutrition (per serving):
49.5 calories;
47% calories from fat;
2.8g total fat;
0.0mg cholesterol;
44.3mg sodium;
206.9mg potassium;
5.4g carbohydrates;
1.9g fiber; 2.4g sugar;
1.7g protein.

Recipe Type:
Bread, uses fermented foods, dairy-free, sprouted, vegan, vegetarian

Yield: 1 large loaf

Prep time: 45 min.

Inactive prep time: 12-16 hrs.

COOKING TIPS

The sourdough starter needs to be highly active to get maximum rise from the flour. If you find the bread is a little too heavy for your liking, then next time try adding 1-2 tsp barley malt or even honey. The extra sugars will cause the wild yeast to become more active and generate additional carbon dioxide necessary to rise the bread.

Optional ingredients you can add to boost taste and/or nutrition could be 1/2 cup minced nuts or dried fruit, 1/3 cup wheat or oat bran or even dried shredded coconut.

NUTRITION FACTS

Nutrition (per serving):
98.5 calories;
13% calories from fat;
1.5g total fat;
0.0mg cholesterol;
20.5mg sodium;
71.9mg potassium;
18.8g carbohydrates;
2.1g fiber; 0.1g sugar;
3.1g protein.

Modified Essene Bread

Not as dense as traditional Essene Bread, Modified Essene Bread is moist and chewy, lighter with the addition of flour and sourdough starter.

3 cups organic sprouted grain, wheat, spelt, or rye (see page 154)
1½-2 cups organic spelt or whole wheat pastry flour
1/4 tsp Celtic or sea salt
1/2 cup sourdough starter (see page 152)
2 Tbsp coconut oil
purified water

Start with sprouted grain that is dry, spreading on a towel for 1-2 hours, if necessary.

With a meat grinder or food processor at medium to high speed, grind dry grain sprouts until pebbly or coarsely chopped.

Add sourdough starter and coconut oil and stir or process until a fairly soft "dough" has formed, which may be varigated in color. Transfer to a lightly floured board or kneading surface.

Mix flour, salt, and any herbs in a small bowl. Knead small amounts of this flour mixture into the dough, a little at a time. Add additional water or flour as needed to create a doughy consistency that isn't either too wet or has excess flour on the surface.

Optimally, at this point, dough should be placed in bowl and refrigerated or left to ferment for 12 hours to convert anti-nutrients in the flour.

When ready to prepare, knead in any optional ingredients.

Shape your bread into a small loaf. Put into an oiled loaf or cake pan suitable for baking or create a flat loaf to dehydrate. Cover with a moist towel and leave at room temperature until doubled in size. from 1-4 hours, depending upon conditions.

Bake 45 minutes at 325°F.

Recipe Source
www.rejoiceinlife.com/recipes/essene.php

Seeded Sourdough Crackers

Homemade crackers are delicious. Easy, healthier and much more interesting than the ones usually available in the store.

Recipe Type:
Appetizer or snack, bread, dairy-free, uses fermented foods, vegan, vegetarian

Yield: 50 - 1½ in. squares
Prep time: 45 min.

2 cups organic whole wheat flour
1 tsp Celtic or sea salt
½ cup raw, cultured butter or coconut oil (see page 129)
1 cup sourdough starter (see page 152)
2 Tbsp sesame seeds, natural
2 Tbsp poppy seeds, whole
2 Tbsp caraway seeds, whole
2 Tbsp fennel seeds, whole

Preheat oven to 375°F. In a large bowl, mix together flour and salt. With a fork or pastry cutter, cut in the butter or coconut oil until the size of small peas.

Stir in room temperature sourdough starter. Dough should be able to hold together and be workable. If using coconut oil in high heat, you may have to add a little more flour.

In a small bowl or large cup, combine seeds and stir to mix. Oil the bottom of 2 cookie sheets or use a baking sheet that has no edges.

Divide dough into 2 pieces, covering one with towel while you work with the other. Flatten dough evenly on bottom of 1 cookie sheet. Press half of seed mixture into dough, then carefully roll cracker dough out to about ¼" thick. Repeat with second batch of dough.

Score dough into 1½-inch cracker-size pieces. Cut through with knife and prick with fork.

Bake 10-15 min until lightly browned. Immediately remove from baking sheet to wire rack to cool.

COOKING TIPS

To make a single seed cracker, like a sesame seed cacker, substitute ½ cup sesame seeds for the mixed seeds. You may also used other seeds such as flax, hemp, mustard, black sesame, coriander, or sunsé seed mix. Experiment to see which combinations you like best.

NUTRITION FACTS

Nutrition (per serving):
46.3 calories;
44% calories from fat;
2.4g total fat;
4.9mg cholesterol;
51.4mg sodium;
41.4mg potassium;
5.6g carbohydrates;
1.2g fiber; 0.1g sugar;
1.2g protein.

Recipe Type:
Basic fermented
formula, side dish,
starch, vegetarian

Sourdough Egg Noodles or Dumplings

Homemade egg noodles or dumplings are delicious,
unlike anything you've tried.

Yield: 2 cups

Prep time: 1½ hr.

Inactive prep
time: 2-3 days

2 cups organic soft wheat flour
6 egg yolks
1 cup liquid whey

COOKING TIPS

These are so much
more delicious and
digestible than
commercial or
unfermented noodles,
but are labor intensive,
so probably more of a
"when you're in the
mood" or special
occasion treat.

Sift the flour, pour it onto the table and make a well in the center.

In a small bowl mix eggs yolks, salt, and whey carefully together until blended.

Pour egg mixture into the well in the flour and begin to mix all together with hands until the mass forms a ball. It should be elastic, but not too stiff. Knead and work the dough until it no longer sticks to hands or to the table.

Place dough in bowl, cover with a clean towel. Let it remain at room temperature for 2 to 3 days, adding a bit of flour and kneading at least once a day.

To prepare noodles, roll out on lightly floured board to ¼-inch thickness. Cut into thin strips.

Or to create dumplings, roll dough into long rope and pinch off small pieces.

To cook noodles or dumplings, fill a 1 qt or larger saucepan with water and 1 tsp sea salt. Or use chicken broth as liquid for more flavor. Bring to a boil, then reduce heat to simmer. Drop noodles or dumplings into the simmering liquid, in batches, if necessary to avoid crowding. Cook for 4-5 minutes, or until firm. Depending upon size, dumplings may float to the surface when done.

Remove with slotted spoon to colander. Drain. Serve plain, buttered and sprinkled with chopped parsley. Or add favorite sauces.

NUTRITION FACTS

Nutrition (per serving):
72.4 calories; 9% calories
from fat; 0.8g total fat;
18.0mg cholesterol;
4.0mg sodium;
44.5mg potassium;
13.5g carbohydrates;
0.5g fiber; 0.2g sugar;
2.7g protein.

Spent Grain Beer Bread

You can use the spent grains from either a mash or from an extract recipe to make wonderful bread!

1¼ qt spent barley or wheat grains
2 cups beer
½ cup molasses or barley malt
½ cup coconut oil
1 cup sourdough starter
1 tsp sea salt
5 lb whole wheat bread flour

Place wet spent grain into a large bowl, and add enough beer, about 2 cups, to allow blending into a mash. Add about ½ cup of molasses, 3 or 4 cups of whole wheat flour, about ⅓ to 1/2 cup coconut oil, a tsp of salt, and 1 cup sourdough bread starter. Mix to yield a dough. Cover with a towel and let set for half an hour to give the sourdough time to get going.

After half an hour, add 1/2 to 3/4 cup rolled oats, and a bit more oil. In total, counting the 3 to 4 cups of flour above, all of a 5.5 lb bag of flour. Basically just keep adding flour until you can knead without the dough sticking to your hands.

Once it forms a nice dough, let it rise (covered) for about 1/2 an hour, then divide into four loaves and put into well-greased bread pans. Cover and let rise again 1/2 - 1 hour. Bake at 370°F. for 30 to 40 minutes.

Recipe Type: Appetizers, uses fermented food, dairy-free, gluten-free, raw, vegetarian, vegan

Yield: 4 loaves
Prep time: 20 min.
Inactive prep time: 3-4 hrs.

NUTRITION FACTS

Nutrition (per serving):
181.2 calories;
11% calories from fat;
2.5g total fat;
0.0mg cholesterol;
33.9mg sodium;
95.0mg potassium;
33.6g carbohydrates;
1.4g fiber; 1.7g sugar;
4.9g protein.

Recipe Type:
Basic fermented formula, bread, uses fermented food, breakfast, starch, sweets and desserts, vegetarian

Yield: 2 loaves
Prep time: 15 min.
Inactive prep time: 1-3½ hrs.

COOKING TIPS

Feed your starter the night before with 2 cups flour and 2 cups water. Cover and leave on the counter overnight so it will be energized and prepared in the morning.

NUTRITION FACTS

Nutrition (per serving):
143.5 calories;
14% calories from fat;
2.4g total fat;
5.1mg cholesterol;
106.0mg sodium;
96.5mg potassium;
27.2g carbohydrates;
2.8g fiber; 2.2g sugar;
4.2g protein.

Sweet Sourdough Bread with Variations

Wouldn't your family love homemade rolls or sweet bread some weekend morning?

2 cups room temperature sourdough starter, (see page 152)
3 Tbsp organic sugar or evaporated cane juice
1 tsp Celtic or sea salt
3 Tbsp melted organic butter
3 cups whole wheat pastry flour, organic

Melt butter in small pan.

In a medium size bowl, mix room temperature sourdough starter, sugar, salt and 2 Tbsp melted butter. Reserve the other 1 Tbsp butter for brushing on finished loaves. Add flour and stir to mix in well.

Add in dried fruit and/or other ingrediients for desired variation from list below..

Knead on a floured board until finger punched into dough leaves an impression.

Place in a greased bowl, rotating dough so that dough has been greased on top. Cover with moistened kitchen towel. Put in a warm place and let rise until doubled in size about 2 hours.

Mix 1/4 cup sugar with the desired flavoring in a measuring cup. Grease 2 loaf pans.

With floured hands punch dough down. Divide dough in half putting one of the halves aside in the greased bowl.

Roll each piece of dough into 18-inch x 9-inch" rectangle. Sprinkle with half of flavored sugar. Sprinkle with water. Roll up jelly-roll style into a 9-inch roll, pinching ends to seal Place in greased loaf pan seam side down. Brush lightly with melted butter. Cover with moist kitchen towel and let rise until doubled about 1 hr.

Preheat oven to 425°F. When hot, place in oven and bake 30-40 min. When fully baked, bread will sound hollow when thumped.

Remove from oven. Brush loaves with butter. Put on wire rack to cool.

Variations:

Cinnamon Raisin: 1 cup raisins, ¼ cup sugar, 2 Tbsp ground cinnamon
Orange Cranberry: 1 cup dried cranberries, ¼ cup sugar, 2 Tbsp grated orange zest
Lemon Poppyseed: ⅔ cup poppy seeds, ¼ cup sugar, 2 Tbsp grated lemon zest
Maple Nut: ⅔ cup walnut pieces, ½ cup maple syrup

Whole Wheat Sourdough Bread or Pizza Dough

Nothing smells lovin' like freshly baked, wholegrain sourdough bread -- from your own starter.

4 cups sourdough starter (see page 152)
3 Tbsp cultured butter, melted (see page 129)
1½ tsp Celtic or sea salt
4½ cups whole wheat flour

In a large ceramic or metal bowl, mix 4 cups room temperature sourdough starter, tepid melted butter and whole wheat flour.

Knead on a lightly floured board until dough is spongy and resilient.

Wash and dry the bowl (or use a clean one). Grease with butter. Place dough into greased bowl, rotating so that top surface has been greased. Cover with a moist kitchen towel and place in a warm place, out of draughts like on top of refrigerator. Let rise until doubled in size, about 1-2 hours.

Grease two loaf pans. Knead gently, shape into loaves, then place dough into greased loaf pans. Cover again with moist kitchen towels and set aside to rise until doubled. Preheat oven to 375°F.

Bake for 45-60 minutes. Bread will be golden brown and should sound hollow when thumped gently with a fist.

Remove from oven. Let pans rest on wire rack to cool slightly. Then turn pans over, tap lightly to release bread. Let bread loaves rest on wire rack until completely cool.

Whole Wheat Pizza Dough

Follow steps 1, 2, and 3 of the whole wheat sourdough bread recipe.

Pull off piece of dough about the size of a large grapefruit. Using a rolling pin, roll out in all directions to create a thin, round sheet.

Place on greased pizza pan and cover with toppings. Preheat oven to 425°F. Let dough rise for 20-30 minutes. Bake for 10-12 minutes, until crisp and cheese is melted. Remove from oven, slice and serve immediately. Makes 4 pizzas, or 2 deep dish pizzas.

Recipe Type:
Bread, breakfast, uses fermented foods, starch, vegetarian

Yield: 2 large loaves
Prep time: 60 min.

COOKING TIPS

Remember, you can feed and keep a sourdough starter, once going, for years. Simply refresh or make active with more flour and water and additional fermenting time. Needs to be active to produce desired leavening.

NUTRITION FACTS

Nutrition (per serving):
121.4 calories; 2% calories from fat; 0.3g total fat; 0.1mg cholesterol; 90.3mg sodium; 37.7mg potassium; 25.4g carbohydrates; 0.9g fiber; 0.2g sugar; 3.5g protein.

Condiments

All-Raw Dark Plum Jam

Recipe Type:
Basic fermented
formula, condiment,
gluten-free, raw,
vegetarian

Dark, sweet, succulent ripe plums are the basis of this delicious and healthy, easy raw conserve.

2½ lb fresh, dark red plums
¾ cup local raw honey
2 tsp Kefir whey
½ tsp Celtic or sea salt
½ tsp cardamom seeds
⅛ tsp ground cloves

Wash the plums well, discarding any that are overripe or damaged. Chop into small pieces, putting aside the center stones.

Add the raw honey, kefir whey, Celtic sea salt, cardamom and cloves, and mix well.

Transfer the plum jam mixture to clean jars, pressing down with a wooden spoon to remove air bubbles. Fill the jars to within 1-inch of the top to inhibit mold growth. Clean the edge of the jar at the top with a cloth or paper towel.

Leave the jam to ferment in a cool place for 3 days before transferring to the refrigerator. Allow flavor to mature for 1 month in refrigerator, but use before 3 months.

Yield: 10 cups
Prep time: 45 min.
Inactive prep time: 3 days

COOKING TIPS

The kernels are high in vitamin B-17. Remove and discard the hard shell of the pits, remove kernels, grind them into a flour and mix in with the jam for distinctive taste and nutrition.

NUTRITION FACTS

Nutrition (per serving):
32.5 calories; 2% calories from fat; 0.1g total fat; 0.0mg cholesterol; 23.8mg sodium; 48.2mg potassium; 8.5g carbohydrates; 0.4g fiber; 8.0g sugar; 0.2g protein

Bean Sprout Kimchi

Kimchi is not necessarily spicy --- just full of good flavor. Try this recipe and variations for your summertime meal!

Recipe Type:
Appetizer, snack, salad, condiment, gluten-free, uses fermented foods, vegan, vegetables, vegetarian

Yield: 3 cups
Prep time: 10 min.
Inactive prep time: 2 hrs.

COOKING TIPS

See other Kimchi recipes in the Condiment Section.

1½ cups fresh bean sprouts, blanched
1 organic cucumber, seeded and diced
1 green onion, finely chopped
½ cup rice vinegar
1 Tbsp sesame seeds, toasted
½ tsp Celtic or sea salt
1 Tbsp organic extra-virgin olive or sesame seed oil

Bring water to boil in a small saucepan. Plunge bean sprouts in water for 1 minute, optional. Pour sprouts into a strainer and quickly rinse with cold water.

In a medium sized bowl, combine chopped cucumber and green onion, rice vinegar, toasted sesame seeds, salt and sesame seed oil. For hotter version, add 1-2 tsp crushed red pepper. Stir and let set for at least 2 hours.

Drain well and place in a serving bowl.

Variation:

Cucumber Kimchi

Omit bean sprouts and add 4 more med organic cucumbers sliced in half lengthwise, seeded and sliced.

NUTRITION FACTS

Nutrition (per serving):
44.9 calories;
35% calories from fat;
3.1g total fat;
0.0mg cholesterol;
236.1mg sodium;
256.2mg potassium;
11.4g carbohydrates;
0.9g fiber; 1.6g sugar;
1.2g protein

Recipe Source
www.angelfire.com/journal/adoptionhelp/kimchi.html

Brewsky Meat Marinade

Try this quick and easy barbeque sauce with beer.

1- 12 fl oz can or bottle beer
4½ Tbsp dried chopped parsley
3 cloves garlic, minced
⅓ cup wheat-free tamari soy sauce

In a mixing bowl, combine beer, parsley, garlic, and soy sauce.

Marinate meat in the mixture for a few hours to overnight. Cover and refrigerate meat while marinating.

Remove marinated poultry or meat from marinade. Cook as desired.

Recipe Type:
Condiment, barbeque sauce, dairy-free, uses fermented foods, alcoholic

Yield: 2 cups
Prep time: 10 min.
Inactive prep time: 4-6 hrs.

COOKING TIPS

This savory marinade could be used to enhance the flavor of beef, pork, fish, poultry or vegetarian dishes.

NUTRITION FACTS

Nutrition (per serving):
13.2 calories; 0% calories from fat; 0.0g total fat; 0.0mg cholesterol; 176.7mg sodium; 25.0mg potassium; 1.4g carbohydrates; 0.1g fiber; 0.1g sugar; 0.4g protein.

Recipe Type:
Condiment, gluten-free, sauce, uses fermented foods, vegetarian

Yield: 5 cups
Prep time: 5 min.

COOKING TIPS

Omit the garlic for a classic savory buttermilk dressing.

NUTRITION FACTS

Nutrition (per serving):
41.5 calories;
63% calories from fat;
3.1g total fat;
0.5mg cholesterol;
29.1mg sodium;
70.8mg potassium;
2.5g carbohydrates;
1.1g fiber; 0.8g sugar;
1.5g protein.

Buttermilk Flaxseed Dressing

Creamy, healthy and easy, this may turn out to be a favorite salad dressing recipe.

½ cup flaxseeds
½ cup pignoli nuts
2 cups purified water
¼ cup lemon juice
1¼ cup cultured buttermilk (see page 128)
1 clove garlic
1-2 tsp wheat-free tamari or shoyu soy sauce
2 Tbsp fresh dill (optional)

Soak flaxseeds and pignoli nuts overnight in a bowl in two cups purified water.

Combine with remaining ingredients in a blender or food processor. Blend until smooth, adding water if desired to create a pourable consistency.

Recipe Source
Rita Romano, *Dining in the Raw*

Cherry Chutney

Another light and naturally refreshing accompaniament for poultry, fish, omelets or cheese dishes

Recipe Type:
Basic fermented formula, condiment, raw, sauce, side dish, vegetarian

Yield: 1 qt
Prep time: 15 min.
Inactive prep time: 2 days

4 cups ripe cherries, pitted and quartered
½ tsp coriander seeds
½ tsp whole cloves
1 orange, grated rind and juice
2 Tbsp organic evaporated cane juice or Rapidura sugar
¼ cup whey
2 tsp sea salt
½ cup filtered water

Place cherries, coriander, cloves, orange rind and juice, sugar, whey, sea salt and water in food processor and pulse a few times until finely chopped.

Place in a wide mouthed quart jar and press down. Mix salt and whey with water and pour into jar.

Top of chutney should be 1 inch below the top of jar. Water should cover the chutney.

Cover tightly and keep at room termperature for two days.

Keep chutney in refrigerator. Use within two months.

NUTRITION FACTS

Nutrition (per serving):
69.1 calories; 3% calories from fat; 0.3g total fat; 0.1mg cholesterol; 132.6mg sodium; 34.4mg potassium; 17.1g carbohydrates; 1.0g fiber; 2.1g sugar; 0.7g protein.

Recipe Source

Sally Fallon, *Nourishing Traditions*

Recipe Type:
Condiment, raw,
sauce, side dish,
vegetarian, uses
fermented foods

Yield: 3 cups

NUTRITION FACTS

Nutrition (per serving):
68.0 calories;
97% calories from fat;
7.5g total fat;
10.5mg cholesterol;
33.9mg sodium;
6.1mg potassium;
0.2g carbohydrates;
0.0g fiber; 0.0g sugar;
0.3g protein

Creamy Tarragon Mustard Dressing

A delightfully fresh and savory salad dressing you can make for chicken, seafood or green salads.

1 large free-range egg
2 free-range egg yolks
⅓ cup mustard (see page 193)
¼ cup tarragon vinegar
2 tsp dried tarragon or 1 oz fresh tarragon

½ tsp Celtic or sea salt
grinds black pepper
1 cup organic extra virgin olive oil
1 cup organic olive oil

Combine egg, egg yolks, mustard, vinegar, herb, salt and pepper in blender or food processor work bowl and blend or process for 1 minute until mixture becomes a bumpy paste. Scrape down sides.

Replace cover, remove center top or pusher, turn on machine and drizzle oil in a slow, steady stream until blended and creamy.

Shut off motor, remove cover, scrape down sides and taste for seasoning.

Transfer into a covered glass jar and refrigerate until ready to use.

Recipe Source

The Silver Palate Cookbook

Yield: 2 cups

NUTRITION FACTS

Nutrition (per serving):
70.8 calories;
96% calories from fat;
7.8g total fat;
0.0mg cholesterol;
47.4mg sodium;
12.4mg potassium;
0.6g carbohydrates;
0.1g fiber; 0.2g sugar;
0.1g protein.

Lemon Vinaigrette Dressing

A piquant and delicious, homemade salad dressing you can create in minutes.

1 cup extra virgin organic olive oil
⅔ cup fresh lemon juice
½ cup fresh chives
2 Tbsp scallions, minced

2 Tbsp mustard (see page 193)
½ tsp Celtic or sea salt
few grinds fresh black pepper

Combine ingredients in blender and blend until smooth.

Taste for seasoning. Remove to serving bowl or transfer into glass container, cover and refrigerate.

Mint Chutney

Sweet and Savory, this refreshing mint chutney is sure to please.

- 2 cups fresh mint leaves
- 1 small onion, peeled and sliced
- 4 cloves garlic, peeled and chopped
- 4 jalapeno chiles, seeded and chopped
- 2 tsp cumin seeds, toasted in oven
- 1 Tbsp Celtic or sea salt
- ¼ cup whey
- 1 cup filtered water

Place mint, onion, garlic, chiles, cumin seeds, and crispy almonds in food processor and pulse a few times until finely chopped.

Place in a wide mouthed quart jar and press down. Mix salt and whey with water and pour into jar.

Top of chutney should be 1 inch below the top of jar. Water should cover the chutney.

Cover tightly and keep at room temperature for two days.

Keep chutney in refrigerator. Use within two months.

Recipe Source
Sally Fallon, *Nourishing Traditions*

Recipe Type:
Appetizer, condiment, basic fermented formula, rawvegan, vegetarian

Yield: 2½ cups
Prep time: 15 min.
Inactive prep time: 2 days

NUTRITION FACTS

Nutrition (per serving):
13.5 calories; 7% calories from fat; 0.1g total fat; 0.1mg cholesterol; 399.2mg sodium; 77.2mg potassium; 2.8g carbohydrates; 0.4g fiber; 1.8g sugar; 0.5g protein

Miso-Scallion Chutney

Possibly the quickest—and most satisfying—chutney you can make, this relish aids digestion and is great in potato, grain or pasta dishes, or served alongside a meat or fish.

- 2 Tbsp miso
- 2 Tbsp finely grated ginger
- 2 Tbsp sesame or other unrefined oil or fat of choice
- 1 bunch scallions, sliced into thin rounds

Put the miso in a small bowl. Place the grated ginger in the palm of your hand and squeeze it over the miso to extract about 2 tsp juice. Discard the ginger pulp. With a fork, blend the ginger juice and miso and set aside.

Warm oil in a small skillet; add scallions and sauté for about 2 minutes or until their color changes. Stir in the miso ginger mixture and simmer for 1 minute. Scrape into a condiment dish and serve hot or cold.

Recipe Source
Rebecca Wood, www.rwood.com/Recipes/ Miso_Scallion_Chutney.htm

Yield: 1 cup
Prep time: 5 min.

NUTRITION FACTS

Nutrition (per serving):
32.3 calories; 93% calories from fat; 3.4g total fat; 0.0mg cholesterol; 0.7mg sodium; 14.9mg potassium; 0.5g carbohydrates; 0.1g fiber; 0.1g sugar; 0.1g protein.

Mustard

Recipe Type:
Basic fermented formula, condiment, sauce, raw vegan, vegetarian

Yield: 1½ cups

Prep time: 10 min.

Inactive prep time: 2 weeks

COOKING TIPS

You can use herbs such as basil, marjoram, dill, parsley, sage, thyme, rosemary, mint. If using fresh herbs, use about 1/3-1/2 cup.

Even one of our most common, frequently used condiments is a cultured food that can easily be made at home – or in a community kitchen as a unique signature item for your local food circle.

2 oz whole white mustard seed
1 oz black mustard seed
2 oz evaporated cane juice or organic sugar
½ tsp Celtic or sea salt
½ tsp turmeric
2 tsp dry herbs

Place white and black mustard seeds, sugar, salt, turmeric and herbs into food processor or blender. Cover and process.

Pile into clean glass jar or jars. Cover and let sit at room temperature in a dark place for two weeks.

Store unopened in cellar indefinitely or in refrigerator after opening for several months.

NUTRITION FACTS

Nutrition (per serving):
21.5 calories;
39% calories from fat;
1.0g total fat;
0.0mg cholesterol;
39.4mg sodium;
26.4mg potassium;
2.5g carbohydrates;
0.5g fiber; 1.4g sugar;
0.9g protein.

Olive and Caper Tapenade

Delightfully quick, easy and delish, this olive, caper, nut paste instantly tranforms vegetables, meats, and appetizers into healthy gourmet fare.

1 cup cured, pitted black olives, drained
½ cup pitted green olives, drained
½ cup walnuts or pine nuts
3 Tbsp capers, drained
3 cloves fresh garlic
2 Tbsp organic extra virgin olive oil

In food processor workbowl or blender container, process black and green olives until chopped, but chunky.

Add nuts and garlic. Process, on and off, for a few seconds, until nuts and garlic are blended in.

Add capers and olive oil. Blend quickly, pulsing machine, until capers are just chopped, not smooth.

Remove to covered glass jar. Refrigerate up to six weeks or longer.

Recipe Type:
Appetizer or snack, condiment, dairy-free, raw, uses fermented foods, vegan, vegetarian

Yield: About 1½ cups
Prep time: 10 min.

COOKING TIPS

Try this scrumptious spread, about 1 tablespoon per serving, over steamed cauliflower or turnips, chicken breasts or vegetable stir-fry. Or as an appetizing addition to Salad Nicoise or even raw vegetable crudité.

NUTRITION FACTS

Nutrition (per serving):
36.5 calories;
84% calories from fat;
3.6g total fat;
0.0mg cholesterol;
106.3mg sodium;
13.4mg potassium;
1.0g carbohydrates;
0.5g fiber; 0.1g sugar;
0.5g protein.

Recipe Type:
Basic fermented
formula, condiment,
gluten-free, raw,
vegetarian

Yield: 1 gal.

Prep time: 1 hr.

**Inactive prep
time:** 3-5 days

Pickled Ginger

*Sushi lover's favorite pickled ginger is a delightful condiment for a
variety of dishes.*

4 lb fresh ginger root
1 Tbsp pickling salt, without iodine
½ pkg yogurt starter
1 cup distilled, filtered or non-chlorinated water

Peel and cut ginger into very thin slices. Pound ginger slices to expel juices.

Place juices and pounded ginger into a glass jar. Mix with salt and water.

Add yogurt starter and seal. Let set at room temperature for 3 to 5 days.

Store in the refrigerator.

NUTRITION FACTS

Nutrition (per serving):
52.1 calories; 8% calories
from fat; 0.5g total fat;
0.0mg cholesterol;
250.3mg sodium;
269.5mg potassium;
11.5g carbohydrates;
1.3g fiber; 1.1g sugar;
1.2g protein.

Recipe Source
healingcrow.com

Pineapple Chutney

This is a delightfully refreshing, heatlhy pineapple complement to meat, fish or curry.

Recipe Type:
Basic fermented formula, condiment, side dish, raw, vegetarian

Yield: 1 qt
Prep time: 10 min.
Inactive prep time: 2 days

1 small pineapple, peeled and chopped in 1-inch pieces
1 bunch cilantro, coarsely chopped
1 Tbsp freshly grated ginger
2 Tbsp fresh lime juice
1 tsp sea salt
¼ cup whey or rejuvelac
½ cup filtered water

Mix pineapple, cilantro and ginger and place in a quart sized, wide-mouth mason jar. Press down lightly with a wooden pounder or a meat hammer.

Mix lime juice, sea salt and whey with water and pour over pineapple, adding more water if necessary to cover the pineapple. The chutney should be at least 1 inch below the top of the jar.

Cover tightly and keep at room temperature for 2 days.

Store in refrigerator for up to two months.

Hot Pineapple Chutney

Add 1 small red onion, 2 cloves garlic and 1 tsp hot pepper, all chopped finely.

NUTRITION FACTS

Nutrition (per serving):
29.3 calories; 1% calories from fat; 0.1g total fat; 0.0mg cholesterol; 61.1mg sodium; 69.3mg potassium; 7.6g carbohydrates; 0.4g fiber; 6.9g sugar; 0.2g protein.

Raw Ginger Marmalade

While raw jams supply enzymes and nutrients destoryed by cooking, making them can be a challenge, so this recipe is "a mostly" raw compromise.

Recipe Type:
Appetizer, basic fermented formula, condiment, raw, vegetarian

Yield: Approx 3¼ cups

Prep time: 40 min.

Inactive prep time: 3 days

COOKING TIPS

This recipe for ginger marmalade is a compromise in that about 1/4 of the ingredients are cooked to soften the rind without toughening it.

Just make sure you cool the rind mixture before adding it to the bulk of the ingredients to avoid deactivating the kefir whey and the enzymes.

5 med oranges
2 small limes
2 small lemons
2-3 Tbsp fresh grated ginger
¾ cup raw honey
4 Tbsp Kefir whey
1 tsp pectin
¼ tsp Celtic or sea salt
¼ cup water

Quarter 1½ oranges and 1 lemon, then cut the rind into thin strips and mix with flesh and 1/4 cup of water in small saucepan. Bring to a gentle boil, then simmer on low heat for 2 hours, or until the rinds have softened.

Meanwhile remove peel from the rest of the fruit, and compost Quarter and chop the fruit into large pieces. In a large bowl mix the fruit with the kefir whey, ginger and honey. Leave to stand until the fruit has finished cooking on the stove.

Once the fruit and peel is cooked, add the salt and pectin. Stir until the pectin is dissolved, 2-3 minutes. Remove from heat. Cool before mixing with the raw fruit mixture.

Stir well, then spoon the marmalade into glass jars. Use a wooden spoon to press the fruit to the bottom, removing any air bubbles. Leave about 1/2-1-inch of air space at the top.

Wipe the neck clean with a paper towel and cap tightly. Put the jam in a fridge for an hour or so to cool the jam to room temperature. Remove from the fridge then leave to ferment for about 3 days. Store the marmalade in the refrigerator for best results.

NUTRITION FACTS

Nutrition (per serving):
54.2 calories; 1% calories from fat; 0.1g total fat; 0.0mg cholesterol; 20.5mg sodium; 95.7mg potassium; 14.9g carbohydrates; 1.5g fiber; 12.4g sugar; 0.5g protein.

Spicy Ginger Miso Paste

Recipe Type:
Condiment, dairy-free, raw, sauce, uses fermented foods, vegan, vegetarian

This pungently flavored soybean paste can be a handy seasoning to have on hand for adding instant flavor to meats, mains and vegetables.

Yield: 1 cup
Prep time: 10 min.

- 2 Tbsp grated fresh ginger
- 2 Tbsp red or dark brown miso paste
- 4 fresh garlic cloves, mashed
- 2 tsp chile-garlic sauce
- 2 tsp organic sugar or evaporated cane juice
- 2 tsp roasted sesame oil
- 1 Tbsp fresh lime or lemon juice

Combine all ingredients and stir well to blend. May blend together in small food processor to make a smooth paste. Store in covered glass jar for up to 3-4 weeks.

Rub liberally onto skin or surface of poultry, fish, beef or other meats, vegetables or use in beans, filling or other applications.

NUTRITION FACTS

Nutrition (per serving):
14.31 calories; .71g total fat; 0.0mg cholesterol; 102.38mg sodium; 13.79mg potassium; 0.0g carbohydrates; 1.75g fiber; .79g sugar; .37g protein

Spinach Kimchi

This kimchi features 3 of the most popular ingredients in Korean cooking: soy sauce, sesame seeds and garlic and is best served at room termperature. Delicious! Shigumch'I namul

1 lb fresh spinach
2 tsp wheat-free tamari soy sauce
1 Tbsp sesame seed oil
1/2 tsp finely chopped garlic
1 Tbsp toasted sesame seeds
1/2 cup water

Lightly cook spinach in large saucepan, steaming with a little bit of water in the bottom, covered over medium high heat for 2-3 minutes until bright green.

Drain in colander. When cool, gently squeeze out excess water with your hands.

Cut spinach into 2-inch lengths and place in a large bowl.

Add remaining soy sauce, chopped garlic, sesame seeds and water and stir to mix.

Serve at room temperature.

Notes

Main Dishes

Basic Marinated Tempeh | with Variations

Tempeh is a fermented soybean cake, popular in Indonesia, with a nutty, delicious flavor that is much more digestible than its plain bean counterpart.

2 Tbsp wheat-free tamari or shoyu soy sauce
1½ Tbsp apple cider vinegar (see page 120)
1 Tbsp toasted sesame oil
1 tsp pepper sauce, optional
optional seasonings from variations below
1-10 oz tempeh cake (see page 156)

In nonreactive ceramic or glass dish, combine tamari, vinegar oil, and pepper sauce. Stir to combine. Select additional seasonings and add.

Marinate the tempeh in above marinade for at least 20 minutes at room temperature or up to 2 days in the refrigerator.

Preheat oven to 375°F. Place tempeh on lightly oiled cookie sheet, leaving space between pieces. Bake for 12 to 15 minutes, then flip pieces over and bake for another 10 or so minutes.

Or pan-fry tempeh cake lightly in oiled skillet over medium heat for approximately 10-12 minutes, turning once, until golden brown.

Variations:

Additions to Basic Marinade: Spice up or flavor basic recipe with your favorite herbs or 1-3 of the following additions: 1-3 cloves garlic, chopped, 1 tsp black pepper, 1-2 tsp honey, 1 tsp ground coriander, 1 Tbsp prepared spaghetti sauce, 1 to 2 tsp toasted sesame oil, 1/2 to 1 tsp more or other hot sauce.

Teriyaki Tempeh: Add a total of 1/2 cup shoyu, 1 Tbsp fresh grated ginger, 1 minced garlic clove, 1 Tbsp toasted sesame or other oil to marinade. Pan-fry tempeh. Add 2 cups vegetables to the pan fry for a complete meal.

Tempeh Paprikash: Prepare basic baked tempeh. Meanwhile, in large Dutch oven, sauté 1 thinly sliced onion and 4 cloves minced garlic. After onions are softened, add 1 Tbsp caraway seeds, 1 tsp thyme, 1 Tbsp paprika, and 1-6 oz can tomato paste. Add baked tempeh. Reduce heat to low and cook, covered, 10 minutes.

Recipe Source
Crescent Dragonwagon, *Passionate Vegetarian*

202

Recipe Type:
Appetizer, gluten-free, main dish, uses fermented foods, vegan, vegetarian

Yield: 4 servings
Prep time: 20 min.

COOKING TIPS

Toasted sesame oil is a dark brown, very savory condiment that can add a burst of flavor to marinades and sauces.

NUTRITION FACTS

Nutrition (per serving):
251.9 calories;
45% calories from fat;
14.2g total fat;
0.0mg cholesterol;
348.9mg sodium;
559.3mg potassium;
14.8g carbohydrates;
0.1g fiber; 0.2g sugar;
23.2g protein.

Recipe Type:
Appetizer, main dish, meat, uses fermented foods

Yield: 8 servings
Prep time: 1½ hrs.

Choucroute with Summer Sausages

This classic French peasant sauerkraut dish uses lower fat turkey bacon, beef summer sausage, fresh chicken sausages and long, slow cooking for coaxing smoky sweetness out of the ingredients.

2 lb sauerkraut
2 Tbsp coconut oil
½ lb turkey ham, cubed
1 large onion, peeled and coarsely chopped
3 large carrots, peeled and sliced or ½ small bag baby carrots
1 large cooking apple, unpeeled and chopped
1 Tbsp caraway seeds
10 juniper berries
½ bunch parsley
2 tsp peppercorns
2 bay leaves
1 cup white wine
1 qt organic chicken stock
1 lb beef summer sausage, cut into large chunks
6 chicken and apple sausages

Preheat oven to 325°F. Rinse and drain sauerkraut. Squeeze very dry in paper toweling.

In large heavy skillet, melt coconut oil over medium heat. Add turkey ham pieces and sauté for 1-2 minutes. Add chopped onion and carrots, increase heat and sauté until lightly browned. Remove from heat. Hold.

In large enamel roaster or heavy enameled casserole, combine drained sauerkraut, turkey bacon, sautéed vegetables, chopped apple, and caraway seeds and stir to mix.

Combine juniper berries, parsley, peppercorns, and bay leaf in cheesecloth bag, burying it in the kraut. Pour in wine and chicken stock, cover and bake in the oven for 4 hours, adding a little more stock if necessary.

Forty minutes before serving, sauté fresh chicken sausages in 1 Tbsp coconut oil and brown on both side. Uncover casserole and arrange chicken sausages on top of dish. Bake about 1/2 hour more. Sauerkraut should be dry and brown.

NUTRITION FACTS

Nutrition (per serving):
279.7 calories;
50% calories from fat;
15.6g total fat;
50.3mg cholesterol;
898.9mg sodium;
512.3mg potassium;
14.5g carbohydrates;
2.5g fiber; 7.3g sugar;
16.0g protein.

Recipe Source
adapted from *The Silver Palate Cookbook*

Corned Beef
or Tempeh Reuben

The penultimate cultured food plate: paired with open barrel pickles, this quick and easy sandwich combo boasts six different fermented foods!

Recipe Type:
Main dish, sandwich,
meat or vegetarian,
uses fermented foods

Yield: 4-6 servings
Prep time: 15 min.

1 lb Corned Beef (see page 214) OR
1-10 oz block whole grain tempeh (see page 156)
2 tsp wheat-free tamari or shoyu soy sauce
8 slices whole grain, sprouted or sourdough bread (see page 183)
⅓ cup Thousand Island Salad Dressing
1 cup sauerkraut, drained (see page 151)
8-1 oz slices Swiss or Farmer's cheese (see page 134)
4 wedges open vat sour dill pickles, garnish (see page 148)

Follow directions for making corned beef on page 214. Slice corned beef to desired thickness. Heat in oven or on top of the stove in covered skillet, additng a little brine or water to steam.

If using fresh tempeh, make 2-3 thin slices per sandwich. Proceed to step 2. If using frozen tempeh, unwrap. Place in lightly oiled, 10-inch stainless or cast iron skillet. Add about 1/4 cup water and turn heat to high. Steam will defrost tempeh as water boils away. Keep an eye on this so tempeh doesn't burn, as you prepare other ingredients.

Turn heat to medium and sauté lightly on both sides to brown. For deeper flavor, sprinkle soy sauce over tempeh and swish till it evaporates. If not already sliced, remove tempeh from pan. and with asbestos fingers, cut in quarters, tip each piece on end and carefully slice through tempeh to make 2-3 thinner slices for each sandwich.

Spread bread slices with 1 Tbsp each, more or less, Thousand Island dressing. Arrange tempeh slices on 4 bread slices.

Layer about 3-4 Tbsp drained sauerkraut over tempeh slices on each sandwich. Press with fingers.

Top with 1 slice cheese and second piece of bread. Press lightly together. Sandwiches may be broiled, open faced, to melt cheese under broiler or toaster oven. OR spread/brushed lightly with oil or butter and gently sauté in skillet on both sides until golden brown and cheese is melted.

Remove to serving plate or platter. Cut each sandwich in half on the diagonal. Serve accompanied by healthy sour dill pickles and Confetti Coleslaw, if desired.

NUTRITION FACTS

Nutrition (per serving):
483.1 calories;
42% calories from fat;
22.7g total fat;
53.2mg cholesterol;
1243.1mg sodium;
43.3g carbohydrates;
6.4g fiber.

Coconut-Crusted Tempeh

A savory version of tempeh with a delightful coconut crust that will make your next homemade Thai or Southeast Asian dinner a hit.

2-10-oz.pkg tempeh, cut into 12 strips (see page 156)
¼ cup or 1 oz thinly sliced fresh ginger
3 large cloves garlic, minced
1 cup loosely packed fresh basil, coarsely chopped
1 tsp Celtic or sea salt
4 pieces star anise or 1 tsp 5-Spice powder
1- 14 oz can coconut milk
1 cup vegetable broth
1 cup unsweetened dried coconut flakes
1 cup plain dry bread crumbs
¼ cup sesame seeds
1 Tbsp kudzu, dissolved in 2 Tbsp cold water

Preheat oven to 325°F. Line cookie sheet with parchment paper.

In large Dutch oven, arrange tempeh slices with ginger, garlic, basil, 3/4 teaspoon salt and star anise.

In small bowl, combine coconut milk and broth and pour over tempeh. Cover and cook over medium heat, stirring occasionally approximately 30 minutes. Reduce heat, if cooking too rapidly.

Meanwhile, prepare coconut breading: In medium bowl, combine coconut flakes, bread crumbs, sesame seeds and remaining 1/4 teaspoon salt; toss to mix.

With slotted spoon, transfer tempeh to plate. There should be at least 1 cup cooking liquid left in pot. If not, add more broth or water to equal 1 cup liquid. Strain tempeh cooking liquid, discard solids and return to pan.

Dissolve kudzu completely in water. Whisk kudzu mixture into strained cooking liquid and bring to a simmer over medium-low heat. Pour thickened liquid into shallow bowl.

Dip tempeh slices first in kudzu mixture and then in coconut breading, turning to coat. Arrange breaded tempeh on prepared baking sheet and bake 15 minutes. Turn and bake another 10 minutes. Let sit 5 minutes, then serve.

Recipe Type: Appetizer, snack, main dish, side dish, uses fermented foods, dairy free, vegan, vegetarian

Yield: 9 servings
Prep time: 60 min.

COOKING TIPS
Try this delish dish with Chinese Broccoli and Cabbage or served hot with a spicy peanut dipping sauce.

NUTRITION FACTS
Nutrition (per serving):
473.5 calories;
60% calories from fat;
34.1g total fat;
0.3mg cholesterol;
457.8mg sodium;
650.6mg potassium;
27.5g carbohydrates;
5.4g fiber; 3.2g sugar;
21.6g protein.

Recipe Type:
Main dish, snack,
meat, dairy-free,
gluten-free, uses
fermented foods

Yield: 4 servings
Prep time: 20 min.
**Inactive prep
time:** 3-4 hrs.

Slow Cooker Lentils with Summer Sausage

An easy lentils, vegetables and sausage crockpot makes a warm and inviting comfort food meal at the end of a long, cold day.

2 cups brown or green lentils
2 Tbsp coconut oil
1 large yellow onion, peeled and crescent-sliced
2 cloves fresh garlic, chopped
2 stalks celery, diagonally cut
2 med carrots, sliced
2 small potatoes or kohlrabi, cut into 1/2-inch cubes
Celtic or sea salt
pepper
2 tsp thyme leaves
purified water to cover
4 sausages, grass-fed beef, chicken or turkey
1½ Tbsp wheat-free tamari soy sauce

Wash lentils with running water in colander or strainer. Drain.

In crock pot, turned to high, melt coconut oil. Add chopped garlic and onions.

Add cut up celery, carrots and potatoes or kohlrabi, salt, pepper and thyme leaves. Saute lightly for 3-4 minutes just until vegetables start to soften and flavors meld.

Add lentils and cover with water or stock, about 3-4 cups. Cover, reduce heat to low and simmer for 2-3 hours min or up to 8 hours.

Sausages may be pan fried at the last minute, or added with the water. Just before serving, add soy sauce and stir to combine.

NUTRITION FACTS

Nutrition (per serving):
474.8 calories;
44% calories from fat;
24.0g total fat;
67.7mg cholesterol;
853.3mg sodium;
935.0mg potassium;
43.9g carbohydrates;
11.6g fiber; 5.6g sugar;
24.3g protein.

Recipe Type:
Main dish, gluten-free, meat, uses fermented foods

Moussaka

This savory variation on the Greek classic main dish uses sliced zucchini instead of eggplant. The yogurt-egg topping is quicker, healthier.

Yield: 1 - 13x9 inch pan

Prep time: 60 min.

COOKING TIPS

Though this recipe has many ingredients and steps to construct it, the result is well-worth the time and effort. Make it when you're in the mood to create something memorable.

A truly delightful meal, accompanied by a salad of mixed greens with Balsamic viniagrette and Greek Retzina or a dry red, slightly fruity wine.

NUTRITION FACTS

Nutrition (per serving):
217.2 calories;
47% calories from fat;
11.9g total fat;
81.8mg cholesterol;
391.7mg sodium;
599.3mg potassium;
19.1g carbohydrates;
2.4g fiber; 12.8g sugar;
11.2g protein

¼ cup organic extra virgin olive oil
5 cloves garlic, minced
2 large onions, chopped
2 lb ground lamb or beef
½ tsp allspice
1 tsp thyme or oregano leaves
1-1lb 12 oz can organic stewed tomatoes
1 cup dry red wine
½ cup currants

1½ lb russet potatoes, thinly sliced
2 lb zucchini, sliced ¼ inch thick
¾ cup grated Parmesan cheese
3 cups whole, plain organic yogurt
3 eggs
1 tsp nutmeg
1 cup mozzarella cheese, grated

In large skillet or frying pan, sauté garlic and chopped onions in about 2 Tbsp oil over medium heat until translucent. Add ground lamb and sauté, stirring with a wooden spoon, until no longer pink.

Add spices, tomatoes, wine, and currants, cooking slowly until excess moisture is absorbed. Remove to bowl for later assembly.

Rinse out skillet and return to stove. Heat over medium, add remaining olive oil and sauté sliced potatoes until they begin to soften. Sprinkle with salt and pepper.

Preheat oven to 350°F. In large 13 x 9-inch ceramic or glass rectangular casserole, brush lightly with oil and layer potatoes. Sprinkle with about 1/2 cup Parmesan cheese. Spread 1/2 reserved seasoned meat mixture evenly over top.

Layer zucchini, overlapping slices over top of casserole. Sprinkle with salt and pepper. Top with remaining seasoned meat. Cover with foil. Bake for roughly 1-1/2 hours.

Remove from oven and remove foil. Beat yogurt, eggs and nutmeg together with a fork to blend.

Pour evenly over top of moussaka. Sprinkle with grated mozzarella and remaining Parmesan cheese.

Bake, uncovered, for another 30 minutes, until top begins to brown. Remove from oven and let rest for 10 minutes before serving.

Recipe Source
adapted from *Simply Slow Easy Cooking*

Three Cheesy Polenta with Black Beans

One of the original comfort foods, creamy polenta layered with black beans and cheese means dinner delish.

Recipe Type:
Main dish, snack, vegetarian, uses fermented foods

Yield: 2- 8 or 9-inch pans
Prep time: 1½ hr.

1½ cups coarse ground organic polenta or cornmeal
6 cups filtered water
2 tsp Celtic or sea salt
3 Tbsp grass-fed, organic, or raw butter
1- 15 oz can organic black beans, drained
2 tsp cumin powder
2 tsp thyme leaves
1 Tbsp wheat-free tamari soy sauce
½ cup Italian mascarpone cheese
¼ lb or 1 cup grated organic mozzarella or monterey jack cheee
¾ cup grated Parmesan cheese

COOKING TIPS

In a pinch, you can purchase and substitute an already prepared roll of polenta, slicing into 18 rounds (after unwrapping) and dividing into two layers.

Or next time, make a double batch of polenta, use half to make the dish, then wrap and freeze the remainder for a quick assembly meal, without worrying about the layering, when you're really pressed for time.

In large, heavy saucepan, bring water to boil over high heat. Add salt. Then add polenta slowly, in a steady stream, stirrring vigorously with wire whisk until incorporated. Reduce heat to medium low.

Continue whisking for about 30 seconds to prevent lumps. Then continue to cook, stirring every few minutes to keep from sticking, for about 35-40 minutes, until polenta is thick and stiff. Add butter and stir to blend.

Divide the hot polenta into two 8 or 9-inch greased glass or ceramic baking dishes. Spread to distribute evenly. Set aside to cool.

Preheat oven to 350°F. Drain black beans. Spread over polenta in one pan. Sprinkle with ground cumin, thyme leaves and tamari soy sauce. Top with dollops of mascarpone and half the mozzarella cheese.

Cut second pan of polenta into two or four pieces. Remove from pan with flat spatula and place on top of casserole. Sprinkle with remaining mozzarella and Parmesan cheeses.

Bake for 20-30 minutes until cheese is bubbly. Turn up oven to 450°F. for the last few minutes to brown cheese, if desired. Remove from oven and let rest for 5-10 minutes before serving.

NUTRITION FACTS

Nutrition (per serving):
349.3 calories;
45% calories from fat;
18.1g total fat;
51.3mg cholesterol;
1188.8mg sodium;
245.2mg potassium;
32.5g carbohydrates;
5.0g fiber; 0.6g sugar;
15.4g protein.

Meats, Poultry and Fish

Chinese Soy-Glazed Chicken

Recipe Type:
Appetizer or snack, dairy-free, main dish, meat, fish, poultry, uses fermented foods

Yield: 6 servings
Prep time: 1-2½ hrs.

A simpler version of a Chinese duck favorite, featuring several cultured ingredients and two options for the classic deep fried crispy skin and a healthier lower fat version.

1 3-4 lb organic, free-range roasting chicken
1 Tbsp ground peppercorns
2 Tbsp grated fresh ginger
2 Tbsp honey
3 Tbsp Mirin, mild rice wine vinegar
1¼ cups organic tamari or shoyu soy sauce
2 Tbsp organic dark or barley miso
1 Tbsp roasted sesame oil
oil for frying, *see notes in procedure**
2 cups organic chicken broth

Rinse and drain the chicken, pulling off excess fat and cutting off the fatty end of the tail. Rub with peppercorns and ginger inside and outside of carcass.

Combine honey, vinegar, soy sauce, miso, toasted sesame oil and chicken broth in medium bowl. Stir well to blend. Pour marinade over chicken in shallow pan and marinate in refrigerator for 3 hours. Drain chicken and reserve marinade.

Choose deep-frying or pan-frying variations and follow directions below.

Remove from marinade. Using cleaver or large butcher knife, cut through bones to cut chicken in half lengthwise. Then cut up chicken into 2-3-inch cross-cut pieces. Transfer to platter and serve with some reserved marinade spooned over top.

Variations:

Deep-frying Variation: Heat wok on high. Add 2 cups peanut oil and heat until very hot. Drain marinade from chicken and reserve. Cook chicken for 8-10 minutes until brown. Remove to casserole. Add marinade and chicken stock. Cover. Simmer for about 2 hours on low. Let set off heat for 30 minutes.

Lower fat Pan-frying Variation: Preheat oven to 350°F. Heat a heavy skillet over high and add only 2 Tbsp oil. Drain marinade off chicken and reserve. Add chicken and brown, turning frequently to brown on many sides. Add marinade and chicken stock. Remove to oven and cook for about 30 minutes.

COOKING TIPS

This dish is typically marinated and then deep fried in peanut oil in a wok, producing a succulently crisp skin. A somewhat healthier, though not quite as crispy, version can be made by browning the bird in a small amount oil, then finishing in the oven, simmered in the marinade and stock.

NUTRITION FACTS

Nutrition (per serving):
333.7 calories;
42% calories from fat;
16.4g total fat;
87.7mg cholesterol;
3690.3mg sodium;
497.2mg potassium;
13.6g carbohydrates;
0.8g fiber; 6.8g sugar;
35.3g protein.

Classic Beef Bourguignon

The classic French beef in burgundy wine stew.

Recipe Type:
Main dish, meat, uses fermented foods

Yield: 10 servings
Prep time: 45 min.

COOKING TIPS

*For fresh Bouquet Garni: wrap the following ingredients in double layer cheesecloth and tie with string:
1 4-inch piece celery, 1 California bay leaf, 3 fresh thyme sprigs, 2 fresh parsley sprigs, 8 black peppercorns, 1/4 tsp slightly crushed fennel seeds, 6 whole cloves. Substitute dried herbs, if necessary.

+You can create non-gluten oat flour, by processing organic rolled oats in food processor workbowl fitted with S-blade until they yield a fine flour. Make some ahead to have on hand for recipes. If celiac, use bean flour or non-gluten flour mix.

NUTRITION FACTS

Nutrition (per serving):
506.7 calories;
61% calories from fat;
34.4g total fat;
101.3mg cholesterol;
180.0mg sodium;
577.4mg potassium;
12.1g carbohydrates;
2.1g fiber; 2.6g sugar;
24.8g protein.

3½ lb organic beef chuck or blade roast
1 bottle organic red wine, preferably burgundy
3 cloves garlic, minced
1 bundle Bouquet Garni*
¼ cup all-purpose or oat flour*
4 Tbsp organic or raw butter
2 med onions, chopped
2 med carrots, cut into 1/4-inch pieces
1 lb small pearl onions or 4-5 French shallots, peeled
1 lb button mushrooms, quartered

Cut the beef into small cubes with a sharp knife. Place meat in large bowl, pour in wine, add chopped garlic and bouquet garni. Marinate in refrigerator for at least 3 hours or overnight.

Remove from refrigerator, drain the meat, reserving the marinade. Dry the meat with paper toweling.

Sprinkle salt, pepper and all purpose or oat flour+ over meat and stir or shake to coat.

Place 3 Tbsp butter in large 6-8 quart heavy iron clad casserole or frying pan and heat on high until melted, but not smoking. Reduce heat a bit, and brown the meat on all sides, in batches, if necessary, Remove meat from pan to bowl.

Preheat oven to 325°F. Add chopped onions and carrots to pan, sauté for several minutes until onions are pale brown. Add marinade, bouquet garni, meat and juices. Bring to boil, stirring, then cover. Place pan into oven and cook for 2-1/2 - 3 hours, until beef is tender.

Meanwhile, melt remaining 1 Tbsp of butter in a clean frying pan. Add pearl onions or shallots and sauté for 7-8 minutes until onions are softened. Add mushrooms quarters and sauté for 2-3 minutes to brown. Add to pan in oven and cook approximately 10 minutes more.

This dish can be prepared a day ahead, and refrigerated, allowing flavors to develop and meld. Fat can be skimmed or lifted off top when solidified. Reheat for 20 minutes to bring back up to temperature.

Recipe Source
Simply Slower Cooking

Corned Beef

Recipe Type:
Basic fermented
formula, meat

Your own corned beef at home or made and shared with your local circle is delicious and practical.

2 qt water
1 cup kosher salt
½ cup brown sugar
2 Tbsp saltpeter
1 cinnamon stick, broken into several pieces
1 tsp mustard seeds
1 tsp black peppercorns
8 whole cloves
8 whole allspice berries
12 whole juniper berries
2 bay leaves, crumbled
½ tsp ground ginger
2 lb ice
1 4-5 pound organic beef brisket, trimmed

Yield: 20 servings
Prep time: 1 hr.
Inactive prep time: 10 days

Place the water into a large 6 to 8 quart stockpot along with salt, sugar, saltpeter, cinnamon stick, mustard seeds, peppercorns, cloves, allspice, juniper berries, bay leaves and ginger. Cook over high heat until the salt and sugar have dissolved.

Remove from the heat and add the ice. Stir until the ice has melted. If necessary, place the brine into the refrigerator until it reaches a temperature of 45°F.

Once it has cooled, place the brisket in a 2-gallon zip top bag and add the brine. Seal and lay flat inside a container, cover and place in the refrigerator for 10 days. Check daily to make sure the beef is completely submerged and stir the brine.

After 10 days, remove from the brine and rinse well under cool water.

Recipe Source
Alton Brown, *Good Eats*

NUTRITION FACTS

Nutrition (per serving):
389.1 calories;
52% calories from fat;
22.7g total fat;
57.9mg cholesterol;
1619.1mg sodium;
799.7mg potassium;
35.8g carbohydrates;
12.7g fiber; 5.6g sugar;
18.6g protein.

Recipe Type:
Appetizer or snack,
basic fermented
formula, meat

Yield: 60-3 oz

portions

Prep time: 2 hr.

**Inactive prep
time:** 3-4 months

Dry Beef Salami

*Making your own salami or summer sausage at home is actually a
fairly simple process requiring only a few special items like casings
that you can obtain by direct mail.*

9 lb grass-fed beef, trimmings okay
1 lb coconut oil
½ cup plus 2 Tbsp Celtic or sea salt
3 Tbsp sugar
2 Tbsp white or black pepper
2 tsp ground mace
2 tsp ground ginger
Starter culture or whey, optional

Grind beef in grinder using 1/8-inch plate. Or process in batches in food processor, removing to a large bowl. Put coconut oil in a warm area until it is spoonable.

Add coconut oil, spices and any starters to meat. Mix all ingredients for 5 minutes or until evenly distributed.

Transfer the mixture to deep trays or pans (ideally 8-10 inches deep to minimize contact with air) for 2 to 4 days at 40°-45°F.

Stuff meat mixture into 5-inch fibrous casings, sewed bags or suitable-sized collagen casings.

Hold or hang salami for 9 to 11 days at 40°F. and 60% relative humidity. This product may be cooked to internal temperature of 148°F. to shorten drying cycle.

Refrigerate or place in cool, dry place after curing until ready to use. Holds for 3-4 months.

NUTRITION FACTS

Nutrition (per serving):
203.3 calories;
73% calories from fat;
16.5g total fat;
47.6mg cholesterol;
1460.2mg sodium;
199.9mg potassium;
0.8g carbohydrates;
0.1g fiber; 0.6g sugar;
12.1g protein.

Recipe Source
A. E. Reynolds, Extension Meat Specialist, Michigan State University

Gravlax

Traditional Gravlax or Lox is delicious sliced with bagels and your own homemade cream cheese, or with Tarator Soup and a mixed greens salad.

1 lb wild Alaskan salmon filet
2 Tbsp Kosher salt
2 Tbsp organic sugar or evaporated cane juice
2 tsp black pepper, ground
8-10 fresh whole dill sprigs

Remove all bones from salmon. As you drape the salmon over your hand you can remove bones with needle nose pliers. Place the salmon on a large piece of plastic wrap (about three to four times the length of the filet) with the skin side down.

Mix salt, sugar, and black pepper and a bowl. Cover the exposed salmon as evenly as possible with the salt and pepper mixture. Place the dill on top of the salmon. (Dill will be removed prior to serving).

Wrap your salmon and toppings into a package using additional wrap to wrap again. Place in a container to catch fluids which will leach out.

Place salmon in refrigerator for at least 2 days; longer refrigeration will increase flavors.

When ready to serve your delicacy, open package, remove dill and rinse in water. Pat dry with a paper towel.

Slice the gravlax thinly and on an angle across the salmon, beginning at the tail. Remove skin prior to serving.

Serve gravlax the way you would serve smoked salmon. Garnish with lemon slices and some fresh dill.

Recipe Type:
Appetizer or snack, basic fermented formula, brunch, dairy-free, gluten-free, seafood

Yield: 4 servings
Prep time: 25 min
Inactive prep time: 2 days

COOKING TIPS

For gravlax, use filets that do not go through the backbone.

NUTRITION FACTS

Nutrition (per serving):
27.3 calories; 1% calories from fat; 0.0g total fat; 0.0mg cholesterol; 2820.8mg sodium; 17.0mg potassium; 7.0g carbohydrates; 0.3g fiber; 6.3g sugar; 0.1g protein.

Recipe Source
www.cookingforengineers.com/recipe/132/Gravlax

Peppered Chicken

Recipe Type:
Main dish, poultry,
uses fermented foods

This quick, beautiful tri-color red, yellow and green main dish will be a hit with family or at a neighborhood gatheirng

Yield: 4 servings
Prep time: 30 min.

5-6 free-range chicken thighs, boneless
12 fresh shiitake mushrooms
5 red, green and yellow bell peppers
¼ cup rice vinegar
¼ cup shoyu soy sauce
½ tsp black pepper

Remove excess fat from chicken. Leave skin on.

Remove hard ends of mushrooms, and cut into halves or quarters. Clean, de-seed and cut peppers into 2-inch strips.

Heat a non-stick fry pan. Cook chicken skin side down until skin browns and crisps. Turn chicken over and cook until other side is brown.

Add mushrooms and peppers to pan. Toss chicken and vegetables while cooking.

When meat and vegetables are cooked, add rice vinegar, black pepper, and soy sauce. Continue to cook as sauce thickens.

Cut into bite-sized pieces and place on serving platter.

NUTRITION FACTS

Nutrition (per serving):
441.1 calories;
17% calories from fat;
9.3g total fat;
74.3mg cholesterol;
616.1mg sodium;
1059.4mg potassium;
76.9g carbohydrates;
11.9g fiber; 21.6g sugar;
29.5g protein.

Recipe Type:
Main dish, meat,
dairy-free, uses
fermented foods

Yield: 12 servings
Prep time: 20 min.
**Inactive prep
time:** 3 hr.

COOKING TIPS

*Adding flour to thicken
juices at the end would
add gluten

Pot Roast with Sauerkraut

*Slow simmered with sauerkraut and vegetables, even tougher cuts of
meat become tender and flavorful.*

4 lb organic bottom round or beef brisket
1 Tbsp coconut oil
1 Tbsp thyme leaves
2 whole bay leaves
1 Tbsp shoyu or tamari
4 cups sauerkraut (see page 151)
1 large yellow onion, chopped
3 stalks celery, cut diagonally
½ lb baby carrots
2 med potatoes, cut in 1-inch chunks
1½ cups rejuvelac (see page 149)

In large crockpot or heavy oven casserole, sauté beef on high or medium high in coconut oil until brown on both sides. If cooking in oven, preheat to 325°F.

Sprinkle beef with thyme leaves, bay leaves, tamari or shoyu. Cover and pack with sauerkraut.

Add chopped onions, celery, baby carrots, and potato chunks. Pour over rejuvelac. Cover. Simmer in crockpot on low or remove to preheated oven and cook for approximately 2 hours. Test for doneness to see if meat fibers separate easily. Poor off liquid and reserve.

Remove cover and continue cooking for approximately 1/2 hour, or until meat forks tender.

If desired, blend hot juices with approximately 1/2 - 2/3 cup of the vegetables or 2 Tbsp whole grain flour in blender until smooth for sauce or gravy. Add more thyme and pepper to taste. Remove roast and surround with vegetables on serving platter, if desired. Top or serve with gravy.

NUTRITION FACTS

Nutrition (per serving):
536.3 calories;
70% calories from fat;
41.7g total fat;
110.4mg cholesterol;
444.4mg sodium;
1016.1mg potassium;
11.9g carbohydrates;
4.7g fiber; 5.4g sugar;
27.7g protein.

Notes

Salads

Calabrese Salad

This quintessentially Italian summer salad is not only delightful, but beautiful with its vibrant red, white, green, and black colors.

4 large ripe tomatoes, cut into 1/8-inch slices
1 lb fresh mozzarella cheese, cut into 1/8-inch slices
½ cup chopped fresh basil
½ cup organic Kalamata or Nicoise olives
½ cup Lemon Vinaigrette (see page 191)
2-3 grinds fresh black pepper

On large serving platter, arrange alternating slices of tomato and mozzarella cheese.

Sprinkle with basil and arrange olives decoratively.

Drizzle with viniagrette salad dressing and grind fresh black pepper generously over platter. Serve.

Recipe Type:
Appetizer or snack, gluten-free, raw, side dish, vegetable

Yield: 6 servings
Prep time: 10 min.

NUTRITION FACTS

Nutrition (per serving):
195.1 calories;
93% calories from fat;
20.4g total fat;
0.0mg cholesterol;
596.4mg sodium;
30.2mg potassium;
3.4g carbohydrates;
0.3g fiber; 0.6g sugar;
0.2g protein.

Recipe Source
The Silver Palate Cookbook

Recipe Type:
Condiment, dairy-free, gluten-free, raw, salad, vegan, vegetables, vegetarian, uses fermented foods

Yield: 1 cup
Prep time: 15 min.

Cucumber Seaweed Salad

To Wakame No Sunomono is the traditional Japanese name of this delicious cucumber salad.

¼ cup wakame seaweed
1 long Japanese cucumber, unpeeled
4 Tbsp rice vinegar
2 Tbsp sugar
3 Tbsp shoyu or wheat-free tamari soy sauce

Pour water over 1/4 cup dried wakame. After 1/2 hour, rinse, drain and chop.

Slice cucumber in half lengthwise and then cut into thin slices. You may remove seeds if you wish. Lightly salt. After 5 minutes drain off excess liquid.

Combine the vinegar, sugar, and shoyu in a small saucepan. Stir over medium flame until the sugar dissolves. Set aside.

Combine wakame, cucumber and dressing. Mix well and serve.

NUTRITION FACTS

Nutrition (per serving):
44.3 calories; 1% calories from fat; 0.2g total fat; 0.0mg cholesterol; 496.0mg sodium; 229.3mg potassium; 15.7g carbohydrates; 0.6g fiber; 7.5g sugar; 1.3g protein.

Recipe Type:
Salad, gluten-free, dairy-free, uses fermented foods, vegetables, vegan, vegetarian

Yield: 6 servings
Prep time: 20 min.

COOKING TIPS

Use ½ cup Golden Sunsé™ Seed Mix (see page 167)

Oriental Confetti Coleslaw

Very unique, this multi-colored cabbage salad is rated "Ah So Good" with its toasted sesame/sunflower flavor and crunch.

½ cup sunflower seeds
¼ cup sesame seeds
1 med head green cabbage, shredded
½ med head red cabbage, shredded
2 organic carrots, shredded
½ bunch parsley, chopped
2 scallions
1 Tbsp toasted sesame oil
¼ cup rice wine vinegar or 3 Tbsp apple cider vinegar
1 tsp vegetable seasoning salt

Toast sunflower and sesame seeds lightly in dry cast iron skillet in oven at 375°F until lightly golden brown with nutty smell, 7-10 minutes.

In large salad bowl, combine shredded green and red cabbage, carrots, scallions, and parsley.

Drizzle over remaining ingredients, and toss to mix well. Toss in most of toasted seeds, reserving some for garnish.

Brighten up any humdrum winter day with this beautiful, savory salad, paired with chili or onion cheese cornbread and soup.

NUTRITION FACTS

Nutrition (per serving):
216.3 calories;
56% calories from fat;
15.6g total fat;
0.0mg cholesterol;
377.2mg sodium;
437.3mg potassium;
20.0g carbohydrates;
3.6g fiber; 4.6g sugar;
7.0g protein.

Greek Tzatziki Salad

This savory traditional Mediterranean salad can stand on its own or become a cool, saucy accompaniment for lamb, gyros, spicy curries or stuffed vegetables.

4-5 med cucumbers
½ tsp Celtic or sea salt
2 Tbsp garlic, fresh minced
1 qt yogurt (see page 159)
3 Tbsp fresh mint leaves, chopped

Peel cucumbers. Cut in half and scoop out seeds. Cut into crescents or cubes, or coarsely grate on large holes of grater.

Place cucumbers in strainer, lightly salt and let drain for 15 or so minutes.

Place cucumbers in serving bowl. Add garlic, yogurt and mint; stir to combine. Season to taste. Refrigerate for half an hour and serve.

Recipe Type:
Salad, raw, vegetables, vegetarian, uses fermented foods

Yield: 6 servings
Prep time: 20 min.
Inactive prep time: 60 min.

COOKING TIPS

If there's no fresh mint available, use 1 Tbsp dried mint or even 1/8 tsp mint extract. If none of these are in your kitchen, substitute chopped parsley or fresh dill.

NUTRITION FACTS

Nutrition (per serving):
127.8 calories;
38% calories from fat;
5.6g total fat;
21.2mg cholesterol;
236.4mg sodium;
525.6mg potassium;
12.9g carbohydrates;
1.4g fiber; 10.2g sugar;
7.0g protein.

Recipe Type:
Appetizer, condiment, dairy-free, gluten-free, raw, salad, uses fermented foods, vegan, vegetarian

Yield: 2 cups
Prep time: 25 min.
Inactive prep time: 35 min.

COOKING TIPS

Daikon is a large Korean radish, available at stores with a large or Asian produce selection or sometimes at a Farmer's Market. You could also substitute the thin Japanese cucumber.

NUTRITION FACTS

Nutrition (per serving):
17.4 calories; 6% calories from fat; 0.1g total fat; 0.0mg cholesterol; 594.9mg sodium; 154.5mg potassium; 4.0g carbohydrates; 1.1g fiber; 2.7g sugar; 0.5g protein.

Radish Salad

Crushed red pepper, preferred by Koreans, makes a very hot salad. Adjust to your preference and serve as salad or condiment.

1 lb daikon, large Korean radish
2 tsp Celtic or sea salt
2 tsp crushed red pepper
2 tsp sugar
1½ tsp rice vinegar
2 tsp minced green onion
1 tsp minced fresh garlic

Peel radish or cuke and cut into match stick pieces about 2-inch long.

Sprinkle with salt and let stand for 10 minutes. Rinse to remove excess salt and drain well.

Wrap radish in several thicknesses of cheesecloth or paper towel and squeeze out as much liquid as possible.

In bowl, combine radish with red pepper, sugar, vinegar, green onion and garlic, mixing well.

Serve at once or refrigerate to blend flavors.

Panzanella Italian Bread Salad

Recipe Type:
Main dish, salad, raw, side dish, vegetarian

This hearty and delightful Italian summer bread salad can be the center of the meal for a summer picnic.

Yield: 4 servings

Prep time: 20 min.

Inactive prep time: 2 hr.

1 qt sourdough bread cubes, ½-inch
⅓ cup organic extra virgin olive oil
2 Tbsp Balsamic vinegar
½ tsp cane juice, organic evaporated
½ tsp Celtic or sea salt
¼ tsp freshly ground black pepper
1 lb fresh plum tomatoes, cut into ½-inch chunks (2½ cups)
1 large cucumber, peeled, halved, seeded and sliced ½-inch thick
8 oz mozzarella, part-skim, cut into ½-inch chunks
½ cup olives, brine-cured such as Kalamata, pitted and slivered
¾ cup basil leaves, fresh and packed, diagonally halved

Preheat oven to 400° F.

Toast bread cubes in even layer on baking sheet, tossing once or twice, 7 minutes, or until lightly browned.

In large bowl, whisk together oil, vinegar, sugar, salt, and pepper. Add tomatoes, cucumber, mozzarella, olives, and basil, and toss well.

Cover wet ingredients and let stand at room temperature for 1 hour or up to 8 hours in refrigerator for flavors to meld before serving.

Add bread cubes and toss all ingredients just before serving. Pile into large glass or crystal bowl or wooden salad bowl. Stunningly beautiful and delicious!

NUTRITION FACTS

Nutrition (per serving):
274.5 calories;
71% calories from fat;
22.2g total fat;
0.1mg cholesterol;
595.7mg sodium;
132.6mg potassium;
16.7g carbohydrates;
1.4g fiber; 1.2g sugar;
2.8g protein.

Recipe Source
Hearst Communications, Inc.

Notes

Soups

Notes

Recipe Type:
Soup, gluten-free, uses fermented foods, vegetarian

Yield: 6 cups

Prep time: 15 min.

Inactive prep time: 50 min.

Borscht | Russian Beet Soup

Russian Borscht varies from region to region and mother to mother, but this basic one is cool, refreshing and tasty on a hot summer day, warming and hearty with more vegies and meat in winter.

3 cups fermented beets, chopped (See page 255)
1 qt beef broth
1 med whole onion, peeled and sliced
2 tsp organic sugar or evaporated cane juice
1 Tbsp lemon juice, or more to taste
1 tsp Celtic or sea salt
3-4 grinds black pepper
2/3 cup cultured sour cream (See page 152)
2 Tbsp fresh dill or chives, finely minced

In medium saucepan, simmer onion and beef broth on medium low for 10-15 minutes until onion is soft. Remove from heat. Remove onion and discard.

Add chopped fermented beets. Add sugar, lemon juice and stir. Add salt and pepper, a little at a time, adjusting to your preference.

Refrigerate until chilled. Serve with a round spoonful of sour cream. Garnish with dill or chives.

NUTRITION FACTS

Nutrition (per serving):
99.2 calories;
49% calories from fat;
5.6g total fat;
11.3mg cholesterol;
482.5mg sodium;
233.1mg potassium;
11.7g carbohydrates;
2.0g fiber; 6.7g sugar;
2.0g protein

French Onion Soup

This ultra-quick version of the delectable French classic is the ultimate, elegant comfort food, featuring several cultured ingredients.

¼ cup cultured butter (see page 129)
4 med yellow onions, peeled and sliced thinly
1 large red onion, peeled and sliced thinly
5 cloves fresh garlic, minced
¼ cup all-purpose flour
1 cup red wine
2 qt stock, organic beef, chicken or vegetable
1 whole bay leaf

2 sprigs fresh thyme or 1 Tbsp dried thyme leaves
⅓ cup high quality, wheat-free tamari soy sauce
12 slices sourdough baguette, day-old bread
4 oz gruyere, camembert, mozzarella or swiss, shredded or cut in chunks
2 oz grated Parmesan cheese, optional

In large enameled, cast iron saucepan or stainless steel stockpot, melt butter over medium heat. Add thinly sliced red and yellow onions. Sauté over low heat for 25 minutes, stirring occasionally, until onion is starting to brown.

Add garlic and flour, raise heat to medium and stir for 2-3 minutes, being careful not to burn. Slowly stir in wine, stock, bay leaf and thyme. Cover and simmer for another 15 or so minutes. Stir in tamari.

Toast baguettes under broiler on both sides. Brush with oil or butter, if desired. Place toasted baguettes in large oven proof serving dish or individual serving bowls. Ladle onion soup over. Top with shredded cheeses and Parmesan. Broil for 3-4 minutes under broiler until cheese is golden brown. Serve immediately.

Variations:

Ultra Quick-In-a-Hurry Version: Slice onions quickly in food processor. Sauté garlic and onions in butter over medium heat, stirring frequently, for a few minutes until translucent and soft. One at a time, stir in wine, stock, bay leaf, thyme and tamari. Bring to a boil, reduce heat and simmer for a few minutes. Toast bread, and cut into croutons. Serve soup bowls with several croutons, sprinkled with cheese.

Classical Slow Cooked for the Most Flavor Version: Sauté onions over very low heat, stirring occasionally for about 2 hours until onions have become very soft and are carmelly, golden brown. Stir in garlic and flour. Increase heat and sauté a few minutes until onions are brown, not burned. Add wine, stock and herbs. Cover and simmer 20-25 minutes longer. Add soy sauce. Toast baguettes under broiler. Place in serving bowls or ramekins. Top with grated cheese. Broil, if desired, until cheese bubbles.

Golden Miso Squash Soup

Recipe Type:
Appetizer or snack,
gluten-free, dairy-free,
soup

Adding coconut milk to a classic squash and miso soup recipe like this one intensifies its rich, sweet flavor and makes it even creamier.

Yield: 4 servings
Prep time: 25 min.

1 Tbsp sesame or coconut oil
1 cinnamon stick
1½ Tbsp minced fresh ginger root
½ tsp ground turmeric
3 cups organic butternut squash, cubed
1 large onion, peeled and diced
1- 14 oz can coconut milk
2½ cups water
½ tsp Celtic or sea salt
2 Tbsp sweet light miso
freshly ground black pepper to taste
½ cup shredded unsweetened coconut, lightly toasted

COOKING TIPS

When using organic yellow or red, tender-skinned squash like butternut or red kuri, it's okay to leave the skin intact, trimming any tough or warty pieces. Let it soften and it will blend right into the soup, yielding more flavor and nutrients.

Heat the oil in a 4-quart stockpot over medium heat. Add cinnamon stick, ginger and turmeric and sauté for 1 minute. Add onion and squash, sautéing for 5 minutes or until vegetables soften.

Add coconut milk, 2½ cups water and salt and bring to a boil. Reduce the heat to medium-low, cover, and simmer for 15 minutes, or until the squash is tender. Remove cinnamon stick.

Stir ¼ cup soup broth carefully into miso in small bowl with a fork. Add to soup and simmer for 1 minute, taking care not to let soup boil. Season with pepper. Remove from the heat.

Lightly purée the soup using a potato ricer or foley food mill, or purée in a blender or food processor, taking care to not burn yourself.

Divide the soup between four bowls, garnishing each with 1 tablespoon lightly-toasted coconut. Serve immediately with a small bowl of extra coconut to pass around.

NUTRITION FACTS

Nutrition (per serving):
343.3 calories;
71% calories from fat;
29.4g total fat;
0.0mg cholesterol;
259.9mg sodium;
686.7mg potassium;
23.1g carbohydrates;
5.6g fiber; 4.2g sugar;
4.0g protein

Recipe Source
Rebecca Wood

Recipe Type:
Appetizer or snack,
gluten-free, raw, soup,
uses fermented foods,
vegetarian

Yield: 1 qt
Prep time: 15 min.

Tarator

This delicious cold yogurt-cucumber soup from Bulgaria makes a refreshing warm-weather meal.

1-2 cloves fresh garlic
½ tsp Celtic or sea salt
1 Tbsp olive oil
1 med cucumber, peeled, seeded and grated
2 cups yogurt (see page 159)
1-2 cups water
½-¾ cup fresh dill, finely chopped
½ cup walnuts, finely chopped

Crush garlic with salt in mixing bowl. Then add oil and mix well.

Add cucumber to garlic mixture; mix well. Stir yogurt and pour over garlic/cucumber mixture. Add water, if desired.

Mix walnuts and dill into soup, reserving some dill for garnish. Chill, for 1 hour, for best flavor.

Serve individual bowls topped with chopped, fresh dill.

NUTRITION FACTS

Nutrition (per serving):
212.9 calories;
59% calories from fat;
14.9g total fat;
7.3mg cholesterol;
380.6mg sodium;
461.8mg potassium;
12.5g carbohydrates;
1.5g fiber; 10.0g sugar;
9.2g protein

Recipe Source
WestonA.Price.org

Notes

Sweets
and
Desserts

Notes

Chocolate Nut Torte

A sinfully rich, decadent dessert that's easy, even foolproof.
Can't "fall" because it doesn't rise.

Recipe Type:
Sweets and desserts,
uses fermented foods,
vegetarian

Yield: 8-inch pan

Prep time: 15 min.

**Inactive prep
time:** 30 min.

COOKING TIPS

Soak and/or ferment nuts for a healthier version. If you do this, make sure nuts are dry before grinding in food processor.

Torte will not rise, but will look like brownies. Best undercooked so texture is soft and moist. You can serve leftovers (ha ha) in lunchbox as brownies.

NUTRITION FACTS

Nutrition (per serving):
373.0 calories;
63% calories from fat;
27.5g total fat;
132.2mg cholesterol;
110.9mg sodium;
138.5mg potassium;
27.8g carbohydrates;
2.7g fiber; 13.4g sugar;
7.2g protein.

½ cup (1 stick) butter, raw or organic
4 oz semi-sweet or bittersweet organic chocolate
1 cup almonds, walnuts, cashews, or pecans, preferably raw, organic
½ cup organic, rolled oats
½ cup sugar or evaporated cane juice, organic
3 eggs, free-range
2 tsp vanilla extract
¼ tsp salt
½ cup mascarpone or cream cheese

Into small metal or glass bowl add chocolate squares and butter. Place bowl over medium saucepan 2/3's full of simmering water, until chocolate and butter are melted. Don't overheat or let water splash in bowl. Stir together gently with spatula to create a creamy blend.

Preheat oven to 325°F. In workbowl of food processor fitted with S blade, grind nuts and rolled oats together to a fine powder. Remove to bowl.

Grease a square 8- or 9-inch square ceramic or glass pan or pie plate. Metal is okay, but just avoid aluminum. Pour about 1/4-1/3 cup ground nuts and oat mixture into pan, shaking to cover the bottom. Shake off excess.

Pour sugar into food processor work bowl, and pulse a few times to fine consistency. Add slightly cooled chocolate-butter mixture, eggs, vanilla and mascarpone. Process on medium high until mixture is thoroughly blended and a little fluffy. Do not overbeat.

Pour mixture into prepared pan, scraping down work bowl with rubber spatula, unless the kids are around. Transfer to oven and bake for approximately 30 minutes. Remove from oven and let cool slightly. Cut into wedges or squares when no one is near to snitch. Serve on individual plates topped with whipped cream, ice cream or mascarpone. Go to heaven.

Recipe Type:
Sweets and desserts

Yield: 10 servings
Prep time: 75 min.

Classic New York Cheesecake with Easy Nut Crust

The rich, creamy classic dessert that just about everyone loves in an easy, crunchy nut crust.

1 recipe nut crust (see page 245)
1lb 10 oz cream cheese (see page 125)
1 cup organic evaporated cane juice
¼ cup organic white pastry flour
2 tsp grated organic lemon peel
4 large free-range eggs
⅔ cup raw organic cream
1 tsp real vanilla extract

Prepare basic nut crust on page 245. Preheat oven to 300°F.

In mixing bowl or food processor workbowl, add cream cheese, sugar, flour, lemon zest and blend until smooth.

Add eggs, one at a time, blending after each. Add cream and vanilla and blend.

Pour into nut crust. Bake for 1 hour and 15 minutes until almost set. Remove from oven. Let cool.

Refrigerate, if desired, before serving. Top with powdered sugar, chocolate or desired fruit topping.

NUTRITION FACTS

Nutrition (per serving):
540.7 calories;
66% calories from fat;
41.2g total fat;
175.4mg cholesterol;
247.1mg sodium;
295.1mg potassium;
35.1g carbohydrates;
2.8g fiber; 27.5g sugar;
11.3g protein.

Creamy Strawberry Dream

You don't have to tell your kids that this sweet, heavenly concoction is quick and healthy, too. Bet they'll never guess...

½ cup raw cashews, soaked 4-6 hrs
1 cup fresh, whole organic strawberries
1 med banana
¼ cup rejuvelac, kefir, yogurt or water

Coarsely grind cashews in blender or food processor workbowl for 5-10 seconds.

Add strawberries, banana and liquid. Blend until thick and creamy. Refrigerate, if desired. You can also add a couple of ice cubes to cool this down.

Pour into serving glass or dish. Enjoy.

Recipe Type:
Sweets and desserts

Yield: 4 servings
Prep time: 10 min.

COOKING TIPS

Serve this scrumptious fruit dream by itself as a soft pudding, or as topping for sliced fresh fruits in season. No matter how you serve it, it'll be a hit!

NUTRITION FACTS

Nutrition (per serving):
369.0 calories;
61% calories from fat;
27.1g total fat;
0.9mg cholesterol;
18.2mg sodium;
573.8mg potassium;
26.1g carbohydrates;
3.4g fiber; 9.8g sugar;
11.7g protein.

Easy Raw and Baked Nut Crusts

These two versions of quick, easy, healthy, and very tasty pie crusts need no rolling. Simply blend in food processor and pat into pie plate.

Recipe Type:
Sweets and desserts

Yield: 8 servings

Prep time: 15 min.

Inactive prep time: 20 min.

COOKING TIPS

These delicious, no wheat, healthier pie crusts work equally well for sweet desserts, as for savory applications like quiches and meal pies.

NUTRITION FACTS

Nutrition (per serving):
140.2 calories;
65% calories from fat;
11.0g total fat;
0.0mg cholesterol;
1.1mg sodium;
170.9mg potassium;
10.3g carbohydrates;
2.7g fiber; 7.1g sugar;
2.9g protein.

Easy Raw Nut Crust Ingredients
¾ cup crispy almonds (See Crispy Nuts, (see page 127)
½ cup crispy pecans (See Crispy Nuts, (see page 127)
¾ cup organic pitted dates
⅔ cup unsweetened coconut

Easy Baked Nut Crust Ingredients
½ cup flax seeds
1 cup regular organic rolled oats
⅔ cup crispy pecans
½ cup crispy almonds
3 Tbsp coconut oil
3 Tbsp raw cultured or organic butter (see page 129)

Easy Raw Nut Crust Procedures

Grind the nuts as finely as possible in a grain mill, blender or food processor. Into food processor, add dates and process until mixture is blended and sticks together. Add coconut and pulse until blended.

Press the date, nut, coconut mixture into an oiled pie plate with your fingers and bottom of a measuring cup to form a thin, even crust. Fill with desired filling.

Easy Baked Nut Crust Procedures

Grind flax seeds into meal in small coffee grinder or food processor. Grind oats in food processor or dry blender into a fine powder. Dump into mixing bowl. Preheat oven to 375°F.

Add pecans and almonds to food processor and grind into fine meal. Add oat flour, flax meal, butter, coconut oil and ½ tsp ground cinnamon or nutmeg, if desired, to ground nuts in food processor. Process in pulses only until mixture begins to stick together.

Pat into 8-inch or 9-inch square pan or pie plate. Bake as is at 375°F. for 20 minutes until lightly brown. Remove from oven. Cool. Fill with prepared sweet or savory filling. Or fill unbaked crust with filling such as quiche and bake until filling is set.

Melt-In-Your-Mouth Coconut Oil Fudge

Recipe Type:
Sweets and desserts, raw, vegetarian

Yes, chocolate is a fermented food! The cocoa bean gets a week of fermenting on the way to becoming one of the foods we know and love.

1½ cups organic coconut oil
1½ cups organic evaporated cane juice, sugar, or 1 cup honey
1 cup organic cocoa powder or carob
½ tsp Celtic or sea salt
⅛ vanilla bean or 1 tsp real vanilla extract
2 Tbsp mesquite powder or Maca, optional

Yield: 18 servings
Prep time: 15 min.

Melt the coconut oil, if very hard, by placing in a small bowl over hot water.

In food processor work bowl, process cane juice or sugar until it becomes a fine powder.

Add remaining coconut oil, cocoa powder, vanilla, and maca to food processor and process together until smooth.

Pour into a greased 9x12-inch pan. Let set up at room temperature, below 70°F, or in the refrigerator until hard. Cut into small candy-sized pieces.

Store in covered container in the refrigerator for up to 12 months. Ha ha.

COOKING TIPS

Mix in ⅔ cup shredded coconut for a tasty variation. You can find the toasty, nutty Maca powder, a South American root that is said to enhance libido, in most health or natural food stores.

NUTRITION FACTS

Nutrition (per serving):
258.8 calories;
62% calories from fat;
18.8g total fat;
0.0mg cholesterol;
54.5mg sodium;
90.3mg potassium;
26.1g carbohydrates;
1.6g fiber; 23.5g sugar;
1.0g protein.

Raw Almond and Coconut Balls

These delightful candies are quick, healthy, raw, naturally sweet, and delicious.

Recipe Type:
Sweets and desserts, raw, vegan, vegetarian

Yield: 48 servings

Prep time: 15-20 min.

COOKING TIPS

The great thing about these balls is you can make them hours in advance, even the day before. They make a delicious raw dessert, and the leftovers make a great snack.

For a sweeter confection you can add raw, unfiltered honey or agave nectar for vegans.

NUTRITION FACTS

Nutrition (per serving):
63.1 calories;
89% calories from fat;
6.6g total fat;
0.0mg cholesterol;
0.1mg sodium;
40.1mg potassium;
1.0g carbohydrates;
0.6g fiber; 0.2g sugar;
0.9g protein.

2 cups raw organic almonds, soaked
1 cup shredded coconut
½ tsp vanilla
¼ cup raw cocoa nibs

In a food processor, combine almonds, shredded coconut, and vanilla.

Blend in food processor until ingredients resemble almond butter.

Shape the mixture into balls about 1/4 inch in diameter, and place them on a non-stick cookie sheet, evenly spaced apart.

Refrigerate until firm or at least a couple of hours.

Raw Kefir Cheesecake

Recipe Type:
Sweets and desserts,
gluten-free

If you want to enjoy a delicious live, raw dessert, try this luscious cheesecake made with kefir cream.

Yield: 8 servings
Prep time: 4 hrs.

2 cups kefir cream (see page 137)
½ cup raw honey or agave nectar
¾ cup raw, organic milk, preferably from pasture-fed cows.
1 Tbsp gelatin or 1½ Tbsp psyllium seed powder
2 med eggs from pasture fed chickens, separated, at room temperature
½ tsp real vanilla extract
2 tsp lime or lemon juice
pinch Celtic or sea salt

COOKING TIPS

Put kefir in bottom of food processor first to prevent honey from sticking. Do not over process, Overprocessing turns the cream to butter.

Prepare kefir and kefir cream on page 137.

Prepare the easy raw or baked crust page 245.

Put milk into a small saucepan, sprinkle with the gelatin or psyllium seed and warm slightly, over lowest heat, stirring with a flat wooden spoon or wire whisk until the gelatin is dissolved. For vegan raw version, sprinkle with psyllium husk powder and stir. Cool.

At this point you will need to work quickly. In a food processor, combine the milk mixture, kefir cream, raw honey, egg yolks, vanilla and lime/lemon juice, and process at low to medium speed for 20-30 seconds, or until smooth, being sure that all the honey has been mixed in and has not stuck to the bottom.

Beat egg whites with a pinch of salt until they form peaks. Set aside.

Transfer the kefir custard mixture to a bowl then gently fold in the egg whites with a spatula. Pour the mixture onto the crust and refrigerate for several hours before serving.

NUTRITION FACTS

Nutrition (per serving):
180.6 calories;
22% calories from fat;
4.5g total fat;
73.1mg cholesterol;
147.0mg sodium;
159.6mg potassium;
31.2g carbohydrates;
0.0g fiber; 27.2g sugar;
5.5g protein

Sour Cream Sourdough Chocolate Cake

Have healthier, life-giving foods and eat your cake too!

Recipe Type:
Sweets and desserts, uses fermented foods, vegetarian

Yield: 2-8 or 9-inch cakes

Prep time: 50 min.

Inactive prep time: 35 min.

¾ cup butter, preferably raw, organic, grass-fed or cultured
1½ cup Turbinado sugar
½ cup sourdough starter (see page 152)
3 eggs, free-range organic
1 tsp real vanilla extract
1¼ cups sour cream (see page 152)
¼ cup water, purified
½ cup organic cocoa powder
2 cups whole wheat pastry flour, organic
1 tsp baking soda
¼ tsp Celtic or sea salt

Preheat oven to 375°F. Grease and flour two 8-inch square pans.

Cream butter and sugar. Add sourdough starter, eggs, vanilla, sour cream, and water. Mix well.

In separate bowl, mix flour, salt, soda and cocoa. Add liquid mixture to flour mixture and beat 2-3 minutes until creamy and blended. Pour cake batter into the two prepared pans.

Bake 30-35 min until wooden toothpick comes out clean. Turn oven down if cake begins to brown.

NUTRITION FACTS

Nutrition (per serving):
129.5 calories;
42% calories from fat;
6.3g total fat;
38.1mg cholesterol;
66.6mg sodium;
60.7mg potassium;
16.9g carbohydrates;
1.1g fiber; 9.5g sugar;
2.3g protein.

Recipe Source
Patricia A. Duncan, *Pat's Sourdough Favorite Recipes*

Chocolate Chip Cookies with Spent Grains

⅓ cup almond butter

2 Tbsp oil

1 cup organic evaporated cane juice or organic sugar

⅓ cup raw milk

1 tsp vanilla

1 cup whole wheat pastry or spelt flour

1 tsp baking soda

½ tsp salt

1½ cup (or more) spent barley grains

½ cup chocolate chips

½ cup walnuts

Mix first five ingredients until smooth in mixing bowl.

Stir in flour, baking soda, salt, spent grains, chocolate chips, walnuts.

If using wet grains, put enough flour so dough retains shape when plopped on pan. Do a test cookie to make sure consistancy is right. Bake on oiled cookie sheet at 425°F for 8 minutes. Let sit on pan for a couple of minutes.

Recipe Source

Seven Bridges Cooperative Brewing

Recipe Type:
Sweets and desserts

Yield: 36 cookies
Prep time: 25 min.

COOKING TIPS

Spent grains are high in fiber, and still have plenty of protein and carbohydrates, making them a nutritious food source. We would love to share more recipes with everyone, so if you have a favorite recipe for cooking with spent grains that you would like to share, please let us know at www.TrulyCultured.com

NUTRITION FACTS

Nutrition (per serving):
82.87 calories;
4.47g total fat;
0.0mg cholesterol;
74.69mg sodium;
63.38mg potassium; .
70g carbohydrates; .
79g fiber; 6.14g sugar;
1.2g protein.

Vegetables

Notes

Recipe Type:
Vegetables, side dish, vegan, vegetarian

Yield: 4 servings
Prep time: 15 min.
Inactive prep time: 10 min.

COOKING TIPS

You can make this quickly for everyday by steaming cauliflowerettes on top of the stove and spooning rich black olive paste over the top of them in the serving dish.

For more elegant preparation, steam the whole head of cauliflower intact, or roast it in a 350°F. oven for 35-40 min., covering with a crown of black olive paste during the last five minutes. Serve on a flat serving plate or dish with low sides.

NUTRITION FACTS

Nutrition (per serving):
70.7 calories;
24% calories from fat;
2.0g total fat;
0.0mg cholesterol;
116.2mg sodium;
643.0mg potassium;
11.6g carbohydrates;
5.5g fiber; 5.1g sugar;
4.4g protein.

Cauliflower with a Crown

This is a beautiful and delicious way to serve normally mild cauliflower, resplendent with a shimmery crown of rich Olive and Caper Tapenade from the Condiment Section.

1 large head fresh organic cauliflower
½ cup Olive and Caper Tapenade (see page 194)

Remove outer leaves from cauliflower head. Wash cauliflower under running water.

For quick preparation, cut cauliflower into large cauliflowerettes by starting with the back side of the head, and cutting in a funnel-shaped circle cut into the core. Lift out core and discard. Cut off 2 or 3-inch flowerettes from the back or underside of the head.

For more elegant whole head presentation, simply remove core and steam or roast cauliflower head intact, see directions in tips.

Steam lightly, covered, for 8-10 minutes in colander or steamer over boiling water, or in a pan with a small amount of water in the bottom. Drain and save cook water for soup.

Remove to flat serving plate or serving dish with low sides, spread or top with Black Olive and Caper Tapenade. Serve immediately.

Recipe Source
Dr. Mercola's TOTAL HEALTH Program

253

Chinese Broccoli and Cabbage in Oyster Sauce

Chinese Broccoli, also known as gai tan, is available from Oriental groceries, but you can substitute Italian broccoli rapini.

Recipe Type:
Side dish, vegetables

Yield: 4 servings
Prep time: 20 min.

1 head Chinese broccoli or gai tan
½ head Chinese cabbage, cut lengthwise
1½ Tbsp coconut or sesame oil
2 med scallions, finely chopped
2 Tbsp grated fresh ginger root or 1 Tbsp ground ginger
3 cloves fresh garlic, finely chopped
3 Tbsp Oyster sauce
2 Tbsp wheat-free tamari or shoyu soy sauce
2 Tbsp rice wine vinegar
1 tsp organic sugar or evaporated cane juice
1 Tbsp toasted sesame oil
⅓ cup organic chicken or vegetable stock or ⅓ cup bean liquor
1½ Tbsp arrowroot

Wash broccoli and Chinese cabbage well. Remove tough stems. Cut brocolli and cabbage up diagonally into bite size pieces, strarting from the stem end.

Plunge broccoli into saucepan of simmering water, to blanch, 1-2 minutes, optional. Remove to bowl of cold or ice water to retain green color.

In large spun-steel wok or frying pan, heat oil until very hot. Stir-fry the chopped scallions, ginger root, and garlic for a few seconds. Add the broccoli and cook until heated through. Add shredded cabbage and stir-fry lightly until slightly wilted, but not limp.

Mix remaining Oyster and soy sauces, rice wine vinegar, sugar, sesame oil, chicken stock and arrowroot together in small bowl. Pour over the brocolli and and cabbage and stir until the sauce thickens. Toss to coat all ingredients. Serve immediately.

NUTRITION FACTS
Nutrition (per serving):
121.3 calories;
57% calories from fat;
8.8g total fat;
0.0mg cholesterol;
722.4mg sodium;
287.3mg potassium;
12.7g carbohydrates;
1.8g fiber; 1.6g sugar;
2.1g protein.

Fermented Beets

*Like pickled beets, only alive, they can also be used to create a quick
borscht, beet soup.*

5 lb fresh raw beets, cleaned, peeled and sliced
½ lb shredded green or red cabbage
2 Tbsp Celtic or sea salt
1 Tbsp whole anise seed
1½ tsp ground allspice

Pack in glass jars or a crock, assuring that beets are below fluid level. If using
crock, place plate and weight on top to hold down contents.

Ferment 2 weeks or more at 75°-80°F. Should keep for the year in fermentation
container at room temperature.

Variations:

Add 2 Tbsp fennel or tarragon, ½ tsp whole cloves or other spices for more
interesting flavor.

Leafy Greens Gala

Dark, leafy greens like kale or swiss chard are nutritional powerhouses that can stand as trusted centerpoints for quick winter meals.

Recipe Type:
Vegetables, side dish, gluten-free, uses fermented foods, vegetarian

Yield: 4 servings
Prep time: 20 min.

2 large bunches kale
2 large bunches red and yellow swiss chard
2 Tbsp butter, raw or organic
3 cloves garlic, peeled and sliced
1 med red onion, peeled and slivered
1 lb mushrooms, shitake or combination, quartered or chopped
1 Tbsp wheat-free tamari or shoyu soy sauce
2 tsp mustard (see page 193)

Wash and drain greens. Tear kale off stems into 2-3-inch pieces. Chop swiss chard, starting from stem end, into ½-inch cross cuts increasing to larger 2-3-inch leafy pieces.

Heat a large, heavy enameled cast iron or stainless steel pot over medium heat. Melt butter and add chopped garlic, stirring. Add red onion slivers, stir to coat and sauté 2-3 minutes until they start to become translucent.

Stir in chopped or quartered mushrooms and continue cooking. After 2-3 minutes pour tamari or shoyu over mushrooms and stir to coat.

Cover with torn leafy greens. Cover pan and sauté for 7-10 minutes, just until greens are wilted. Splash with a little water to create more steam. Volume will be greatly reduced. Add in your homemade mustard and stir to coat greens.

Serve, topped with a sprinkling of pine nuts, sunflower seeds or, for protein types, chopped or sliced beef summer sausage. Or try topped with my delicious Sunsé Seed Mix[TM] (see page 167)

COOKING TIPS

This tried and true technique for cooking greens quickly keeps them tasty and succulent, without strong, sulphury off flavors from overcooking. Pile this savory delight on baked polenta squares or seasoned lentils.

NUTRITION FACTS

Nutrition (per serving):
106.0 calories;
51% calories from fat;
6.2g total fat;
15.3mg cholesterol;
338.1mg sodium;
677.3mg potassium;
11.5g carbohydrates;
3.3g fiber; 1.1g sugar;
3.7g protein

Recipe Type:
Vegetables, side dish, dairy-free, gluten-free, vegetarian

Yield: 4 servings
Prep time: 10 min.
Inactive prep time: 30 min.

Oven Roasted Steak Fries

Easy classic steak fries oven roasted with a savory tamari and oil coat.

3 med organic russet or baking potatoes
3 Tbsp coconut oil or organic extra virgin olive oil
2 Tbsp wheat-free tamari or shoyu soy sauce
¼ tsp coarsely ground pepper

Preheat oven to 400°F. In 9 x12-inch baking pan or cookie sheet, melt coconut oil.

Cut each unpeeled potato lengthwise into quarters, then cut each quarter lengthwise into 2-3 wedges. You can also cut potatoes crosswise into 1/4-inch-thick slices.

Remove pan from oven, add potato wedges. Toss to coat with oil.

Pour tamari over potatoes. Sprinkle with pepper, toss potatoes again to coat thoroughly.

Spread potatoes evenly over pan, return to oven and oven-fry for 25-30 minutes or until tender and browned. Turn potatoes once or twice through cooking.

Variation:

Lemony Oven Fries: Prepare Classic Oven Fries as above in steps 1 and 2. In step 3, mix 1 tsp grated fresh lemon peel, 2 Tbsp fresh lemon juice, 1 Tbsp dried oregano, and 1 large garlic clove, crushed, with salt, pepper, and oil in bowl. Add potatoes and toss to coat. Complete recipe as in step 4.

NUTRITION FACTS

Nutrition (per serving):
152.9 calories;
57% calories from fat;
10.3g total fat;
0.0mg cholesterol;
506.5mg sodium;
333.5mg potassium;
14.1g carbohydrates;
1.1g fiber; 0.6g sugar;
2.6g protein.

Spinach with Feta

A quick and delicious spinach side dish that could work for a weekday dinner or a weekend party.

2 bunches fresh spinach
3 Tbsp cultured butter (see page 129)
1 clove garlic, minced
½ tsp Celtic or sea salt
¼ tsp freshly ground black pepper
6 oz organic feta cheese

Wash spinach carefully. Drain.

In large skillet over medium high, melt butter. Add chopped garlic and sauté lightly.

Add spinach and sprinkle with salt and pepper. Stir. Cover. Cook gently for 3-5 minutes until wilted.

Crumble feta cheese over spinach and heat for 1-2 minutes more to soften cheese. Remove to serving dish. Serve immediately.

Recipe Type:
Vegetables, side dish, gluten-free, vegetarian, uses fermented foods

Yield: 4 servings
Prep time: 10 min.

COOKING TIPS

This could also be served as a light vegetarian main dish served with a mixed green vegetable salad for two people.

NUTRITION FACTS

Nutrition (per serving):
151.0 calories;
56% calories from fat;
9.7g total fat;
38.3mg cholesterol;
889.7mg sodium;
840.8mg potassium;
7.8g carbohydrates;
3.2g fiber; 2.9g sugar;
10.5g protein.

Turnips with Garlicky Tahini Sauce

A quick and savory dish for a warm winter meal, served as a side dish for four or a main dish with a salad for two.

Recipe Type:
Vegetables, side dish, dairy-free, gluten-free, vegetarian

Yield: 4 servings

Prep time: 12 min.

Inactive prep time: 7 min.

2 lb fresh, white turnips
⅔ cup Garlicky Tahini Dip (**see** page 163)

Peel and quarter turnips. Steam lightly **or** plunge turnips into boiling, salted water for 5 to 6 minutes until tender.

Transfer to serving dish and pour Garlicky Tahini Sauce, made with a little extra water, over top. Serve immediately.

NUTRITION FACTS

Nutrition (per serving):
63.5 calories; 2% calories from fat; 0.2g total fat; 0.0mg cholesterol; 152.0mg sodium; 433.2mg potassium; 14.6g carbohydrates; 4.1g fiber; 8.6g sugar; 2.0g protein.

Notes

Glossary & Vocabulary

Acetobacter: any of several rodshaped aerobic bacteria of the genus Acetobacter, certain species of which are used in making vinegar.

aerobic: in the presence of oxygen.

agave: the sweet, low glycemic syrup produced from the cactus plant, used as an ingredient sweetener and in the production of certain fermented beverages.

alchemy, alchemist: A medieval chemical philosophy aimed at the transmutation or transformation of base metals into gold, discovery of the panacea, and the preparation of the elixir of longevity; those medieval scientist philosophers who practiced this work, considered the forerunners of chemists.

alkaline or alkalinizing: a measure of the basic or high pH end of the hydrogen ion scale, above 7.

anaerobic: a term coined by Pasteur, used to describe organisms or living conditions capable of existing without oxygen.

anti-nutrient: a substance that interferes with the utilization of one or more nutrients by the body, as oxalate and phytate, which prevent calcium absorption.

archetype: the original pattern or model from which all things of the same kind are copied or on which they are based; a model or first form; prototype, or a collectively inherited and or connected unconscious idea, pattern or thought in Jungian psychology.

Aspergillus: A genus of fungi that includes many common molds, include many which are contaminants. food spoilage organisms and/or food ingredient substrates.

bacteria: one of several types of microbes or microorganisms along with yeasts and molds, involved in the fermentation and spoilage of food.

buttermilk: The sour liquid that remains after the butterfat has been removed from whole milk or cream by churning; a cultured sour milk made by adding certain microorganisms to sweet milk.

Candida albicans: the most common of the Candida yeast, which causes thrush or a yeast infection.

Candidiasis: commonly called yeast infection or thrush, is a fungal infection of any of the Candida species, of which Candida albicans is the most common.

charcuterie: from the French, meaning gourmet delicacies such as sausages, ham, pâtés, and other cooked or processed meat foods; a delicatessen specializing in such foods.

chi, ki, or prana: essentially equivalent terms in Chinese, Japanese and Hindu systems reflecting the vital force thought to be inherent in all things; the unimpeded circulation of chi and balance of its negative and positive forms in the body are held to be essential to good health in traditional Chinese medicine.

E. Coli/escheresci coli: one of the many bacteria normally present in minute quantities in the intestinal tract, that can proliferate and cause disease problems when inner ecology is unbalanced.

culture: the totality of socially transmitted behavior patterns, arts, beliefs, institutions, and all other products of human work and thought; predominating attitudes and behavior characterizing a group or organization's functioning; enlightenment arising from the development of the intellect through training or education; the growing of microorganisms, tissue cells, or other living matter in a specially prepared nutrient medium, including a growth or colony, as of bacteria; cultivation of soil; tillage.

dahi or dadhi: in sanskrit is a popular Indian fermented milk product mentioned in the ancient Vedic scriptures, 3000 B.C.

enzyme: highly specific protein compounds produced in living cells that accelerate, catalyze or speed up metabolic processes of an organism, functioning within a tight range of temperature and pH, involved in such processes as the digestion of large food molecules, and creation of DNA.

fermentation: tranformative process that increases the nutritional and or sensory characteristics of a food material.

food circle™: a local or focally based, sustainable food system; a local or focal community of people who work cooperatively together to increase the availability and access to high quality, nutrient-dense food and/or nourishment.

FOS, fructo-oligosaccharides: a type of prebiotic often derived from jerusalem artichokes or other high inulin tubers.

functional foods: a contemporary category of conventional foods that have physiological benefits and or reduce the risk of chronic disease beyond minimum nutritional functions.

gastrointestinal: pertaining to the GastroIntestinal Tract (GIT) often called the GUT, the entire mucosal lined "food tube" from mouth to anus.

heterofermentation: a mixed fermentation containing a variety of microrganisms.

homofermentation: a mono or single fermentation involving one predominant microorganism, generally in the third stage of vegetable fermentation.

iatrogenic: physician-created or induced illness.

isoflavones: One of a family of phytoestrogens found chiefly in soybeans under investigation for preventive health benefits as a nutritional supplement.

kefir: a tart, fermented milk beverage produced by a symbiotic combination of lactic acid bacteria, yeasts and acetic acid originating in Russia.

kimchi: an ancient fermented vegetable condiment or salad dating back as far as 1145 AD, popular in Korea, made from a wide variety of vegetables, highly spiced or flavored with ingredients such as garlic, scallions, radish, chiles or red pepper.

kumiss or kumys: an ancient fermented drink made from mares' milk or a sparkling lactic acid beverage originating in Mongolia, widely consumed in Eastern Europe and the Asiastic regions.

kvass: a traditional fermented beverage popular in the Balkans, Eastern Europe and Russia made with bread, raisins or other carbohydrates.

lactic acid: the primary acid created by the fermentation process, facilitated by microorganisms that turn lactose into lactic acid.

Lactobacillus plantarum: often the dominant species of Lactobacillus bacteria in traditional lactic acid fermented foods based on plant materials.

leben: traditional Middle Eastern fermented milk containing yogurt bacteria from which the whey is drained.

Leuconotstoc mesenteroides: a species of bacteria which generally initiates the fermentation process, producing the lactic and acetic acids that quickly lower the pH in the production of sauerkraut and other fermented vegetables.

microflora: pertaining to beneficial microorganisms in the GUT or gastrointestinal tract, particularly the large intestine.

miso: a rich, fermented soybean and grain paste which originated in oriental cultures.

mold: one of three classes of microorganisms often involved in the fermentation process and / or spoilage of foods.

natto: an oriental and southeastern Asian fermented whole bean product made using Bacillus subtilis, which is similar to miso with numerous reported health benefits, translated from the Japanese as "contributed beans."

neutraceutical: a subclass of functional foods created to possess higher nutrient density and / or unique benefits to address specific nutritional functions.

Pasteurization: the rapid heating of a food mixture, especially dairy products, to temperature of 72°F. for 15 seconds to kill pathogenic and spoilage bacteria.

pathogenic: capable of causing or originating disease.

pH: a symbol representing the concentration of hydrogen ions used to describe the acidity and alkalinity of a solution.

post fermentation: describing a second or subsequent stage of the fermentation process.

prebiotic: nondigestible food ingredients capable of improving health by stimulating the growth of beneficial bacteria in the intestines.

probiotic: live microorganisms or the foods containing them that confer a positive health benefit upon the host through presence in the gastrointestinal tract.

putrefactive: fermentation of protein foodstuffs, producing off flavors and tastes.

quark: a soft creamy acid-cured cheese of central Europe made from whole milk.

reductionist: the practice of simplifying a complex idea, issue, condition, or the like, esp. to the point of minimizing, obscuring, or distorting it.

rennet: an enzyme from calf's stomach used to coagulate milk in the cheesemaking proces.

respiration: The process by which organisms exchange gases, especially oxygen and carbon dioxide, with the environment; the conversion of oxygen by living things into energy; a part of metabolism.

starter cultures: Starter cultures are those microorganisms that are used in the production of cultured dairy products such as yogurt and cheese.

synthesize: to form a material or abstract entity by combining parts or elements, such as to synthesize a statement. In chemistry. to combine constituent elements into a single or unified entity.

vitalism: a theory or doctrine proposed by the alchmists of the Middle Ages, that life processes arise from or contain a nonmaterial vital principle and cannot be explained entirely as physical and chemical phenomena.

whey: the liquidy portion of milk products high in lactose, whey proteins and minerals, usually removed during the cheesemaking process, but also sometimes used as a starter for fermentation processes.

wort: an infusion of malt that is fermented to make beer.

yeast: one of the class of microrganisms involved in secondary phases of fermentation.

yogurt: one of the earliest fermented or soured milk products, containing lactobacilus acidophilus or lactobacillus bulgaricus bacteria, prescribed by ancient physicians of the Near and Middle East for curing or alleviating disorders of the stomach, intestines and liver and now one of the most popular cultured foods.

ONE GOOD WORD

This is not
the age of information.
This is not
the age of information.
Forget the news,
and the radio,
and the blurred screen.

This is the time
of loaves
and fishes.
People are hungry,
and one good word is bread
for a thousand.

David Whyte

Sources and Resources

Some Additional Key Reference Books On The Subject Of Fermented And Cultured Foods

Nourishing Traditions, Sally Fallon, www.newtrendspublishing.com

Wild Fermentation: The Flavor, Nutrition and Craft of Live-Culture Foods, Sandor Ellix Katz, www.wildfermentation.com

The Body Ecology Diet, Donna Gates, www.bodyecology.com

Dr. Mercola's TOTAL HEALTH Program, Dr. Joseph Mercola, Brian Vaszily, Dr. Kendra Pearsall and Nancy Lee Bentley
www.mercola.com

The Metabolic Typing Diet, William Wolcott, www.metabolictyping.com

Traditional Food Preparation Workshop with Maureen Diaz, motherhen@myfam.com

Restoring Your Digestive Health, Jordan S Rubin, NMD and Joseph Brasco, MD
www.gardenoflifeusa.com/wol_books_restore_health.shtml

Dr. Cass Ingram's How to Eat Right and Live Longer, www.p-73.com

Fermented Food Making Supplies and Cultures

Truly Cultured™ Starter Kits	www.TrulyCultured.com
Leener's	http://www.leeners.com
Caldwell BioFermentation	www.BioLacto.com
G.E.M Cultures	www.gemcultures.com
New England Cheesemaking Supply Company	www.cheesemaking.com
Tempeh cultures, The Farm	email: thefarm@usit.net
Kefir info, Dom's Kefir-in site	http://users.sa.chariot.net.au/~dna/kefirpage.html
Kombucha cultures, Worldwide Kombucha Exchange	www.kombu.de
Salt, Celtic Sea Salt, The Grain and Salt Society	www.celtic-salt.com
Dr. David Fankhauser's Cheese page, University of Cincinnati, Clermont College	http://biology.clc.uc.edu/fankhauser/Cheese/CHEESE.HTML

Equipment

Lehman's Hardware	www.Lehmans.com, 877-438-5346
Ball Corporation glass jars	www.freshpreserving.com
Harsch Fermenation Crocks	www.CanningPantry.com, 800-285-9044
Sprouters	www.sproutpeople.com
Fermentation Troubleshooting, Sandor Ellix Katz,	sandorkraut@wildfermentation.com
Support Networks	www.westonaprice.org, Local Chapters, Shopping Guide

For Additional Information, Sources and Updates, Visit www.TulyCultured.com

Bibliography

Appleton, Nancy. (2002). *Rethinking Pasteur's Germ Theory: How to Maintain your Optimal Health*. Berkeley, CA: Frog, Ltd.

Bach, A.C., Ingenbleek, Y. and Frey, A. (1996). *The Usefulness of Dietary Medium-Chain Triglycerides in Body Weight Control: Fact or Fancy?* Journal of Lipid Research. 37:708-726

Ballentine, Rudolf. (1978). *Diet & Nutrition: A Holistic Approach*. Honesdale, PA: The Himalayan International Institute.

Be'champ, A. (2002). *The Blood and its Third Element*. USA/Australia: Metropolis Ink.

Be'champ, A. *Fermentation, The Missing Link*. Kessinger Publishing's Rare Reprints. *www.kessinger.net*

Beard, F. & Beard, A. (1936). *Fresh and Briny: The Story of Water as Friend and Foe*. New York: Frederick A Stokes Company.

Bentley, Nancy Lee (May 2007) *Diabesity: A Big, Pinkish White Elephant*, Nutritional Outlook Magazine.

Bentley, Nancy Lee (Jan 2005) Low Carb Lifestyle, New Jersey: BarCharts, Inc.

Bentley, Nancy Lee (2004) *The Incredible Health Benefits to You of Traditionally Fermented Foods*, Mercola E-Healthy News You Can Use. www.mercola.com.

Bentley, Nancy Lee, (1994) *To Everything There is a Season.. An Introduction to The Food Circle: A Stewardship Technology for the New Paradigm*, OR: EcoCity Journal.

Bentley, Nancy Lee (May 2004*). Find Out What Type of Raw Diet is Best for You*. Mercola E-Healthy News You Can Use. www.mercola.com

Berry, Wendell, (1977). *The Unsettling of America, Culture and Agriculture,* San Francisco, CA, The Sierra Club.

Blume, David, (2006), *Alcohol Can Be a Gas, Too*, Soquel, California International Institute for Ecological Agriculture.

Brandt, L. (Sept 1996). *Pickled to Perfection*. http://www.vpico.com/articlemanager/print erfriendly.aspx?article=77386.

Bratman, Stephen Dr. (2001). Health *Food Junkies: Orthorexia Nervosa: Overcoming the Obsession with Healthful Eating,* New York: Broadway Publishing.

Buhner, Stephen H. (2003). P: adi Lost: Of Healing, the Sacred, and Beer. www.gaianstudies.org

Carper, Steve. Carper's SuperGuide to Dairy Products, Lactose Tolerance Clearinghouse.

Caulfield, C.R. & Goldberg, B. (1993). *The Anarchist AIDS Medical Formulary: A Guide to Guerrilla Immunology*. Berkeley, CA: North Atlantic Books.

Cherniske, S. (2003). *The Metabolic Plan: Stay Younger Longer*. New York: Random House Publishing Group.

Cicero, Providence. (Dec 2003) *Belly Up to the Olive Bar at Local Supermarkets*, Seattle: The Seattle Times.

Cohan, R. (1972). *How to Make It on the Land*. New York: Galahad Books.

Colbin, A. (1986) *Food and Healing. New* York: Ballentine Books, Div. Random House.

Cole, Carol. (1993) *Microbial Microcosm*, Context Institute, www.context.org

Conway, P.L., Gorbach, S.L., Golden, B.R., (1987). *Survival of Lactic Acid Bacteria in the Human Stomach and Adhesion to Intestinal Cells*. J. Dairy Science: 70: 1-12. Medline.

Crook, William H, (1994), *The Yeast Connection and Women's Health,* Jackson, TN, Professional Books.

Cousens, G. (1986). *Spiritual Nutrition and the Rainbow Diet*. Boulder, CO: Cassandra Press.

Culinary Institute of America. (1993). *The Professional Chef's Techniques of Healthy Cooking*, New York, Van Nostrand

D'Adamo, Peter. J. (1996) *Eat Right 4 Your Type. New York*: G.P. Putnam's and Son.

Daniel, Kaayla. T. (Feb 2005) The *Soy Myth Exposed: Soy is Not a Health Food*. Mercola E-Healthy News You Can Use. http://www.mercola.com/2005/feb/26/soy_myths.htm

Daniel, Kaayla, T. (2005) *The Whole Soy Story: The Dark Side of America's Favorite Health Food*. Washington, DC: New Trends Publishing.

Dokken, Larry. (1992). *Fermentation in the Food Industry: An Introduction to Biotechnology*, Workshop, University of Wisconsin – River Falls.

Douaund, C. (15/11/2006). *US get worst health marks*. Breaking News on Supplements & Nutrition. Nutra Ingredients/Europe. Decision News Media SAS. http://www.nutraingredients.com/news/printNewsBis.asp?id=72091.

Duncan, P. A. (1990). *Pat's Sourdough Favorite Recipes*. Douglas, WY: T.A.P. Publishing CO.

Eisenstein. C. (2003). *The Yoga of Eating: Transcending Diets and Dogma to Nourish the Natural Self*. Washington D.C.: New Trends Publishing, Inc.

Enig, M.G. (Summer 2005). *Know Your Fats: Vitamin A for Fetal Development*. Wise Traditions in Food, Farming and the Healing Arts, 6, 47, 51.

Enig, M. (2006, Fall). *Know your Fats*. Wise Traditions in Food, Farming and the Healing Arts, 7, 50-51.

Erochenko, Tatiana, MD. (2006). *Ketosis: Mystery or Misconception?* Bella Online, www.bellaonline.com.

Erlandson, K. (1989). *Home Smoking and Curing: How to Smoke-cure meat, Fish & Game*. London: Ebury Press.

Estella, M. (1985). *Natural Foods Cookbook: Vegetarian Dairy-Free Cuisine*. Tokyo & New York: Japan Publications, Inc.

Fallon. S. (2005, Summer). *A Campaign for Real Milk: Recent Research on Human Milk*. Wise Traditions in Food, Farming and the Healing Arts, 6, 68-69. Daniel, K. (2006, Fall). *Soy Alert!*. Wise Traditions in Food, Farming and the Healing Arts, 7, 69-73.

Fallon, S. (Aug 2007) *President's Message: On the Omnivore's Dilemna*. Wise Traditions, D.C. Weston A Price Foundation.

Fallon, S. & Enig, M. (2005, Summer). *Caustic Commentary*. Wise Traditions in Food, Farming and the Healing Arts, 6, 8-10.

Fallon, S. & Enig, M. (2006, Fall). *Caustic Commentary*. Wise Traditions in Food, Farming and the Healing Arts, 7, 10-13.

Fallon, S. and Enig M.G. (2001). *Nourishing Traditions: The Cookbook that Challenges Politically Correct Nutrition and the Diet Dictocrats (rev. 2nd ed.)*. Washington DC: New Trends Publishing, Inc.

Fankhauser David B, PhD. Fankhauser's Cheese Page, http://biology.clc.uc.edu/Fankhauser/Cheese/buttermilk.htm

Farnworth, E.R. (ed.). (2003). *Handbook of Fermented Functional Foods*. Boca Raton, FL: CRC Press.

Fisher, M.F.K, (1976). *The Art of Eating*, New York: Vintage Books div. Randwm House.

Fisher,S. (2004, Winter). *The Quest for Nutrient-Dense Food: High Brix Farming and Gardening*. (An interview with Rex Harrill). Wise Traditions in Food, Farming and the Healing Arts, 5, 18-29.

Food and Agricultural Organization. *Fermented vegetables: A Global Perspective*. www.fao.org/docrep/x0560e/0560e06.htm#1.4

Forristall, L. J. (2004, Winter). *Ultrapasteurized Milk*. Wise Traditions in Food, Farming and the Healing Arts, 5, 57-59.

Gail, P.A. (1994). *The Dandelion Celebration: A Guide to Unexpected Cuisine (2nd ed.)*. Cleveland, Ohio: Goosefoot Acres Press.

Gates, D. & Schatz, L. (2006). *The Body Ecology Diet: Recovering your Health and Rebuilding your Immunity (9th ed.)*. Decatur, GA: B.E.D. Publications.

Gehman, R. (1969). *The Sausage Book*, New York: Weathervane Books.

Gly, Joanne. (2003) *Simply Slow Cooking*, New York: Barnes and Nobles Books.

Golden, B.R., Gorbach, S.L. (1992) *Probiotics for Humans* in Probotics: The Scientific Basis. London: Chapman & Hall.

Gordon, James, MD (Ed.) (Jun 2006) Food As Medicine: Integrating Nutrition into Clinical Practice and Medical Education. Baltimore, MD. Seminar Conference. Baltimore: Center for Mind Body Medicine.

Harkins, Don. (Apr. 1999) *JAMA stats tell the tale: Doctors Kill More People than guns and traffic accidents*. ID: Idaho Observer. http://proliberty.com/observer/19999

Hartman HartBeat (Jul 2007) *Demon Ingredient: High Fructose Corn Syrup*. Bellevue, WA: The Hartman Group.

Hartman HartBeat (Jun 2007) *Globalization of Food Choices*. Bellevue, WA: The Hartman Group.

Hartman HartBeat (Sept 2007) *Report on Sustainability*. Bellevue, WA: The Hartman Group.

Heinberg, Richard (2003) The Party's Over: Oil, War and the Fate of Industrial Societies. Vancouver, BC: New Society Publishers.

Home Nest Yogurt Conspiracy (2006) *Fermenting is Fun*. The Healing Crow, www.healingcrow.com

Howell, Edward MD, (1995) *Enzyme Nutrition*. New York: Avery Publishing.

Herter, G.L. & Herter, B. E. (1960). *Bull Cook and Authentic Historical Recipes and Practices*. Wasesa, Minnesota: Herter's, Inc.

Hughes, P. (ed.). (1977). *Pueblo India Cooking: Recipes from the Pueblos of the American Southwest*. NM: Museum of New Mexico Press.

Hume, Douglas & Bechamp, Antoine. *Bechamp or Pasteur: A Lost Chapter in the History of Biology*. Kessenger Publishing. www.kessinger.net.

IFOAM International Newsletter (Sept 2007) *First IFOAM International Conference on the Marketing of Organic and Regional Values Concludes Local and Regional Development Must be Strengthened by All Means*. International Federation of Organic Agriculture Associations, www.ifoam.org/press/positions/pdfs/Conference_Declaration.pdf

Jones, Peter J. (2002) *Clinical Nutrition: Functional Foods – More Than Just Nutrition*, CMAJ-JAMC, Canadian Medical Association.

Juttelstad, A. (May 1999). *The Best of the Wurst*. Retrieved 11/04/2006, Food Product Design, Virgo Publishing. http://www.vpico.com/articlemanager/printerfriendly.aspx?article=78276.

Katz, S.E. (2006) *The Revolution Will Not Be Microwaved*, White River Junction, VT., Chelsea Green Publishing Company.

Katz, S. E. (2003). *Wild Fermentation: The Flavor, Nutrition, and Craft of Live Culture Foods*. White River Junction, VT: Chelsea Green Publishing Company.

Kazuko, Emi & Fukuoka, Y. (2003). *Japanese Cooking*. London SE1 BHA: Aness Publishing Limited.

Kiahorst, S.J. (Mar 1997). *Designer Enzymes Create New Forms and Functions*. Food Product Design Magazine, Virgo Publishing. www.vpico.com/articlemanager/printerfriendly.aspx?article=77357.

Kushi, Micho, *The Macrobiotic Way*, 1985, Wayne, NJ: Avery Publishing Group.

Laign J. (Ed.) (2000). *Healing Secrets from Around the World*. Lincolnwood, IL: Publications International, Ltd.

Lister, Joseph (1878). *On the Lactic Fermentation and Its Bearing on Pathology*, London. Transactions of the Pathological Society of London, Vol 29.

Livingston, A.D. (1995). *Cold-Smoking & Salt-Curing Meat, Fish, & Game*. Guilford, Connecticut: The Lyons Press.

Longstreet, S. & Longstreet, E. (1996). *A Salute to American Cooking*. New York, NY: Hawthorne Books, Inc.

Lopez, D.A., Williams, R.M., & Miehlke, M. (1994). *Enzymes: the Fountain of Life*. Charleston, SC: The Neville Press, Inc.

Manning, Richard, 2004, *Against The Grain*, How Agriculture Has Hijacked Civilization, New York, NY, North Point Press, div. of Farrar, Straus and Giroux.

Margulis, Lynn, (1998) *Symbiosis, A New Look at Evolution*, Amherst, MA:. Science Writers.

Margulis, Lynn, & Sagan, Dorion. (1986) *Microcosmos: Four Billion Years of Microbial Evolution*, Berkeley, CA. University of California Press.

Massey, G. (1998). *Man in Search of His Soul during Fifty Thousand Years, and How He Found It!*. Retrieved 01/10/07, http://www.theosphical.ca/ManSearchSoul.htm. www.gaianstudies.org

Medved, E. (1981). *The World of Food*. Lexington, MA: Ginn and Company, Xerox Corporation.

Mercola, Joseph, Vaszily, Brian, Pearsall, Kendra & Bentley, Nancy Lee. (2005). *Dr. Mercola's Total Health Program*, Schaumburg, IL: www.Mercola.com.

Miczak, M. (1999). *Nature's Weeds Native Medicine: Native American Herbal Secrets*. Twin Lakes, WI: Lotus Press.

Pennybacker, Mindy (Ed.) (1997) *The Green Food Shopper*, New York, NY. Mothers & Others For a Livable Planet.

Mitchell, Stacy, (2006) *Lecture on Globalization*. Croton-on-Hudson, NY: E.F.Schumacher Society Lecture Series,

Nestle, Marion. (2002) *Food Politics: How the Food Industry Influences Nutrition and Health*. Berkeley, CA: University of California Press.

Netzer, Corinne, (2003) The Complete Book of Food Counts, New York, NY: Dell Publishing, Div of Random House.

No name. No date. *Alcoholic fermentation by Yeast cells*. Retrieved 11/3/2006, http://www.yobrew.co.uk/fermentation.php.

FF Journal Publications, APA Format

O'Brien, Christopher, 2007 *Fermenting Revolution*, Vancouver, BC, New Society Publishers.

O'Brien, Robyn (2007) *Testimony of a Mother - AllergyKids and GMOS: A Complex Truth*. Chicago, IL: BioVISION2020. www/BioVISION2020.org

O'Donnel, K. (Feb 2000). *Simple Steps to Artisan Breads*. http://www.vpico.com/articlemanager/print erfriendly.aspx?article=77912.

Organic Gardening Magazine Editors. (1982). *Home Food Security*. Emmaus, PA: Rodale Press, Inc

Pepper, Penny (2006) *Simply Slower Cooking*. AZ: Self published.

Pfeiffer, Dale Allen, (2006). *Eating Fossil Fuels: Oil, Food and the Coming Crisis in Agriculture*, Vancouver, BC: New Society Publishers.

Poggi, B. (2005, Summer). *Soy Alert! The Effects of Antenatal Exposure to Phytoestrogens on Human Male Reproductive and Urogenital Development*. Wise Traditions in Food, Farming and the Healing Arts, 6, 61-66.

Prentice, Jessica. (2006) *Full Moon Feast*. White River Junction, VT: Chelsea Green Press.

Prentice, Jessica. (Mar 2003). *Heaven's Leaven*. Wise Food Ways, www.stirringthecauldron.com

Price, Weston A., DDS. (1933). *Nutrition and Physical Degeneration*. Van Nuys, CA: Price-Pottender Nutriiton Foundation

Rapp, Doris J. MD, (2004) *Our Toxic World: A Wake Up Call*, Buffalo, NY: Environmental Medical Research Foundation.

Rubin, Jordan S. NMD and Brasco, Joseph, MD, (2003) *Restoring Your Digestive Health*, New York, NY: Twin Streams Books, Kensington Publishing Corp.

Russo, Julee & Lukins, Sheila. (1982). *The Silver Palate Cookbook*, New York, Workman Publishing.

Santillo, H. (1991). *Food Enzymes: The Missing Link to Radiant Health*. Prescott AZ: Hohm

Press.

SASNET-Fermented Foods (2004) *Collection of Data on Fermented Foods of South Asia*. Swedish South Asian Network for Fermented Foods. www.fermented-foods.net/News-Sasnet.html.

Savard, Tony PhD. (2006). *Lecture on Fermentation*. Wise Traditions Conference. Virginia. Weston A. Price Foundation.

Schechter, S.R. & Monte, T. (1988). *Fighting Radiation with Foods, Herbs, & Vitamins*. Brookline, Massachusetts: East West Health Books.

Schleyer, M.B. (1987). *The High Integrity Diet*. No copyright page.

Schmid, R. (2003). *The Untold Story of Milk: Green Pastures, Contented Cows and Raw Dairy Foods*. Washington DC: New Trends Publishing, Inc.

Schmidt, G. (1980). *The Dynamics of Nutrition*. Wyoming, RI: Bio-Dynamic Literature.

Sheldrake, R. (1995). *A New Science of Life: The Hypothesis of Morphic Resonance* (2nd ed.). Rochester, VT: Park Street Press.

Sardi, W. (November 1,2006). *New Book Touts Red Wine Pill as Tonic for Aging Adults*. Retrieved 11/02/2006, http://www.prweb.com/printer.php?prid=46 7467.

Schultz, M. (April 2005). *What's Sauce for the Sushi?* Retrieved 11/04/2006, http://www.vpico.com/articlemanager/print erfriendly.aspx?article=77798.

Shurtleff, W., & Aoyagi, A., (2004). *A Brief History of Fermentation, East and West*. Unpublished. *History of Soybeans and Soyfoods: 1100 BC to the 1980s*. Lafayette, CA: Soyfoods Center.

Smart Brief (11/15/2006). *Food Lineage Grows More Important for Consumers*, National Restaurant Association from The New York Times.

Smith, Jeffrey, M. (2003) 3rd edition. *Seeds of Deception: Exposing Industry and Government Lies about the Safety of the Genetically Engineered Foods You're Eating*, Fairfield, IA. Yes! Books. www.seedsofdeception.com

Smith, Jeffrey, M. (2007) *Genetic Roulette: The Documented Health Risks of Genetically Engineered Foods*. Fairfield, IA: Yes!Books

www.seedsofdeception.com.

Staff Reporter. (11/16/2006). *Flat pickle market could see boost from health*. Food USA Navigator. Decision News Media SAS. http://www.foodnavigator.com.

Starling, Shane (July/Aug 2007) *Special Healthy Food Report: Healthy Ingredients Power Up the Healthy Foods Trend*, Functional Foods and Neutraceuticals. www.ffnmag.com.

Storl, W.D. (1979). *Culture and Horticulture: A Philosophy of Gardening*. Wyoming, RI: Bio-Dynamic Literature.

Stone, R.B. (1989). *The Secret Life of Your Cells*. Atglen, PA: Whitford Press.

Symons, M. (2000). *A History of Cooks and Cooking*. Champaign, IL: University of Illinois Press.

Tannahill, R. (1973). *Food in History*. New York: Three Rivers Press.

Terebelske, D. & Ralph, N. (2003). *Pickles of Asia*. Food Product Design. http://www.myfoodmuseum.org/pasia.htm.

Tiwari, Maya. (1995) *A Life of Balancez;The Complete Guide to Ayurvedic Nutrition* VT Healing Arts Press.

Tocci, Peter G. (1998). *The Dark Closet of Medical Biology*, MT: Gemini Press.

Toussant-Samat, Maguelonne, (1987) *History of Food*. Malden, MA: Blackwell Publishing.

Trebing, W.P. (2006). *Goodbye Germ Theory: Ending a Century of Medical Fraud and How to Protect Your Family* (6th ed.). USA: Xlibris Corporation.

Voss, Neil R. (2003) *Lecture on Nutrition*: /personal communique. Sheboygan, WI

Waugh, Alec. (1968) *Foods of the World: Wine & Spirits*. New York: Time-Life, Inc.

Weston A. Price Foundation. *Proceedings of Wise Traditions 2006 7th annual conference*. [DVDs]. USA: Fleetwood OnSite Conference Recording.

Wigmore, A. (1982). *Be Your Own Doctor: Let Living Food be Your Medicine*. Wayne, NJ: Avery Publishing Group.

Wolf, R. (ed.), Organic Gardening and Farming. (1977). *Managing your Personal Food Supply*. Emmaus, PA: Rodale Press, Inc.

Yeager, S. and the Editors of Prevention. (1988). *The Doctors Book of Food Remedies*. USA: Rodale Inc.

truly *Cultured*
isn't just a book ...

TrulyCultured.com

**Just like microorganisms,
this work keeps growing and evolving ...**

So join us in a little more interactive format and
setting — on the web.

• Sign up for our email newslist to stay in touch with all things Truly Cultured™

• Find starter kits and e-course class support, more about using, storing, and
  creating these healthy foods and food community

• Keep up-to-date on news, trends, sources and resources at our
  TrulyCultured.com blog

Did you like the quotes in Truly Cultured?
Visit the website and select from a variety of quotes
and colored circle mandalas on your own beautiful,
custom framable mattes, Truly Cultured™ T-Shirts
and other items.

**Create your own local
community food circle.**™
Get community building kits at *thefoodcircle.com*.

Keep checking for developments on
the upcoming The Full Circles
Community Network™ at
fullcirclescommunity.com.

Attend *Truly Cultured*
author Nancy Lee Bentley's teleclasses, appearances and workshops

Learn how to create Project Messenger Nancy Lee's signature, versatile Sunsé™ Seed Mix and other foods for your family or as your own local food circle business.

For more information visit *TrulyCultured.com*

ap10

About the Author

Nancy Lee Bentley is a dynamic, nationally-known Wholistic Health Expert — Chef, Food Scientist, Nutrition Specialist, Natural Foods Marketing Consultant, Writer, Teacher, and Minister of Healing — who has done just about everything you can do with food.

From a Cornell foods, nutrition and communications degree and Madison Avenue food photography styling, she has gone full circle — with spoon in one hand and mouse in the other — from developing gourmet organic food products and farm-to-chef market programs to co-authoring the breakthrough *Dr. Mercola's TOTAL HEALTH Program* and recently being honored as one of the first 15 top, national Project Messengers.

Completing the whole circuit around what she calls "The Food Circle," wearing hats as Food Systems Development Specialist, Specialty Grain Broker, Food Editor and Healthy Foodservice Specialist, this new

paradigm innovator has lots of stories and wisdom to tell about teaching MasterCard® chefs, baking Prince's purple flowered birthday cake, organizing the first organic trade association and developing wheat-free recipes for Cher.

A visionary activist and champion for healthy foods and sustainable communities who has been sowing the "seeds of health," making the connections and building the food, agriculture, nutrition, health and wellness soil-to-spirit bridge for over 25 years, Nancy Lee has been called a pioneer in the fields of natural and organic foods, sustainable foodsystems and holistic health.

Her passion, unquestionably, is healthy food. Whether teaching, writing or nurturing with it, through it, this food ambassador sees food and nourishment as a metaphor for life, an inspiriting path to community, good health and well-being, a bridge to satisfying deeper hungers, to peace and to REMEMBERING who we are.

I want to thank all of those who've assisted in the seeding and nurturing of this labor of love, most especially Sally Fallon for her inspiration and courage and my editor, Jean Stanley for her patience and perseverance.

As microorganisms are constantly evolving, so is this book.
Consider this a starting point for discussion and action.
Please let us know if you find errors or inconsistencies.

Join with US
LETS GET A ROUND TO IT!

One in the Work,

Nancy Lee Bentley

www.TrulyCultured.com